JONATHAN EDWARDS,

RELIGIOUS TRADITION,

AMERICAN CULTURE

. . .

Jonathan Edwards,
Religious Tradition,
&
American Culture

. . .

JOSEPH A. CONFORTI

THE UNIVERSITY OF NORTH CAROLINA PRESS

CHAPEL HILL AND LONDON

Publication of this work was made possible in part through a
grant from the Division of Research Programs of the National Endowment
for the Humanities, an independent federal agency whose mission is to award grants
to support education, scholarship, media programming, libraries, and museums in
order to bring the results of cultural activities to a broad, general public.

The paper in this book meets the guidelines for permanence and durability
of the Committee on Production Guidelines for Book Longevity of the Council
on Library Resources.

Library of Congress Cataloging-in-Publication Data
Conforti, Joseph A.
Jonathan Edwards, religious tradition, and American culture / by Joseph A.
Conforti.
p.   cm.
Includes bibliographical references (p.   ) and index.
ISBN 0-8078-2224-8 (cloth : alk. paper). — ISBN 0-8078-4535-3 (pbk : alk. paper)
1. Edwards, Jonathan, 1703–1759—Influence.   2. United States—Civilization—
19th century.   3. United States—Church history—19th century.
4. United States—Church history—20th century.   5. United States—
Civilization—20th century.   I. Title.
BX7260.E3C64   1995
285.8'092—dc20   94-49526
CIP

Portions of this work appeared earlier, in somewhat different form, in
"Jonathan Edwards's Most Popular Work: 'The Life of David Brainerd' and Nineteenth-
Century Evangelical Culture," *Church History* (June 1985); "David Brainerd and the
Nineteenth-Century Missionary Movement," *Journal of the Early Republic* (Fall 1985);
"The Invention of the Great Awakening, 1795–1842," *Early American Literature* (Fall 1991);
and "Mary Lyon, the Founding of Mount Holyoke College and the Cultural Revival of
Jonathan Edwards," *Religion and American Culture* (Winter 1993); and are reprinted
here with permission.

99 98 97 96 95   5 4 3 2 1

To the memory of

ORLANDO C. CONFORTI, *my father,*

and

WILLIAM G. MCLOUGHLIN, JR., *my teacher*

CONTENTS

• • •

ILLUSTRATIONS

• • •

PREFACE

• • •

This study examines Jonathan Edwards's place in American cultural history. It is an extension of my earlier work on the New Divinity clerical followers of Edwards. After completing that study in 1981, I watched revisionist scholarship emerge that restored the New Divinity men to their rightful place as legitimate Calvinist theological heirs of Edwards. At the same time, it seemed to me that this new scholarship and my earlier work had approached Edwardsian tradition too narrowly, both in terms of the longevity of Edwards's influence and of the "thickness" of a religious culture that bore his imprint and that a vibrant New Divinity movement only partially represented. My initial efforts to come to terms with this religious culture focused on Edwards's most popular work, the *Life of David Brainerd*, and its importance to nineteenth-century evangelical America. I soon realized that many of Edwards's other works were enormously popular; an emergent evangelical print culture extensively republished his writings and appropriated and widely disseminated his interpretations of theology, conversion, revivalism, and personal piety. Most surprising of all, I found that even after the post–Civil War retreat of the evangelical "empire" that had so markedly affected antebellum America, Edwards endured or was "reinvented" as a cherished icon – a cultural artifact who met the needs of a new generation that, among other things, "discovered" colonial antiques.

How had scholarly interpreters of Edwards, who have produced such a capacious body of literature on this prolific and brilliant thinker, overlooked impressive evidence of his abiding importance in nineteenth-century American culture? I have concluded my analysis with a brief examination of how Progressive and then neo-orthodox intellectuals appropriated Edwards for their own cultural needs and thereby deflected scholarly attention away from the vital nineteenth-century Edwardsian traditions that this study examines.

I have chosen not to end my analysis with a full rehearsal of Progressive and neo-orthodox lines of interpretation. For several reasons, I have only sketched the twentieth-century appropriation of Edwards. The twentieth century witnessed the increasing academization of Edwards's cultural figure. In particular, the neo-orthodox "recovery" swelled the tide of publications on Edwards. It would have required a lengthy, heavily historiographical analysis to chart in detail the course of that scholarship. In any case, it seemed to me that a handful of key works, especially the publications of Perry Miller, overdetermined mid-twentieth-century scholarly interpretations of Edwards. I have tried to map the influence of these major works and plot the interpretive lines that connect the initial neo-orthodox recovery and the expansion of academic scholarship on Edwards in the post–World War II era.

In many respects, scholarly inquiry about the Edwardsian legacy remains entangled with the powerful neo-orthodox construction of Edwards. There has been no new Edwards – no contemporary recovery and appropriation of Edwards comparable to the neo-orthodox, Progressive, colonial revival, and antebellum evangelical cultural constructions that this study examines. Scholars have recovered the New Divinity movement and begun to show how Edwards's clerical disciples successfully carried some of his ideas into the early nineteenth century. Students of Edwards continue to produce a steady current of books, essays, and dissertations. Two national conferences, in 1984 and 1994, provided forums for assessing contemporary scholarship on Edwards. This scholarship increasingly focuses on the voluminous unpublished writings of Edwards, a development that will continue as Yale accelerates the pace of its publications in the *Works of Jonathan Edwards*.

Yet all of this scholarly activity has not actually produced a clear cultural appropriation that we might label a post-neo-orthodox or a postmodern Edwards. Having participated in the most recent national scholarly conference on Edwards, held at Indiana University in June 1994 and cosponsored by the *Works of Edwards* at Yale, I can attest to the continuing vitality of Edwardsian scholarship and to the ongoing pursuit of the "essential" Edwards in a mid-eighteenth-century context. In reaction to neo-orthodox claims for the prophetic Edwards, who stood as an isolated genius in the American wilderness, recent scholarship has tended to cut the theologian down to more manageable size by emphasizing his ties to Puritan heritage and to an eighteenth-century transatlantic intellectual world. My tack is rather different, for it seems to me that neither contemporary scholars nor neo-orthodox interpreters have adequately addressed the issue of Edwardsian tradition. I focus on the one hundred and fifty years after Edwards's death, and, in contrast to much contemporary scholarship, my analysis enlarges Edwards's figure in American religious and cultural history. At the same time, I take issue with inflated claims, perpetuated or invented by neo-orthodox scholars, concerning the colonial awakening and Edwards's relationship to the American Revolution and to the nineteenth-century literary renaissance. While I draw on recent cultural theory, criticize some attempts to "essentialize" Edwardsian tradition, and focus on the constructed Edwards, I am not trying to invent a postmodern Edwards. Rather, and I hope more modestly, I simply want to contribute to a renewed contemporary examination of Edwards's legacy and to do so in an up-to-date, interdisciplinary way.

·   ·   ·

I want to acknowledge the support, encouragement, and assistance of a variety of individuals. Philip F. Gura took a strong interest in my work, affirmed the direction of my analysis, and urged me to send an early draft of Chapter 1 to *Early American Literature*. The essay won the Richard Beale Davis Prize for the best article in that journal for 1991. Similarly, Stephen Stein encouraged my work and provided me with the opportunity to make two presentations, including the post-banquet address, at the conference on Edwards that he organized at Indiana University. I have profited from conversations with Allen C. Guelzo about Edwardsian tradition and from the superb example of his own work. Richard D. Brown chaired two panel sessions at professional meetings, commented on papers that were early drafts of chapters of this study, and in the process encouraged the larger project. Stephen Nissenbaum participated in one of those sessions and has continually stimulated me to think about the invention of tradition. Irene Quenzler-Brown also participated in one of those sessions and made a number of helpful comments and suggestions about David Brainerd and evangelical piety that strengthened Chapter 3. Sue Gerry gave a late draft of the manuscript a careful reading, as only an ex–English teacher can. At UNC Press, from the initial review of the manuscript to final revisions, Lewis Bateman has provided encouragement and sound advice. Portions of this book have appeared in *Church History, Early American Literature, Journal of the Early Republic,* and *Religion and American Culture.* I am grateful to the editors of those journals for permission to use previously published material.

I began this study while a faculty member at one institution and completed it while holding a faculty-administrator appointment at another institution. Administrative responsibilities temporarily diverted me from Edwards. But I have benefited from working with a lively group of colleagues in building a strong interdisciplinary program at the University of Southern Maine. Ardis Cameron has been an especially stimulating colleague, and I have learned and received support from Donna Cassidy, Joel Eastman, Joseph Grange, Nathan Hamilton, Faith Harrington, Kenneth Severens, and Allan Whitmore. The University of Southern Maine also granted a sabbatical leave that enabled me to complete the book. In addition, the university has provided me with an excellent administrative assistant. Dorothy Sayer has typed and corrected countless drafts of this book and is still trying to figure out if it's Edwardsian or Edwardsean. Her patience, sense of humor, and efficiency were essential to the timely completion of this book.

Numerous librarians provided assistance, but three deserve special mention. Clifton Davis of Bangor Theological Seminary opened the holdings of Moulton Library to me, responded to my requests for photocopies of material, and answered questions about Enoch Pond and the Seminary. Harold Worthley of the Congregational Historical Society also answered numerous questions, furnished me with material, and helped me track down Puritan monuments. Elise Bernier-Feeley of the Forbes Library in Northampton is an Edwards specialist in her own right. She provided excellent advice and steered me to sources on Edwards and Northampton in the late nineteenth century.

I thank my wife, Dorothy, for her patience during my preoccupation with Edwardsianism, for her understanding of my reluctance to take a vacation until I had finished the manuscript, and for contributing so much to the quality of my life. I thank my daughter Tonia for some of the photographs in the book.

I have dedicated the book to two important men in my life, who died within one month of each other while I was still working on the manuscript. I owe both of them far more than a book dedication can possibly acknowledge.

JONATHAN EDWARDS,

RELIGIOUS TRADITION,

AMERICAN CULTURE

INTRODUCTION

• • •

EDWARDS, CULTURE, AND TRADITION

Jonathan Edwards – the name has evoked lofty appraisals of America's Augustine, America's Aquinas, and America's Kierkegaard. Most recently he has been presented as "America's theologian,"[1] a kind of white whale of American religious history. Edwards sounded the depths of human thought and experience. Moreover, his majestic, though tragic, intellectual figure has inspired a scholarly chase that has nearly inundated the academy with books, articles, and dissertations. Edwards's clerical career was cut short by his death (from a smallpox inoculation) at age fifty-four, but not before he had produced a voluminous body of unpublished writing that has provoked a kind of epic scholarly pursuit of his seemingly empyrean religious-philosophical significance.

Edwards blazed a brilliant, though largely conventional, path into one of the most prominent pulpits in mid-eighteenth-century New England. Born in East Windsor, Connecticut, in 1703, Edwards displayed his discerning intelligence at Yale, where between 1716 and 1722 he earned his bachelor's degree and completed postgraduate studies in divinity. In 1727, after an eight-month ministry in New York and an appointment as a tutor at Yale, Edwards became assistant to his grandfather, Solomon Stoddard, in Northampton, Massachusetts. Later that year he married seventeen-year-old Sarah Pierpont of New Haven, with whom he had fallen in love when she was only thirteen. Upon Stoddard's death, two years after Edwards's arrival in Northampton, the grandson became pastor of the church. In the mid-1730s, he led a series of revivals in Northampton and in other towns of the Connecticut River Valley, forerunners of a later "season of grace" that has come to be known as the Great Awakening. Edwards drew on his superior intelligence and his intense personal religious experience to defend, interpret, and publicize the spiritual authenticity of revivalistic religion. But as early as 1743, religious zeal had diminished dramatically, and the revival seemed to end suddenly, even while supporters and critics continued to wrangle over its significance.

By 1750, Edwards had so alienated his church that the members voted overwhelmingly to dismiss him. Retreating to the Indian mission at Stockbridge on the Massachusetts frontier, Edwards confronted poverty, the machinations of whites who wished to appropriate tribal lands, and missionary work for which he was ill fitted. Edwards turned to theological projects that he had started or contemplated. During his Stockbridge exile, he completed the major Calvinist works upon which his reputation as a theologian and philosopher principally rests. Summoned to the presidency of the College of New Jersey (later renamed Princeton) in 1757, Edwards died after serving less than two months.

Edwards's closest clerical followers, a small group of New Divinity men who were natives of Connecticut and graduates of Yale, edited and posthumously published some of his works; other writings were not published until the nineteenth century; and still other unpublished material has been and continues to be prepared for publication by twentieth-century scholars. The depth, complexity, and sheer volume of his writings help explain why no other figure in American religious history has been the subject of more study than Edwards. Two book-length bibliographies list hundreds of books, articles, and dissertations on Edwards.[2] Yet these bibliographies, now a decade and a half old, are already in need of supplements. Highly specialized studies examining historical, literary, philosophical, theological, and psychological aspects of Edwards's life and thought continue to roll off presses. Major works debate whether Edwards was a distinctly nationalist religious voice who believed that America was in special covenant with God or a thinker with an eighteenth-century globalist vision who embraced "one holy and happy society" under God.[3]

Yet, in spite of such an ample and ever expanding body of literature on Edwards, we have no broad assessment of his legacy for American religious and cultural history. Aspects of his thought have been traced into the early nineteenth century. The doctrine of disinterested benevolence, for instance, especially as it was reformulated by Edwards's New Divinity disciples, provided a theological underpinning for religious reform in the early republic. Revisionist historians have even begun to recognize that the

New Divinity theological movement as a whole remained a vital presence in early-nineteenth-century American religious life. Several contributors to an important recent volume of essays titled *Jonathan Edwards and the American Experience* point to nineteenth-century American evangelical culture as a fruitful field for exploring Edwardsian tradition.[4]

Still, scholarship on Edwards remains overwhelmingly concentrated on analyzing him in the context of or in relationship to the mid-eighteenth-century revivals that inspired so much of his writing. Not surprisingly, a considerable body of scholarly work has focused on the controversial problem of the contributions of Edwards and the colonial awakening to the American Revolution.[5] At the same time, literary historians have explored the theologian's legacy for the nineteenth century – though not for its evangelical culture, which developed an American literature of its own modeled on such canonical works as Edwards's *Life of David Brainerd*. Instead, scholars of American literature, following Perry Miller's lead, have continued to behold Edwards's shadow in the writings of Emerson and the mid-nineteenth-century literary renaissance.

Such lines of inquiry into the theologian's legacy have obscured how, from the Second Great Awakening to the turn of the twentieth century, Edwards's religious figure and thought were a continual, if changing, part of American cultural discourse. In 1787, nearly thirty years after the theologian's death, President Ezra Stiles of Yale dismissed Edwards's thought and his writings as fossilized remnants of a rapidly receding and archaic religious past. Edwards's works "in another generation will pass into as transient notice perhaps scarce above oblivion," Stiles observed, "and when posterity occasionally comes across them in the rubbish of Libraries, the rare characters who may read and be pleased with them will be looked upon as singular and whimsical."[6] Stiles's fact-filled and often gossipy *Literary Diary* has been cited frequently by scholars to document the dwindling influence of Edwards and his New Divinity adherents in late-eighteenth-century New England. In turn, revisionists have challenged the reliability of Stiles's perspective on his theological adversaries and have argued for the ongoing vitality of Edwardsianism in the late eighteenth century. While Stiles's comments on the feeble state of the New Divinity involved more than wishful thinking, they also represented much less than a suggestive historical guide to the debilitation of Edwardsian tradition.

Most of Stiles's critical remarks on Edwards and the New Divinity were offered in the decades before the Second Great Awakening revitalized

American religious life. Stiles died in 1795; he did not live to see, and perhaps to anguish over, the new religious authority that was invested in Edwards's thought and writings during the Second Great Awakening. The
growth of the New Divinity movement was only one aspect of the renewed
Edwardsianism stimulated by the Second Great Awakening. Much more
interesting and almost totally neglected by Edwards scholars was the way
the new wave of revivals led to the creation of Edwardsian traditions. The
Edwardsianism of the Second Great Awakening was more cultural invention than cultural recovery. Edwards's works were first canonized and
widely republished in the nineteenth, not the eighteenth, century. Moreover, the notion of the "great" colonial awakening that has become almost
universally accepted by scholars was a reification that served the cultural
and polemical needs of the leaders of the Second Great Awakening.

The creation of other Edwardsian traditions was implicated in such
moments of social transformation and their attendant cultural formation.
Consider "*the* New England theology," a powerful systematic body of doctrines derived from Edwards's thought, which has been accepted by scholars as a dogmatic tradition that proceeded by the impetus of its own intellectual energy. In fact, the term New England theology was coined and
propagated at Andover Seminary in the middle of the nineteenth century
when the first efforts were made to assemble one hundred years of theological speculation into a coherent narrative. This narrative of the New
England theology was shaped by the rise of seminaries, the professionalization of theological study, and academic contention over Edwards's doctrinal legacy. The history of the creation of the New England theology
stands as a case study in the persistence of dynamic Edwardsian and
Calvinist traditions in American culture at least down to the Civil War,
long after their alleged demise.

Even with the theological collapse of Edwardsianism and Calvinism after the Civil War, Edwards endured as a cultural figure who was central to
newly constructed narratives about America's religious past. Indeed, Yankee citizens of late-nineteenth- and early-twentieth-century Northampton
summoned Edwards to serve new cultural needs just as their civic ancestors had sought his religious direction. Edwards, as an embodiment of a
laudable, though imperfect, Puritan spirit, was memorialized in speeches
and in bronze and granite monuments. He became a Puritan cultural
icon – his figure caught up in a widespread revival of interest in the colonial past which was a heavily reactionary response to the ethnic, urban,

and industrial transformation of America that altered even relatively small communities like Northampton.

This examination of Edwards's legacy in American religious and cultural history, then, is not an analysis of the lineal unfolding of Edwardsian tradition. Neither is it, in a strict sense, a study of influence, that is, something handed continuously across time like a baton in a cultural relay race. Nor, for that matter, is it a history of Edwards as symbol and image in American culture. Rather, focusing on the publishing history and appropriation of his work, this study examines the construction of traditions around Edwards's writings, thought, and religious and cultural figure. It explores the context in which these formations emerged and the religious and cultural needs they addressed, and it examines the process by which newly created traditions were both contested and institutionalized. This study is informed by the perspectives of what has been called the "new" cultural history, which has been shaped by recent developments in literary and anthropological scholarship.[7]

A brief exploration of my understanding of "Edwardsianism," culture, and tradition will perhaps clarify the approaches employed in this work. Edwardsianism does not refer narrowly to the theologian's doctrinal legacy. Instead, I use it to examine the way in which Edwards's writings and thinking on personal piety, individual conversion, mass revivalism, *and* theology were appropriated in the nineteenth century. I have restricted the term "Edwardsians" to Congregationalists and Presbyterians for whom Edwards represented a special, direct, even denominational heritage. Of course, as we shall see, the individuals I identify as Edwardsians did not all agree on or passively accept Edwards's doctrinal positions. Indeed, this study argues that Edwards's theological legacy, like the larger religious tradition to which it was attached, emerged as complex, ambiguous, and contested, not monolithic, fixed, stable, and consensual. "Edwardsians" refers to Congregationalist and Presbyterian leaders who either helped create or who accepted and attempted to come to terms with Edwards's new authority on personal piety, revivalism, and theology during the Second Great Awakening. Thus, Nathanael Emmons, Lyman Beecher, Edwards A. Park, Charles Hodge, and Mary Lyon were all Edwardsians, though they did not uniformly accept Edwards's doctrinal positions. Still, they contributed to the creation, institutionalization, and perpetuation of a powerful Edwardsian tradition. Furthermore, it was from this nineteenth-century religious tradition – not an earlier Puritanism and

Calvinism – that such prominent mid-Victorians as Harriet Beecher Stowe, Henry Ward Beecher, and Emily Dickinson sought emancipation.

While the label "Edwardsian" is restricted to Congregationalists and Presbyterians, Edwardsianism – that is, Edwards's authority and the use of his writings – extended to Methodists and Baptists. John Wesley, Bishop Francis Asbury, and other Methodist leaders, for example, admired and invoked the authority of Edwards, not as a Calvinist theologian, but as a man of deep personal piety and of seasoned wisdom on individual conversion and mass revivalism. I refer to the "Methodization" of Edwards to describe such selective appropriation of his thought and writings – an appropriation that responded to the evangelical needs of the Second Great Awakening and that shaped the Congregational-Presbyterian construction and use of Edwardsian tradition.

It is tempting to approach Edwardsianism as a cultural system, but this study adopts a post-Geertzian conception of culture. Over the last two decades, Clifford Geertz himself – like Edwards during the Second Great Awakening – has become a canonical authority, whose thought has informed or garnished numerous scholarly studies, including histories of American religion.[8] "All experience," Geertz has argued, "is construed experience." Culture consists of a coherent world view – a system of interdependent values, symbols, rituals, and social arrangements that give meaning to experience. In a well-known summation of his approach to culture, Geertz observed that "man is an animal suspended in webs of significance he himself has spun." Such a perspective encourages the scholarly observer to practice "thick description," that is, to uncover the layers of meaning embedded in symbolic behavior and social arrangements and to "read" these "texts" in relationship to the cultural system of which they are part.[9]

Geertz's semiotic understanding of culture helped make social history more cultural; textualizing social experience encouraged quantitative history to become more anthropological. Thick description offered historians a methodology for accomplishing this end. Moreover, Geertz's practice of thick description and his interpretation of culture as a system of meaning appealed across disciplinary lines as historians, anthropologists, and literary scholars took up his ideas and methods. However, Geertz's views and methods have also been subjected to criticism.

Geertz largely ignored the process of constructing meaning or the history of cultural production. In Geertz's work, historian Aletta Biersack has argued, "Meaning is described, never derived." [10] Geertz's view of systems of meaning represents a rather static and consensual view of culture that ignores the ideological origins and use of cultural meaning. Geertz fails to historicize his notion of culture. He does not sufficiently acknowledge, as Lynn Hunt has suggested, that a cultural system is the "product of historically contingent discursive formations." [11] Furthermore, the failure to historicize leaves culture as a kind of fixed, holistic, expressive object waiting to be decoded rather than as an emergent, constructed, and contested historical process of establishing meaning. Geertz's work reveals what anthropologist James Clifford identifies as a "bias toward wholeness, continuity and growth" in a concept of culture that originated in the late nineteenth century. Such a concept has difficulty incorporating "complex historical processes of appropriation, compromise, subversion, masking, invention, and revival." [12]

Geertz's important insights and his understanding of culture as imbuing experience with meaning need to be modified rather than abandoned. A more historical, contextual, and instrumental understanding of "culture in action" [13] would address many of the shortcomings of Geertz's lines of inquiry. Culture is not a seamless web of meaning; it is a historically contingent and constructed "partial truth." [14] Culture is the product of a dynamic historical process in which a selective interpretation of meaning is reified and naturalized as the "whole" truth. Such a process of constructing or producing meaning is the result of moments of cultural formation – periods when meaning is both created and contested. Since culture is a historically constructed artifact, the meaning and order it imposes on experience is always partial, incomplete, and likely to encounter resistance. Moreover, cultural formation is a historically dynamic process; meaning is continually invented and reinvented to meet new needs. In short, a historical, instrumental approach to culture examines the emergence and use of cultural "truths," not just their semiotic system of meaning or structure of signs.

Tradition, too, is historically constructed, contingent, negotiated, and instrumental, and not an autonomous, lineal evolution of meaning that is passively received as part of a cultural system. "The roots of tradition," James Clifford has remarked, "are cut and retied . . . ; they live by pollination, by (historical) transplanting." [15] Recent literary scholars who work under the rubric of the "new historicism" have especially contributed to an understanding of culture in action and of the invention and reinven-

tion of traditions. These scholars have analyzed the history of canon formation and the way literature or "high culture" is enmeshed in social relations and in decidedly nonliterary, material processes of cultural production. New historicists have also shown how literary traditions are often the
result of recent periods of cultural formation and not the outgrowth of a
long history or of a lineal trajectory.[16]

Such studies reinforce the notion that tradition, like culture, is tempo-
ral and emergent, constructed and contested, and significant not only for
its meaning, but also for its historical creation and use. Traditions are generated, mediated, and maintained by institutions and individuals, who
function as "cultural custodians" and "guardians" of the past.[17] There is a
social history behind the creation and use of tradition. "The past, however
worthy, does not survive by its own intrinsic power," literary historian
Richard Brodhead has written. Tradition is recovered, invented, and reinvented by individuals in response to cultural needs. But tradition is sustained by incorporating "itself into an institution – a transpersonal or cultural structure that can carry it forward from its first rememberers and
establish it in the understandings of others through time."[18]

This study, then, is a cultural history of Edwardsian traditions in action. It examines the publishing history and appropriation of Edwards's
works and the creation of Edwardsian religious traditions between the
Second Great Awakening and the bicentennial of the theologian's birth in
1903. These traditions emerged in moments of cultural formation and
as a response to interpretive needs. The revivalistic controversies of the
Second Great Awakening, the rise of seminaries and the professionalization of theological study, and the ethnic and religious transformation of
post–Civil War America all generated Edwardsian traditions that attempted to impose interpretive order on the past and thus contain the
disorder of the present. The creation and transmission of these traditions
coincided with the emergence of new cultural institutions, organs, and
rituals: tract societies, religious presses, seminaries, theological journals,
historical and literary textbooks, historical societies, and commemorative
celebrations. The social history behind cultural activity reminds one that
knowledge of the origin and use of tradition is essential for a historical understanding of its meaning.

My examination of Edwards's cultural and religious legacy historicizes
texts like the *Life of Brainerd* and explores how historical traditions and
narratives, such as the notion of the "great" colonial awakening, have been

"textualized." [19] The analysis of Edwardsian tradition begins with the Second Great Awakening, during which conservative and radical revivalists appealed to the colonial revivals to legitimate their religious activities. In the process, an Edwardsian revivalistic tradition was codified and contested, and the colonial revivals were transformed into the "Great Awakening" – the magisterial historical event of religious legend.

The Second Great Awakening also witnessed a kind of "reinvention" of Edwards as a founding father of evangelical America's emerging benevolent empire of revivalism, piety, and reform. Chapter 2 examines the broad revitalization of Edwards's cultural and religious authority that paralleled the "invention" of the Great Awakening. In particular, leaders of the Second Great Awakening tended to "Methodize" Edwards for a lay audience; they republished and widely distributed Edwards's works of practical divinity, not his dogmatic texts. Chapter 3 discusses the publishing history and nineteenth-century religious appropriation of Edwards's most popular inspirational work of practical divinity. The popularity of the *Life of Brainerd* reflected the Methodization of Edwardsianism; but the text, with its heroic account of disinterested, self-denying benevolence, was also used to contain populist and perfectionist impulses in antebellum evangelical culture.

The Edwardsian missionary tradition and religious culture of self-sacrifice that the *Life of Brainerd* underwrote found an especially receptive audience at both Mary Lyon's Mount Holyoke Seminary and at the New Divinity–dominated Andover Seminary. Chapter 4 examines how Mount Holyoke evolved as a sort of evangelical nunnery where Lyon institutionalized Edwardsian revivalism and social ethics. Under Lyon's direction, Mount Holyoke emerged as a "sister" institution to Andover Theological Seminary, America's oldest – and the mid-nineteenth-century's largest – postgraduate divinity school. The Edwardsian religious culture and influence of Andover, however, differed in at least one major way from the work of Mount Holyoke. More than any other institution, Andover contributed to the nineteenth-century torrent of publications – the paper war of words – that scrutinized Edwards's theology. Chapter 5 focuses on Andover and the historical work of its preeminent authority on Edwardsian theological tradition, Edwards A. Park. As the distinguished Abbot Professor at Andover, Park organized the theology of Edwards and his New Divinity followers into a coherent historical narrative – the first "genetic" doctrinal history of Edwardsianism. Park's work reveals the contours and texture of a rich, complex academic Edwardsian Calvinist culture that persisted through the middle of the nineteenth century and that coexisted with a more Methodized, popular Edwardsianism.

Even during the post-Calvinist and postrevival decades after the Civil War, Edwards remained a central figure in American culture. Chapter 6 analyzes how late-nineteenth-century "colonial revivalists" created a usable Puritan past that reserved a prominent place for Edwards. The famous theologian and revivalist was recast into a de-Calvinized cultural icon – a kind of totemic figure in heavily nativist colonial revival narratives explaining the Anglo-Puritan origins of American culture. Historic anniversaries, like the bicentennial of Edwards's birth in 1903, culturally licensed nostalgic, filiopietistic reassessments of Puritan tradition – including the intellectuality, sense of duty, and "manliness" of its most formidable representative.

Over the three decades following the bicentennial of his birth, however, Edwards was relegated to the margins of American cultural discourse. Progressive Era reformers and interpreters of America's past devised new narratives that met the cultural needs of the present by devaluing the role of religion in general, and of Puritanism in particular, as nation-shaping forces. As the Epilogue suggests, the cultural and hermeneutic demise of religious, Puritan, and Edwardsian narratives during the Progressive Era set the stage for a neo-orthodox "recovery" beginning in the 1930s. Yet neo-orthodox reinterpreters overreacted to their immediate Progressive predecessors. As a result, the putative neo-orthodox recovery of Edwards tended to portray him as an isolated genius, who was betrayed even by his closest theological followers. Edwards reemerged as a great, but tragic and essentially traditionless, figure in American cultural history. It should not be surprising, then, that twentieth-century scholars have overlooked the vital nineteenth-century Edwardsian traditions that this study examines.

1

· · ·

INVENTING THE GREAT AWAKENING

EDWARDSIAN REVIVALISTIC TRADITION FROM

THE NEW DIVINITY TO NEW MEASURES

The religious outburst known as the Second Great Awakening began in the 1790s, ebbed and flowed for the next generation, swelled into an emotional tidal wave in the early 1830s, and persisted at least down to 1840, the centennial of the start of America's colonial awakening. A diverse, complex, and transformative religious movement, the Second Great Awakening has been the focus of some of the most important recent work in American religious history. No longer viewed by most historians as a clergy-inspired campaign of social control, the revival has been explained variously as an institution-building process, a cultural revitalization movement, a women's awakening, a shopkeeper's millennium, and a democratizing upheaval, to identify some influential interpretations. Such lines of analysis posit that the Awakening marked a sharp break with the past, as evangelical Protestantism responded to an emergent capitalist industrial order, democratic culture, and expansive frontier. It has even been suggested that the Awakening promoted a Jeffersonian "disdain" for tradition and "for the past as a repository of wisdom."[1]

In the course of the new awakening, however, leaders and participants came to possess an acute historical consciousness, not simply a forward-looking millennial expectation and a democratic distrust of religious and cultural authorities. Historians have not examined how the Second Great Awakening provoked a significant, and sometimes acrimonious, debate over *the* American revivalistic tradition – a debate that constituted a major cultural response to the kind of democratic changes that are described so effectively in accounts of the revival.[2] Leaders of and participants in the Second Great Awakening ransacked the annals of colonial revivalism, with important consequences for successive historical understanding of the First Great Awakening. Second Great Awakeners created an Edwardsian revivalistic tradition; in fact, they reified the colonial awakening into a "great," general, and formative event. Not surprisingly, this line of interpretation has proved to be persistently troubling in modern historiography of the eighteenth century. Perhaps no other American religious episode and few other political-military events have been asked to carry the interpretive freight that historians have loaded on the First Great Awakening. It has been viewed as the opening round of the American Revolution, as marking the birth of American nationalism, and as furnishing the religious catalyst for American individualism, to cite some familiar examples.[3]

Jon Butler has suggested recently that this historically entrenched notion of the colonial awakening as a "great," general, and transformative event is an "interpretative fiction" that began in the late nineteenth century and was extended by twentieth-century historians.[4] Such an analysis, however, ignores the critical role of Second Great Awakeners in reifying the colonial revival and creating an Edwardsian revivalistic tradition. If the Great Awakening is an interpretive fiction, as Butler has argued, it originated as a cultural production of the Second Great Awakening, not as a historiographical development of the late nineteenth and the twentieth centuries. The invention of the Great Awakening was initiated by New England–based New Divinity clerical disciples of Jonathan Edwards, who were tied either directly, or through their theological teachers, to the era of the colonial revivals. At the outset of the Second Great Awakening, New Divinity men launched a process of historical interpretation and cultural containment that would be continued by other evangelicals – invoking the social memory, cultural authority, and sacred texts of the past to respond to the democratizing changes and revivalistic conflicts of the present. In the early nineteenth century, conservative Presbyterian leaders joined Edwardsian Congregationalists in creating an American revivalistic tradition. Then, with the rise of Charles Grandison Finney and his controversial new-measures revivalism in the 1820s and 1830s, this influential Edwardsian "Presbygational" alliance used a burgeoning religious periodical press, as well as the institutions and publication organs of the newly established benevolent empire, to invoke the past against their revivalistic foes. The "paper war" over new measures produced a richly textured interpretation of colonial revivalism. By reissuing works from the era of the colonial awakening and by publishing historical accounts and biographical studies that extended the New Divinity's interpretation of an "American" revivalistic tradition, Presbygational leaders, in their attempt to resolve contemporary religious controversies, invested the colonial revival with enormous cultural authority.

.   .   .

Unlike modern historians, commentators on and participants in the mid-eighteenth-century revivals did not conceive of or describe them as a "great" and "general" intercolonial awakening – and for good reason. In different corners of colonial America revivals began and reached a peak of religious intensity in a decidedly unsynchronized way, sometimes even decades apart. Virginia, for example, did not experience an upsurge of revivalism until the 1750s and 1760s, long after religious ardor had waned in New England. More than half the colonies experienced nothing more than occasional revivalism at any time during the era of the so-called great awakening. In addition, where significant revivalism did occur, its religious sources varied from homegrown Calvinism in New England to German pietism and other international influences in the Middle Colonies. It was primarily in New England that revivals occurred in a timely, regionally connected, and partially coordinated way that approximates the conception of a "great" awakening. Still, even in New England, Jonathan Edwards applied the terms "great awakening" or "general awakening" to the Northampton revivals of 1734–35, not to subsequent revivals or to an intercolonial religious movement.[5] The notion of "the Great Awakening" may be understood as a product of New England's cultural imperialism – the way in which the American colonial experience came to be viewed, during the first half of the nineteenth century, as regional history writ large. The historical reification of the colonial revivals and of New England's religious experience into a great, general, and transformative historical episode was a cultural production of the Second Great Awakening that was set in motion by Edwards's New Divinity disciples.

The commencement of the Second Great Awakening usually is dated to the local revivals that revitalized Connecticut churches in the 1790s. "I saw a continued succession of heavenly sprinklings . . . in Connecticut," New Divinity minister Edward Dorr Griffin observed, "until in 1799, I could

stand at my door in New Hartford . . . and number fifty or sixty congregations laid down in one field of divine wonders, and as many more in different parts of New England."[6] Griffin and other Connecticut New Divinity ministers were not only in the forefront of the local revivals that
inaugurated the Second Great Awakening; they also provided the leadership for the *Connecticut Evangelical Magazine*, the Connecticut Missionary
Society, and the moral society movement within the state. The memory of
the behavioral excesses of the colonial awakening encouraged New Divinity ministers to channel and institutionalize the religious fervor stimulated
by the revivals into socially constructive activities.[7]

Moreover, the prominence of New Divinity ministers in the Connecticut revivals contradicts what many historians have described as the evangelical debility of Edwards's closest theological disciples. New Divinity
ministers have been accused of betraying Edwards's evangelicalism by re-
fusing to heed his warning that the laity "did not so much need to have
their heads stored, as to have their hearts touched."[8] The New Divinity
men, it is often argued, became arid scholastics who overintellectualized
the vital piety of the colonial awakening – an assessment of these religious
quislings that was captured by a mid-nineteenth-century opponent who
penned a composite historical portrait of the Connecticut minister of old:
"He was utterly inaccessible to the graces of life; no bird ever sung in his
ear; no flower ever bloomed for his eye. . . . Staggering through life with a
great burden of theologies on his back, which it was his constant burden to
pack into smaller and smaller compasses, let us hope that the burden, like
that of a Christian, slipped away before he entered the celestial presence."[9]
Yet, Edwards's New Divinity disciples embraced the Second Great Awakening and brought to it an acute consciousness of their historical bonds
with revivalism in general and the colonial awakening in particular.

Joseph Bellamy embodied one crucial link between the two awakenings
in New England and helped New Divinity ministers fashion and appropriate an American revivalistic tradition. Though he stands with Samuel
Hopkins and David Brainerd as one of Edwards's closest disciples, Bellamy
has been something of a neglected figure in American religious history.
Unlike Hopkins, Brainerd, and other disciples of Edwards, Bellamy's contributions to nineteenth-century evangelical culture were not primarily in
theology, or personal piety, or religious reform. Rather, Bellamy emerged
as a central historical figure in the American revivalistic tradition that was
created by leaders of the Second Great Awakening in New England.

Bellamy graduated from Yale in 1735, a sixteen-year-old youth from Cheshire, Connecticut. Shortly after graduation, he experienced conversion and began studying for the ministry. In 1736, he made a pilgrimage to Northampton, Massachusetts, where he boarded with the Edwards family and studied theology under the leader of the "frontier" revival of the mid-1730s. His residency in Northampton, though lasting only several months, inspired his later efforts as an Edwardsian teacher and revivalist. Licensed to preach in 1737, Bellamy was called to Bethlehem, Connecticut, the following year and permanently installed as minister in 1740. He remained with his church until his death fifty years later, came to be known as the "Pope of Litchfield County," and was recalled by the leaders of the Second Great Awakening in New England for the judicious revivalism, the ecclesiastical order, and the pastoral stability that characterized his ministry.[10]

Bellamy also was remembered as the most popular teacher of clerical aspirants in New England during the second half of the eighteenth century. Drawing on his experience with Edwards in Northampton, Bellamy welcomed ministerial candidates to his "school of the prophets." He even erected a two-room "Log College," which provided classroom space, while the third floor of his parsonage served as a dormitory. Between 1750 and the revolutionary era, Bellamy instructed approximately sixty ministers, many of whom established their own schools of the prophets modeled after their teacher's. Consequently, New Divinity followers of Edwards and Bellamy dominated postgraduate clerical preparation in Connecticut from the middle of the eighteenth century down to the formation of the Yale Divinity School in 1822.[11]

Bellamy furnished an influential Edwardsian evangelical role model for the numerous students he trained. Unlike some of the metaphysical preachers of the New Divinity movement, Bellamy followed Edwards in distinguishing the work of the study from that of the pulpit, the purpose of the written word from that of the spoken word. Bellamy adhered to his mentor's view that ministers ought to preach extemporaneously, using only brief sermon notes. He achieved recognition as one of the outstanding preachers of mid-eighteenth-century New England, frequently compared with Edwards and George Whitefield. Virtually all contemporary assessments of his preaching agree that he was "to be reckoned among the sons of thunder," and that he spoke "with a prodigious voice, a vivid imagination, great flow of language, and rarely failed to secure an honest attention."[12] As a result of his reputation, Bellamy continued to receive invitations to preach long after the colonial revivals had subsided. Many of these requests were from former students who sought his help in starting or continuing a local revival.

Since he died in 1790, Bellamy did not live to see his students (and their students) assume the leadership of the Second Great Awakening in Connecticut and other parts of New England. Nor did he live to hear them invoke his name and revivalistic record to secure their historical ties to and legitimize their claims on the revivalistic legacy of Edwards and the colonial awakening. As one New England partisan proclaimed in the face of Charles G. Finney's revivalistic practices, "What measures and means have succeeded [are] substantively the same as were employed by Edwards, and Bellamy, and Brainard [sic], about a century ago." [13]

Beginning in the 1790s, well before the emergence of Finney and new measures, New Divinity ministers' personal and secondhand recollections of the colonial revivals were revivified by new outbursts of evangelical piety. In fact, the start of the Second Great Awakening transmuted individual recollections of the colonial revivals into social memory – group pictures of the past that wielded interpretive power over the present. In New England, Edwards's influential New Divinity disciples viewed the Second Great Awakening from the perspective of the images, personalities, conflicts, and texts – the social memory – of the colonial revivals.[14] Even before local revivals swept through Connecticut churches in the late 1790s, New Divinity ministers not only announced the start of a new awakening, but they also reestablished the concert of prayer that had been proposed by Edwards fifty years earlier. Meeting in Lebanon, Connecticut, in 1794, and directly invoking the memory and authority of Edwards, a group of New Divinity ministers agreed that, beginning in January 1795, two o'clock on the first Tuesday of the four quarters of the year would be set aside for a concert of prayer in support of the new awakening. Adopting tactics of the Revolutionary resistance movement, the ministers proceeded to issue circular letters and to establish a committee of correspondence to promote the concert. At the same time Edwards's *Humble Attempt to Promote Explicit Agreement and Visible Union of God's People, in Extraordinary Prayer, for the Revival of Religion and the Advancement of Christ's Kingdom on Earth*, which had encouraged the concert of prayer in 1747, was reissued along with other Edwardsian and New Divinity works from the era of the colonial awakening (including Bellamy's treatise on *The Millennium*). In addition, the promoters of the new awakening began to publish biographical material on Edwards and on important Edwardsian disciples from the era of the colonial revivals, such as David Brainerd.[15] Thus, at the outset of the Second Great Awakening, New Divinity leaders began an interpretive process that continued into subsequent phases of the revival: invoking the past to explain the present and anticipate the future.

New Divinity preachers exploited historical and theological ties to the era of the colonial awakening to appropriate a revivalistic legacy, which they defined as a tradition of sober, clerical-directed, local revivals. Such an interpretation deradicalized the revivalistic legacy of Edwards and the mid-eighteenth-century awakening and enabled New Divinity preachers to contrast colonial tradition with the "disorderly" Kentucky frontier revivals that marked the beginning of the Southern phase of the Second Great Awakening at the turn of the century. Personal claims on the past also encouraged New Divinity men to use the authority of history against a more localized threat: the invasion of Methodist preachers into New England that began when Bishop Francis Asbury sent Jesse Lee to Connecticut in 1789. By the 1790s, Methodist itinerants were leading revivals in Congregational churches, and some members of the Standing Order began to adopt Methodist revival tactics. Samuel Goodrich recalled that his father, who was the Congregational pastor in Fairfield, Connecticut, organized evening meetings at church and then at private houses. "No doubt, also, he put more fervor into his Sabbath discourses," Goodrich noted. "Deacons and laymen, gifted in speech, were called upon to pray and exhort, and tell experiences in the private meetings, which were now called conferences. A revival of religious spirit arose even among the orthodox. . . . Thus orthodoxy was in considerable degree methodized, and Methodism in due time orthodoxed." [16] New Divinity leaders summoned the authority of the past to resist, or at least moderate, the Methodization of evangelical Congregationalism. On the one hand, Edwards's disciples "New Englandized" the colonial revivals, defining their essence in terms of a tradition of temperate, locally based, institutionally mediated revivalism that was compatible with the socioreligious culture of the emergent white Federal villages of post-Revolutionary New England. On the other hand, Edwards's disciples originated the now historically entrenched notion that the colonial awakening was a "great," "general," and transformative event.[17]

The New Divinity's line of analysis was connected to larger processes of New England cultural interpretation in the early republic. The simultaneous reification and deradicalization (or de-Methodization) of the colonial awakening paralleled broader Federalist efforts not only to derevolutionize the Revolution but to find alternative, less problematic formative events in the colonial past. On this level, the reification of the colonial awakening was related to such developments as the invention of the Pilgrims and the transformation of the founding of Plymouth Colony into a major historical event from which the American republic germinated. Indeed, at the height of the Second Great Awakening, Lyman Beecher established a pro-revival journal, the *Spirit of the Pilgrims*, which fashioned a filiopietistic interpretation of New England and American religious history that consistently linked the mid-eighteenth-century forefathers of American revivalism to the founders and spiritual ideals of Plymouth Colony.[18]

Well before such filiopietistic lines of interpretation were fully developed, New Divinity ministers used the *Connecticut Evangelical Magazine*, one of the major organs of the New England phase of the Second Great Awakening, to stake out a claim to the "temperate" and judicious revivalism of the mid-eighteenth century. The *Connecticut Evangelical Magazine* offered its readers not only carefully edited contemporary revival narratives, but also a perspective on the historical importance and relevance of the colonial awakening. In 1808, for instance, two issues of this monthly examined the "Life and Character of Rev. Jonathan Edwards." Northampton was depicted as the epicenter of both the "very great awakening" of the mid-1730s and the "very great revival" of the 1740s. While Edwards avoided learned sermons, the *Connecticut Evangelical Magazine* writer stressed, he did not resort to Methodistical, camp meeting tactics to awaken his audience: "He had a happy faculty of treating the most important subjects in such a way as to be familiar to the most common understanding, without descending beneath the dignity of the pulpit, or debasing the subject by vulgarity of style." Moreover, in his authoritative writings on revivalism, Edwards strove to combat "vulgar" preaching and its attendant religious enthusiasm which "gave an occasion of reproach to adversaries."[19]

In historical accounts and sermons, New Divinity ministers extended the line of interpretation advanced by the *Connecticut Evangelical Magazine*. For example, in the second volume of his influential *Complete History of Connecticut, Civil and Ecclesiastical*, which was published in 1818, New Divinity minister Benjamin Trumbull devoted a chapter of well over a hundred pages to the colonial awakening. He attempted to show how

Connecticut's leadership of the Second Great Awakening represented a historical continuation of colonial revivalism. In the First Awakening, as in the Second, Trumbull argued, "Connecticut was more remarkably the seat of the work than any part of New England or the American colonies." In the "great and general" awakening of the 1740s, Trumbull noted, Edwards recorded some of his most impressive successes in Connecticut.[20]

Trumbull heaped praise not only on Edwards, but also on Joseph Bellamy, whose students dominated the *Connecticut Evangelical Magazine*, the Connecticut Missionary Society, the moral society movement within the state, and the efforts to revive the concert of prayer. Through his students, Bellamy provided a direct and personal connection to the era of the colonial awakening. Not surprisingly, Trumbull singled out Bellamy's contributions to the mid-eighteenth-century revivals. What Edwards introduced in Connecticut, Bellamy sustained and extended, "Preaching in neighboring towns and societies . . . in all parts of the colony." Unlike the unlettered preachers of Trumbull's era, however, neither Bellamy, Edwards, nor their revivalistic coworkers achieved popularity at the expense of religious decorum and clerical dignity. "They were not noisy preachers," Trumbull asserted, "but grave, sentimental, searching, and pungent."[21]

Trumbull took special note of the most famous sermon to emerge from the colonial awakening – Edwards's single most anthologized work in American literature textbooks that has fixed the imagery of the revival as a transforming religious convulsion. In contrast to many modern interpreters of "Sinners in the Hands of an Angry God," however, Trumbull claimed that Edwards calmly read the sermon in a level voice; when members of the audience began to express their spiritual distress, "the preacher was obliged to speak to the people and desire silence, that he might be heard."[22] Edwards's performance, Trumbull suggested, differed drastically from the intemperate preaching of individuals such as James Davenport, who was banished from Connecticut in 1742, and nineteenth-century Methodist itinerants. These rabid revivalists profaned the sober eloquence and respectable evangelical practices and traditions that Edwards and Bellamy nurtured, according to Trumbull. Religious enthusiasm was a vexing, but only minor, aspect of colonial revivalism, particularly in Connecticut. Yet, opponents of evangelical religion, most notably Charles Chauncy, magnified the intemperance of the colonial awakening and helped to undermine it. For Trumbull, then, the local, orderly, institutionally mediated revivalism of Connecticut's Second Great Awakening constituted nothing less than a reenactment of the colonial revival and a continuation of Edwardsian tradition.[23]

Thus, Trumbull and other New Divinity leaders initiated the transformation of the colonial awakening's place in American historical consciousness from personal recollection, to social memory, to full-fledged, if partisan, interpretation of a heroic past.[24] The colonial revival emerged for the first time as a great, general, and formative event. It had retarded the growth of purely moralistic, rational religion, promoted preaching that recognized the importance of religious affections, introduced a generation of Americans to revivalism, and produced sacred texts. In sum, New Divinity men asserted, the colonial revival (or more precisely the New England experience) not only established the historical precedents for the Second Great Awakening, but it also represented the "traditionality" against which contemporary religious events were to be judged.

The New Divinity's perspective on the past was not simply constituted and propagated through historical accounts, religious periodicals, sermons, and reprints of works from the era of the colonial revival. The invention of the Great Awakening became institutionalized at Andover Seminary, America's first postgraduate theological school. Dominated by the New Divinity at its founding in 1808, Andover remained a receptive and important center of Edwardsianism throughout the Second Great Awakening. Both within its official curriculum and its noncurricular religious culture, Andover introduced hundreds of future leaders of the "benevolent empire" to the historical importance of the colonial awakening and contributed to the canonization of key Edwardsian texts, such as the *Personal Narrative*, the *Life of David Brainerd*, and the *Religious Affections*.[25] Andover and its graduates participated in what Nathan Hatch has called the rise of a democratic religious print culture during the Second Great Awakening. Hatch has argued that the religious press "swiftly became a sword of democracy, fueling ardent faith in the future of the American republic." The popular press decentralized religious authority, undermined respect for tradition, education, and station, and elevated populist leaders to "equal footing with Jonathan Edwards or Timothy Dwight."[26] Such an interpretation ignores the way mainline evangelical leaders invoked the past, created a revivalistic tradition, and canonized "classic" religious texts as a response to the religious populism that was stimulated by the Second Great Awakening. The religious press and a popular print culture were as central to the invention of religious tradition as Hatch claims they were to the democratization of religious authority during the Second Great Awakening.

.   .   .

New England Edwardsians entered the decade of the 1820s with a clear vision of their historical descent and with confidence in their ability to use "traditional" revival practices to redeem the young republic. And then Charles Grandison Finney arrived to rescue souls and to reclaim the American revivalistic tradition from his opponents. In the 1820s and 1830s, the controversy over Finney's new-measures revivalism gave increased momentum to the reification of the colonial awakening. Presbyterian opponents of Finney, who saw in him the transmigration of James Davenport, joined New England Congregationalists in extending the kind of cultural construction of a revivalistic tradition that had been underway since the start of the Second Great Awakening. Indeed, at no time before or after the 1820s and 1830s did the colonial awakening loom so large in the Presbygational historical imagination. Even the iconoclastic Finney, in the flush of his most impressive evangelical successes, felt compelled to come to terms with, rather than dismiss, the historical authority of what he acknowledged was "the great revival in the days of President Edwards." [27]

The story of the rise of Finney and new-measures revivalism is well known. After a transforming conversion experience in Adams, New York, in 1821, Finney abandoned a legal career, was ordained as a Presbyterian home missionary, and began traveling by horseback among the towns that would soon comprise a "burned-over district." By the mid-1820s, Finney's remarkably successful preaching announced that the Second Great Awakening had entered a new phase. "If I had had a sword in my hand," Finney reported, "I could not have cut them off . . . as fast as they fell." [28] To the scores of transplanted New Englanders and others who composed his local audiences in western New York, Finney offered familiar Calvinistic images of a stern God and of the horrors of hell reminiscent of the preaching of his native Connecticut. But, while he framed his message in traditional Calvinistic imagery, he also seemed to democratize the morphology of conversion; Finney dwelled on the importance of individual moral initiative and the role of free will in the conversion process.

Finney, like extraordinarily successful revivalists before and after him, inspired emulation. Other revivalists joined him not only in preaching a

new theology, but also in popularizing controversial revival practices that
were dismissed derisively as new measures by opponents: protracted
prayer meetings, identifying sinners by name, using an "anxious seat" for
awakened sinners, denouncing ministerial opponents, and permitting
women to pray and exhort in the presence of men. Such practices encouraged groaning, shouting, fainting, and other indecorous behavior that
threatened the socially respectable tradition of revivalism that New England Congregationalists in particular had been forging since the start of
the Second Great Awakening. For both New Englanders and Old School
Presbyterians, Finneyism was perceived as a menacing frontier revival invasion of mainline evangelical Protestantism.[29] A Presbygational historical
script linked new measures to Methodist revivalism, frontier camp meetings, and the emotional excesses of the colonial awakening. Only the Unitarian cause, it was feared, would profit from the emotional indulgence of
evangelical Protestantism.

At New Lebanon, New York, in the summer of 1827, Lyman Beecher,
conservative revivalist Asahel Nettleton, and Presbygationalists from New
England and New York, who saw themselves as the heirs to an Edwardsian
evangelical tradition, appealed to Finney and the westerners to moderate
their revival practices and to restrain the "disorderly" social behavior that
new measures encouraged. Finney and his supporters, emboldened by
success, remained resolutely committed to their brand of revivalism. In
the aftermath of the New Lebanon conference, Beecher and Nettleton
published their sharply critical *Letters . . . on the "New Measures" in Conducting Revivals of Religion* (1828).[30]

Again, most of the foregoing is well known, as is the fact that Finney
represented the birth of "modern" revivalism − a recognition of the
human role in "getting up" a revival. What has not received adequate
attention is the way in which new-measures revivalism provoked a major
cultural debate over *the* American revival tradition − a debate that
contributed to the ongoing reification of the colonial awakening. Even
Finney, who so defiantly assaulted the religious "tradition of the elders,"
did not feel free to reject either Jonathan Edwards or colonial tradition.[31]
Far from initiating a radical departure from colonial revivalism, Finney
employed historical revisionism to modernize Edwards and to extend the
revival tradition that had been constructed concurrently with the invention of the "great" awakening.

In the year before the dramatic confrontation with Finney at New

Lebanon in July of 1827, the New Englanders had worked privately, through correspondence and personal contacts, to form a Presbygational alliance with New Yorkers against new-measures revivalism and to persuade Finney to reconsider his practices.[32] A shared historical perspective on the Edwardsian revivalistic tradition, as well as the perceived social threat of new measures, fostered the Presbygational counteroffensive. Finney, so defiant toward contemporary religious leaders, found himself inadequately prepared to deal with historical authority. The Reverend Silas Aiken of Utica, where Finney had led a revival in late 1826, reported to Lyman Beecher a few months before the New Lebanon conference that the controversial revivalist had begun to change his ways. "I apprehend that reading those very quotations which you make from Edwards on Revivals was the means of his reformation," Aiken observed. "Until he came to my house (at Utica) he had never read the book, and here it was frequently in his hands during the revival; also other volumes of the great writer; and he often spoke of them with rapture."[33] But Finney did not passively accept his opponents' exegesis of Scripture or their interpretation of history. As early as the Utica revival of December 1826, he began a revisionist process of reconciling Edwards and the legacy of the colonial awakening with new-measures revivalism. Drawing on *Some Thoughts Concerning the Present Revival of Religion in New England* (1742), Edwards's reaffirmation of the authenticity of the colonial revival against critics of its emotional excesses, and on the *Religious Affections* (1746), Finney justified his emotional appeals as necessary in the face of a ministry "at ease in Zion" and wedded to formal, uninspired preaching.[34] During the late 1820s and early 1830s, the meridian of the Second Great Awakening, Finney developed and sharpened his revisionist historical perspective; then, in the phenomenally successful *Lectures on Revivals*, he announced his reclamation of the Edwardsian and American revivalistic tradition.

Between the New Lebanon conference in 1827 and the publication of *Lectures on Revivals* in 1835, the Presbygational alliance conducted a "paper war" over new measures which produced detailed accounts of Edwards and colonial revivalism that compelled Finney to construct his own revisionist interpretation. The era of the colonial awakening provided the major historical arena for the Presbygationalist-Finney debate over religious tradition. The contending parties turned to the past to understand and resolve the religious controversies of the present. "If ministers would read Edwards once a year," a Presbyterian critic of new measures contended, "all the controversy would come to an end."[35] Appeals to the authority of the past, however, only produced competing social memories of the colonial awakening that mirrored and reinforced the conflicts of the present.

At the same time, the often acrimonious debate over an American revivalistic tradition during the 1820s and 1830s abetted the continuing reification of the "great" colonial awakening. As they reissued Edwardsian works from the era of the colonial revivals and published historical accounts and biographical studies that extended the New Divinity's interpretation of an American revivalistic tradition, Presbygationalist leaders contributed to a rhetorical torrent that endowed the eighteenth-century awakening with extraordinary historical significance and cultural authority. Edwards and "many other of the holiest and greatest men whose labors have blessed the church," Presbyterian historian William B. Sprague claimed in 1832, produced "a succession of revivals" in the middle of the eighteenth century that "caused the wilderness to blossom as the rose, and the desert to put on the appearance of the garden of the Lord." Yale's Noah Porter agreed that the colonial awakening was "rapid, powerful, and extensive, beyond example in this or almost any country." Samuel Miller, Presbyterian biographer of Edwards, reflected that not only were "Many thousands of souls . . . brought into the Kingdom of Christ" during the colonial awakening, but a new "impulse and aspect [were] given to the church in American colonies."[36]

The Presbygationalists went on to assess the Second Great Awakening against the authority of colonial tradition, and, not surprisingly, they found cause for both alarm and hope. Thus, in their *Letters . . . on "New Measures,"* published in 1828, Beecher and Nettleton decried what they saw around them and appealed to the lessons of the past: "Whoever has made himself acquainted with the state of things in New England, near the close of the revival in the days of Whitefield and Edwards, cannot but weep over its likeness to the present. It is affecting that the warm friends of Zion should unwittingly betray their best interests. But so it was then. The young itinerants, in their zeal to extend the work, began to denounce all those settled ministers who would not go all lengths with them."[37] Unrestrained enthusiasm aborted the colonial awakening before it fulfilled its spiritual promise. In the Presbygational historical narrative, evangelical excesses, combined with military and political conflicts that redirected American moral fervor, accounted for the decline of revivalism in the second half of the eighteenth century. But now, armed with the lessons and authority of the past, Americans confronted a new providential opportunity to avail themselves of revivalism and to continue the transformation of the nation into a righteous republic that had been set in motion by the colonial awakening.

The Presbygationalists' historical-cultural script cast Edwards in the central role, of course; and the Edwards who was offered to the evangelical audience was a sober, judicious, and humble revivalist. In particular, Finney's opponents were drawn to Part IV of *Some Thoughts Concerning the Present Revival of Religion in New England*, published at the height of the colonial awakening. Edwards devoted Part IV, by far the largest section of *Some Thoughts*, to "Shewing What Things Are To Be Corrected or Avoided, In Promoting This Work, Or In Our Behavior Under It." Citing Biblical injunctions admonishing Christians to "*Be sober, be vigilant, because your adversary the Devil, as a roaring lion, walketh about*," Edwards repudiated distressing manifestations of antinomianism: spiritual pride, immediate revelation, censoriousness, and unregulated lay exhorting.[38] Edwards's condemnation of such behavior gave additional textual support to the humble, self-effacing piety captured in his private writings, like the *Personal Narrative*, and depicted in his important post-awakening works on personal holiness, like the *Life of Brainerd*. All of these works, as we shall see, were first canonized and widely reprinted during the Second Great Awakening.

Finney's evangelical foes not only invoked the authority of *Some Thoughts* to prop up the humble, disinterested piety of other sacred Edwardsian texts; they also employed it as a major historical weapon in the campaign to browbeat new-measures men into cultural submission. Presbygationalists positioned their critique of new measures well within the Edwardsian revivalistic tradition that had been created by New Divinity ministers. They summoned the figure of a courageous Edwards, who, at the height of the colonial awakening, exposed himself to charges of being antirevival by confronting the "'unsightly spots in a blaze of glory.'" New measures were simply a resurrection of antinomian threats to revivalism that Edwards had renounced a century ago. "In such errors of a former day," one evangelical concluded in an article titled "President Edwards on Revivals," "it is not difficult to trace the thoughts of many who discredit the revivals of the present time."[39]

Such a historical perspective disclosed that the chief enemies of revivalism were some of its warmest "friends." Finney's adversaries repeatedly apprised the evangelical public of what Edwards had warned in *Some Thoughts*: Satan worked to undermine revivals primarily from within. By promoting the "indiscreet" zeal of Christians and antinomian "extravagances," Edwards had stressed, Satan encouraged critics of a revival and confused its genuine friends. Thus, Beecher and Nettleton appealed to the authority of *Some Thoughts* to issue a challenge to their antagonist: "before he can plead the example of Edwards, Brother Finney must make the same distinction which Edwards had done, between true and false zeal – true and false affections."[40] Finney's opponents attempted to personalize their campaign of guilt by historical association when their conjuring produced the specter of the colonial awakening's bête noire, who had been declared non compos mentis by Massachusetts authorities in 1742. "It is well known," Presbyterian Albert Dod scowled, "that [James] Davenport . . . is redivivus in Mr. Finney."[41]

In contrast to Davenport and new-measures men, the revivalistic successes of Edwards and his disciples during the "great" colonial awakening were not achieved by trampling on the dignity of the pulpit and exciting "animal" passions. The Presbygationalists continued the interpretation of Edwards as a preacher that Benjamin Trumbull had offered when he claimed that even "Sinners in the Hands of an Angry God" was a sober and controlled sermon, not a fire and brimstone harangue. Sereno Edwards Dwight, the great-grandson and biographer of Edwards, pointed out in 1829 that the distinguished divine did not rely on intemperate appeals to the affections, elaborate gestures, a "graceful delivery, [or] musical voice." Rather, Finney's evangelical foes repeatedly emphasized, Edwards won souls by a "God-inspired" "art or power *of persuading*," which rested on deep personal piety and conviction and which enabled him to appeal systematically and progressively to a sinner's understanding, conscience, and will.[42] Thus, the intemperate preaching and revivalistic gimmicks of the new-measures party were nothing less than betrayals of Edwardsian tradition and the colonial awakening.

Such innovations also betrayed Edwards's sense of himself as a member of a sacred profession. The Presbygationalists brought to their reading of Edwards and the colonial awakening an expanding self-consciousness of and concern for the ministry as a profession. Both colonial revivalism and the Second Great Awakening produced crises of professional authority, of the social authority of the ministry. One of the consequences of the interiorization of authority that revivalistic religion encouraged was an internalization of the qualifications for the ministry. During periods of revivalism, spiritual grace – rather than education, family background, and refinement – became increasingly important as prerequisites for the evangelical ministry. For many pious young men, conversion led directly to thoughts of a clerical career, for which they felt well qualified by the very fact of their conversion. From the colonial era to the Second Great Awakening, revivalism became linked both to the recruitment of ministers and to the democratization of the ministry.[43]

On one level, then, Presbygationalists perceived Finney and new-measures men as a professional threat, as an incursion into mainline evangelical Protestantism of the kind of democratized ministry that characterized the Methodist and Baptist churches. Edwards's clerical figure was invoked to shore up the social authority of the ministry. A sense of professionalism became part of the Edwardsian and American revivalistic tradition that Presbygationalists constructed; and Edwardsian professionalism embraced not only proper pastoral conduct in leading a revival, but appropriate preparation for the ministerial office itself. Hence, Finney's critics deplored the way new-measures men were "rushing into the pastoral office," when the great Edwards "did not think three full years of diligent professional study enough to prepare *him* for this arduous work."[44]

· · ·

Professional dignity, sober but persuasive preaching, judicious revivalism – such were the evocative terms and the aspects of the historical record that Finney's opponents forged into an Edwardsian and American revivalistic tradition. Through numerous and varied publications and redactions, the Presbygationalists contributed to the invention of a "great" colonial awakening, a historical notion that became embedded in the religious polemics of the 1820s and 1830s and that gained currency in public consciousness. The colonial, Edwardsian, and American (the terms became interchangeable) revivalistic tradition not only closely resembled, but also conferred historical legitimacy on, the Presbygational brand of revivalism. Yet, the process of fashioning a tradition seems to have suggested to its creators that the colonial revivalistic legacy was far more ambiguous – that there was not simply *a* tradition – than they publicly acknowledged. Selective proof texting and republishing of Edwards's revivalistic works are only the most obvious examples of this historical awareness. Much more interesting and complex is the way Presbygationalists conflated Edwards's cultural authority and their own. They invoked Edwards's cultural authority to shore up their own and simultaneously asserted their social authority to interpret and define revivalistic tradition.

Thus, in one of the major Presbygational responses to Finney and new measures, William B. Sprague, in *Lectures on Revivals* (1832), appealed to Edwards's revivalistic writings and the colonial awakening to delineate a tradition of judicious American revivalism. But then Sprague turned to contemporary social authorities – prominent ministers and seminary presidents and professors – for cultural and professional endorsement of his interpretation. Sprague included in his *Lectures on Revivals* twenty letters from ministers representing six different denominations, all of whom offered brief observations on the history of revivalism that ratified the Presbygational interpretation of the Edwardsian revivalistic tradition and of a "great" colonial awakening.[45]

Issues of cultural and social authority intersected in the struggle over Edwards's revivalistic legacy because Finney and his new measures challenged both the Presbygationalists' definition of Edwardsian tradition and their professional authority as well. Yet, as iconoclastic as he was, Finney did not feel free to reject the cultural figure of Edwards or the historical importance of the "great" colonial awakening. Rather, Finney sought to redeem a countercultural tradition from the historical reification of his opponents. One of his most important sermons, titled "Traditions of the Elders," subjected the notion of religious tradition to an analysis that revealed the human, and therefore often corrupting, role in its creation: "For many centuries, but little of the real gospel has been preached, that is, it has been so mixed with the traditions of men, so much that is human, so much that is false, has been added to it, and intermingled with it, as to break its power." In a classic Protestant stance, Finney argued that the human role in constructing and corrupting religious tradition required additional human agency – reformers who would restore some of the religious purity to tradition. From this perspective, Finney knit together a sacred history that included Luther, Wesley, Whitefield, Edwards, and himself – countercultural "innovators" who were really religious reformers.[46] In his famous *Lectures on Revivals* Finney answered the Presbygationalists with a countercultural interpretation of the Edwardsian and American revivalistic tradition.

By the time Finney published *Lectures on Revivals* in 1835, he had moved from the "burned-over district" revivalistic circuit to Chatham Street

Chapel in New York City and then to the position of professor of theology at Oberlin Collegiate Institute. The success of Finney's *Lectures on Revivals* paralleled his pulpit triumphs, the most glorious of which now lay behind him. It has been estimated that 12,000 copies sold "overnight";[47] certainly the work quickly became a revivalistic handbook which far outstripped in influence such competing volumes as Sprague's *Lectures on Revivals.*

Finney's *Lectures on Revivals* was both a specific reply to Sprague and a general response to the larger Presbygational historical appropriation of the legacy of the colonial awakening. Finney retrieved a countercultural revivalistic tradition from the same Edwardsian text that the Presbygationalists had used to anchor their interpretation of the temperate Edwards – *Some Thoughts Concerning the Present Revival of Religion in New England.* For while Edwards had deplored and pleaded for the reformation of the antinomian immoderation associated with the colonial awakening, as Presbygationalists stressed, he also reserved some of his sharpest criticism in *Some Thoughts* for ministers and lay people who used behavioral excesses to discredit the authenticity of the revival and who thus "have been great stumbling blocks in others' way."[48] In a long chapter on "Hindrances to Revivals," Finney assumed Edwards's pose at the height of the first awakening and hurled at opponents of new measures Edwardsian condemnations of the critics of the colonial revival. "*Slandering revivals* will often put them down," Finney thundered. "The great revival in the days of President Edwards suffered greatly by the conduct of the church in this respect."[49]

Indeed, Finney reminded his readers, enthusiasts were not the only tools of Satan; rather, as Edwards had suggested, critics of revivalism were even more dangerous dupes of the devil. "It has always been the policy of the devil to turn off the attention of ministers from the work of the Lord, to dispute and ecclesiastical litigations," Finney contended, as he linked himself and Edwards in a history of victimization. "President Edwards was obliged to be taken up for a long time in disputes before ecclesiastical councils; and in our days, and in the midst of these great revivals of religion, these difficulties have been alarmingly and shamefully multiplied."[50] Thus, the decline of the "great" colonial awakening was less the result of religious enthusiasm than of indifference and hostility to revivalism by people who rose to Satan's bait and used "unsightly spots" to place stumbling blocks in the way of "a blaze of glory."

Finney not only seized the historical moment of *Some Thoughts* as his own; he presented his *Lectures on Revivals* as a successor, or at least complement, to Edwards's volume and defended new measures as an extension of Edwardsian New Light tradition. "President Edwards . . . was famous in his day for new measures," Finney boasted. An acceptance of the physical "agony of prayer" displayed by awakened sinners, a refusal to baptize the children of the unconverted, a "defence" of lay exhortation – these were some of the controversial Edwardsian new measures of the colonial awakening.[51] Citing a long passage from *Some Thoughts*, for example, Finney demonstrated how the physical agony that accompanied both his protracted meetings and his use of the anxious seat "was prevalent in President Edwards's day . . . and was one of the great stumbling blocks in those days, to persons who were opposed to the revival." Finney tied the present to the past in a vision that subsumed Scripture, the Protestant Reformation, and American revivalism. "If we examine the history of the church," he concluded, "we shall find there never has been an extensive reformation except by new measures."[52]

Finney's opponents belittled his historical reappropriation of both Edwards and the legacy of the "great" colonial awakening. "Among these new-measure men he introduces the name of President Edwards," Princeton's Albert B. Dod fumed in a lengthy review of Finney's *Lectures on Revivals*. "He has no right to slander the dead, or impose upon the living."[53] But other foes of Finney did not dismiss his historical revisionism so easily. Between the publication of *Lectures on Revivals* and the commemoration of the centennial of the colonial awakening in 1840, evangelical commentary on the Edwardsian and American revivalistic legacy evolved to a level of debate that testifies to Finney's achievements as both a revivalist and revisionist. Since the historical record lent at least partial support to Finney's revisionism, adversaries of new measures such as Charles Hodge, professor of theology in Princeton Seminary, began to focus on the postawakening Edwards, who privately reassessed his leadership of the revival. Smarting from the decline of the revival and the revolt of his own congregation, Edwards anguished over his conduct during the awakening and revealed some of his sober reservations to supporters in Scotland. "His correspondence," Hodge stressed in a lengthy analysis of the colonial awakening in the *Constitutional History of the Presbyterian Church in the United States of America* (1839), "affords abundant evidence how fully sensible he became of the extent to which this revival was corrupted with false religion."[54] In this correspondence, Edwards penitently confessed that he had lacked "experience, and ripeness of judgment and courage" during the "great" colonial awakening. In his own church, he self-laceratingly regretted, his poor judgment encouraged "spiritual pride, and other things that are exceedingly contrary to true Christianity."[55] Hodge's account suggested that an accurate assessment of the Edwardsian and colonial revivalistic legacy needed to reconcile the public and the private Edwards, the revivalist of the awakening and of the post-awakening years.

The first comprehensive history of the colonial revival attempted just such a reconciliation. Joseph Tracy's *The Great Awakening: A History of the Revival of Religion in the Time of Edwards and Whitefield*, which was published in Boston in 1841, was inspired by the importance of the colonial revival in evangelical historical consciousness. In fact, New England churches sponsored commemorations of the centennial of the "great" colonial revival in 1840. Moreover, as Tracy noted, the authority of the past had been consistently invoked in the disputes that divided Second Great Awakeners: "the advocates of all kinds of 'measures,' new and old, have been asserting that the events and results of that [colonial] revival justified thus several theories and practices."[56] Tracy's work, then, was both a serious study and a celebratory account of the colonial revival.

Tracy's history, in its rich detail and its recognition of the complexity and ambiguity of the colonial revivalistic legacy, went well beyond the partisan narratives that controversialists produced at the height of the Second Great Awakening. For that reason, and because of the sheer size of his volume (well over 400 pages), Tracy's work became the new authority on the colonial awakening, still referred to by historians as the "classic" account. Yet Tracy, New England Congregationalist, historian of the missionary movement, and Edwardsian cleric with close ties to Andover Seminary, clung to the interpretive line spun out by Benjamin Trumbull and other New Divinity men in the early stages of the Second Great Awakening. Tracy completed the process of transforming the colonial New England revival experience into a great, general, and formative American historical event.

Through an emphasis on "new birth," Tracy argued, the colonial revival challenged "established and venerated habits of thought, feeling, and action" and stimulated "a revolution in the minds of men, and thus in the very structure of society."[57] Among the "great" historical consequences of the awakening, Tracy numbered the spiritual transformation of the American ministry, a new understanding of experimental religion, the growth of evangelical theology, the origins of the missionary movement, and the preparation of "many minds" for the American Revolution. And of course Edwards, who "had done more than any other man to awaken the ministry and the churches in the first instance, and to produce the movement which had now become general," was the great man of the transformative historical event.[58] But Tracy's account was not an "unmixed eulogy" either for Edwards or for the colonial awakening. At the height of the revival, even its most spiritually discerning leaders had not been exempt from being at least partially blinded by the blaze of glory. Such was the case with Edwards, and, Tracy observed apologetically, "it will not be an easy task to point out an error in all his reasonings." For while Edwards spoke out against the enthusiasm excited by the revival, "it must be admitted that, in the practical application of his own principles, he was too indulgent."[59] Still, Edwards and the other distinguished leaders of the colonial revival later acknowledged their mistakes. In spite of the errors and excesses that accompanied it, Tracy reassured his readers, the Great Awakening profoundly and positively shaped the course of American religious history.

Jon Butler, who has subjected the historiography of the colonial revival to penetrating analysis, singles out Tracy as the first to use the label "the Great Awakening" in the broad, inclusive, and familiar way that historians have come to accept. Butler has also claimed that "not until the last half of the nineteenth century did 'the Great Awakening' become a familiar feature of the American historical landscape."[60] Yet the notion of a "great" colonial awakening fully emerged from the religious polemics of the early nineteenth century and from efforts to codify Edwardsian revivalistic tradition. Thus, Tracy's influential but heavily derivative volume, which was republished in 1845, culminated rather than launched the cultural invention of the Great Awakening.

· · ·

The canonization of Edwardsian texts that focused on the piety inspired by revivalistic religion was central to the nineteenth-century invention of the Great Awakening. The Presbygationalist-Finney wrangling over *Some Thoughts Concerning the Present Revival in New England*, however, disclosed that certain sacred Edwardsian texts presented nineteenth-century evangelicals with a problematic, even ambiguous, religious legacy. Consider, also, the evangelicals' approach to the *Religious Affections*, Edwards's "masterpiece" on experimental religion. A long, wordy, frequently cryptic, hyper-Calvinist defense of the spirituality of the colonial revival, the *Religious Affections* was not canonized and regularly reprinted until the Second Great Awakening. But even then, the accessibility of the *Religious Affections* to a nineteenth-century lay audience was problematic; many evangelical leaders agreed that the *Religious Affections* was a spiritual classic, "which should be read as soon as it was rewritten."[61]

The popular nineteenth-century editions of the *Religious Affections*, issued by newly established denominational and interdenominational presses, were all heavily abridged and edited works. The American Tract Society, for example, first issued its "modernized" edition of the *Religious Affections* in 1833, and by midcentury had distributed upward of 75,000 copies of the work. This abridged edition not only radically reduced Edwards's numerous biblical citations in support of the twelve signs of genuine religious affections, but also made more telling alterations in the original. Edwards's language was edited where it proved to be inappropriate for, and even condescending toward, the lay audience of Jacksonian America. His references to the "common and less considerate and understanding sort of people" were revised to such statements as "Persons of little information, who are not accustomed to reflect." The Tract Society also eliminated Edwards's discussions of controversial theological-philosophical issues, like freedom of the will and moral versus natural ability.[62]

In addition, the Tract Society rewrote some passages and expunged many others with the design of toning down the mystical and aesthetic aspects of Edwards's thought that were deemed inaccessible and potentially perplexing to a lay audience. In the *Religious Affections*, Edwards frequently dwelled on the spiritual beauty of regeneration, attempting to capture intellectually the "inward sweetness" that he had described in the *Personal Narrative*. As a result, several of the twelve signs of genuine religious affections described existential states and aesthetic perceptions. By editing Edwards's descriptions of the converted person's apprehension of the "supreme beauty and sweetness of . . . divine things,"[63] the Tract Society reshaped the *Religious Affections* into a condensed and easily decipherable work of practical divinity.

Another popular edition of the *Religious Affections* followed the tack of the Tract Society but displayed an even sharper editorial knife. John Wesley prepared an abridgment of the *Religious Affections* that was first published in London in 1801 and was being reissued in America as late as 1855. As with the many other Puritan works of practical divinity that composed his so-called *Christian Library*, Wesley strove for clarity, brevity, and an avoidance of Calvinist theology so that important evangelical volumes would become affordable and intellectually accessible to ordinary lay people. Wesley claimed that the *Religious Affections* contained "much wholesome food . . . mixed with much deadly poison."[64] Wesley went well beyond the Tract Society in editing Edwards's hyper-Calvinism and cloud religion. He completely eliminated some of Edwards's signs of genuine religious affections, reducing the number from twelve to eight. Sign three was one of those deleted: "Those affections that are truly holy, are primarily founded on the loveliness of the moral excellency of divine things. Or (to express it otherwise), a love to divine things for the beauty and sweetness of their moral excellency, is the first beginning and spring of all holy affections." Wesley discarded three more signs, shortened and revised Edwards's analysis of others, and rescued from the *Religious Affections* those major elements of Edwardsianism that supported practical Methodist evangelical piety.[65]

Other popular nineteenth-century editions of the *Religious Affections* were abridged and revised works based on considerations and producing results similar to the efforts of the Tract Society and of Wesley.[66] These "improvements" of Edwards restrained the quietistic, aesthetic, mystical, and Calvinistic elements of the *Religious Affections* and accentuated the activist, practical, pietistic, and Methodistical side of Edwardsianism. Orthodox Calvinists, who valued the doctrinal substructure of the *Religious Affections*, objected to alterations of the text and complained that it had come to be "thought of merely as a practical work."[67] But a "modernized" *Religious Affections* bolstered the practical piety of such popular works as Edwards's *Personal Narrative* and the *Life of Brainerd* that were canonized during the Second Great Awakening. In the hands of nineteenth-century evangelicals, the *Religious Affections* was transformed from a wordy, often learned and obscure work into an accessible religious "classic" that promoted the popular piety of the Second Great Awakening. Ironically, then, while the "invention" of the Great Awakening originated in New Divinity efforts to resist Methodist challenges to New England revivalism, the process of historical interpretation during the Second Great Awakening ended with the presentation of an increasingly Methodized Edwards to a popular evangelical audience.

Still, the invention of sacred Edwardsian texts did not simply shore up the popular evangelical religion of the Second Great Awakening. Newly canonized Edwardsian works were invoked to contain Methodistical piety as well. Moreover, the invention of sacred texts and of cultural authorities was essential to the transformation of the colonial awakening into a great, general, and formative event. Lyman Beecher spoke for many Second Great Awakeners when he observed in 1829, "most that is at present desirable in the religious aspect of things among us may be traced to the influence of men who were trained and instructed in the revival of 1740."[68]

Such interest in and respect for personalties and texts from the era of the colonial revival – a historical perspective that even nineteenth-century Methodists embraced – suggests how it is misleading to argue that the Second Great Awakening stimulated a democratizing process that scorned tradition and the wisdom of the past and simply leave it at that. It is precisely during such periods of sweeping democratic change that new traditions are likely to be created.[69] The reification of the colonial awakening, the creation of an American revivalistic tradition of New England origin, and the canonization of particular Edwardsian texts were all part of a cultural response to democratic change during the Second Great Awakening that enabled the past to exert interpretive influence over the present. It is time for scholars to disencumber the colonial revival from the interpretive burden that it has been asked to bear. The "Great Awakening" needs to be recognized as the deus ex machina that it is: a nineteenth-century cultural artifact invented by Second Great Awakeners, who created an Edwardsian revivalistic tradition to resolve contemporary religious conflicts.[70]

2

· · ·

THE SECOND GREAT AWAKENING AND
THE CULTURAL REVIVAL OF EDWARDS

The elevation of Jonathan Edwards to a position of major cultural authority was central to the New Divinity–inspired process of creating an American revivalistic tradition. To trace the trajectory of Edwards's reputation
and influence as well as the publishing history of his works is to recognize
how the eminent theologian did not move toward the center of American
evangelical culture until the nineteenth century. New Divinity men initiated the development of an Edwardsian structure of authority as part of
the effort to transform the largely New England colonial awakening into a
great, general, and formative *American* event that could be invoked to
influence the course of the Second Great Awakening.[1]

The spiritual "harvests" in the Connecticut River Valley in the mid-
1730s had first thrust Edwards into regional prominence. His reputation
then grew with the expansion of revivals in New England in the early 1740s
and with his vigorous defenses of their authenticity. But the sudden decline of religious ardor, beginning in 1743, eroded Edwards's recently established authority, a process that continued when his own congregation
rebelled against him in 1750. Edwards went into exile on the Massachusetts
frontier, a typical obscure settlement for a stigmatized minister. Even Edwards's call to the presidency of Princeton eight years later did little to repair the damage that the demise of revivalistic religion and the antagonism
of his own congregation had done to his reputation. Edwards died within
weeks of returning from his frontier exile.

To be sure, Princeton's summons demonstrated that Edwards was still
highly regarded in some evangelical circles. Yet Edwards's standing in the
decades after the colonial awakening must not be overestimated. High

esteem, bordering on reverence, for Edwards in post-awakening America was limited to the New England wing of the Presbyterian church and to a then small group of New Divinity Congregationalists. In fact, it was in Scotland, not in America, that Edwards continued to speak to a significant audience in the second half of the eighteenth century. During those decades, Scottish Presbyterian leaders, with whom Edwards had conducted a lengthy correspondence in the 1740s and 1750s, reprinted many of the theologian's works. "It is a humiliating fact," Edwards A. Park, professor of theology at Andover Seminary, remarked a century later, "that several of Edwards's writings were sent to Scotland for publication, because our community would not patronize them." Only a few obituaries announced Edwards's tragic death in 1758, and they suggest that there was no great outpouring of grief. Moreover, Samuel Hopkins, Edwards's most devoted New Divinity disciple, who authored the first biography of the theologian and who prepared some of his works for posthumous publication, abandoned plans for a complete edition of Edwards's writings because he feared there would not be enough buyers.[2]

The first American edition of Edwards's works was not published until 1808; by then an Edwardsian cultural renaissance was underway – a phase of the New Divinity reification of the colonial awakening and creation of an American revivalistic tradition. The cultural revival of Edwards – like the transformation of the historical significance of the colonial awakening – offers persuasive evidence of how the New Divinity movement had grown in size and influence to a position of dominance within New England Congregationalism by the early nineteenth century. Once again, what the New Divinity originated, leaders of the benevolent empire extended. Denominational, interdenominational, and commercial presses inundated the antebellum evangelical community with Edwardsian publications; the American Tract Society alone published over a million copies of Edwards's works.[3] At the same time an ever-expanding religious periodical press created an Edwardsian journalistic industry which examined nearly every aspect of the eminent divine's life and thought.

Edwards's new cultural authority and his exalted place in nineteenth-century evangelical hagiography derived from three sources. First, Edwards came to be admired as a man of remarkable, even saintly, piety; his private writings were exhumed and became sacred public property that furnished a model of genuine evangelical spirituality. Second, as the "father" of the Great Awakening, Edwards was invoked as the major

American authority on individual conversion and mass revivalism. Finally, the theological and metaphysical Edwards, admired abroad and vigorously promoted by New Divinity men at home, emerged as a cultural and intellectual icon whose thought was defended, "improved upon," and even occasionally wheeled out simply to "dignify" evangelical theological efforts.[4]

Evangelicals enshrined Edwards as the most distinguished eighteenth-century founding father of America's righteous empire. In the process, they sometimes cut his figure and trimmed his thought to fit the "Methodized" fashions of the day; yet, at the same time, they often summoned Edwards to restrain disquieting expressions of populism and perfectionism in antebellum piety, revivalism, and theology. The revival of Edwards involved far more than a simple rediscovery by antebellum evangelicals of the eminent divine's continuing cultural relevance. Nor was the cultural revival merely the cumulative effect of individual influence, individual interests, and individual texts. Rather, the Edwardsian revival was part of the cultural politics and cultural production of the Second Great Awakening. Edwards's cultural authority was not simply rediscovered; it was created through a process of social and cultural production that involved new religious institutions: presses and periodicals, reform societies and agencies, and theological seminaries. Moreover, the cultural revival of Edwards did not involve the retrieval of an already constituted tradition. Antebellum evangelicals created an American religious tradition around Edwards's figure. They "classicized" Edwards and his writings and in turn used his religious authority to "traditionalize" nineteenth-century piety, revivalism, and theology.

. . .

The contrast between the two most important early biographies of Edwards, one written after the colonial revivals and the other at the height of the Second Great Awakening, reflects the evolution of his standing in America. In 1765, Samuel Hopkins published a slim biography of Edwards that served for more than a generation as the authoritative "life" of the theologian. Hopkins's volume originated as an introductory memoir that accompanied Edwards's *Sermons on Various Important Subjects*. Hopkins completed the memoir in anticipation of the publication of other Edwardsian manuscripts and perhaps even a collected edition of the theologian's works. Such New Divinity editorial projects, however, typically failed to win the support of American publishers in the decades after Edwards's death.[5]

Though Hopkins, like other first generation New Divinity ministers, revered his mentor, he was careful not to deify Edwards. Hopkins's memoir introduced the private Edwards to the public, publishing for the first time confessional and devotional works that would become sacred Edwardsian texts – classics of evangelical spirituality – during the Second Great Awakening. Hopkins included in his life of the theologian the *Personal Narrative*, Edwards's lyrical account of his conversion, written some twenty years after the experience. Hopkins also published for the first time Edwards's youthful "Resolutions" for moral and spiritual development and extracts from his private diary. For a disciple and close friend of Edwards, Hopkins exercised considerable restraint in presenting both the public and private lives of his teacher. Impelled more by familiar religious didacticism than by filiopietism, Hopkins disavowed any desire simply to "tell the world how eminently great, wise, holy and useful President Edwards was." Hopkins endeavored to write not "a mere encomium on the dead, but a faithful and plain narration of matters of fact, together with his [Edwards's] own internal exercises, expressed in his own words." Though not hiding his esteem for Edwards, even in the face of publishers' reluctance to reprint the theologian's works or to issue manuscript material that his New Divinity literary executors possessed, Hopkins saw his biography as not "so much an act of friendship to the *dead*, as of kindness to the *living*; it being only an attempt to render a life that has been greatly useful, yet more so."[6]

Hopkins's brief biography spawned other sketches of Edwards in the late eighteenth and early nineteenth centuries. But neither Hopkins's volume nor the vignettes it inspired met the needs of the cultural work of the Second Great Awakening: the invention of an American revival tradition, the reification of the colonial awakening, and the use of the past to arbitrate the religious controversies of the present. Thus, in an act of personal filiopietism that contributed significantly to the cultural production of the Second Great Awakening, Sereno Edwards Dwight published a lengthy memoir of his great-grandfather in 1829. Dwight's memoir served as the introductory volume to a collected edition of Edwards's works.[7] While other collected editions were already available in America, none provided the kind of biographical information that Dwight, the principal custodian of Edwards's papers, presented. More than 600 pages long, Dwight's volume ranked as one of the most detailed American biographies published up to that point and testified to the enormous evangelical interest in Edwards. Where Hopkins had published only about half of Edwards's youthful "Resolutions" on moral and spiritual development, Dwight included all seventy. Where Hopkins had only partially opened a window on Edwards's domestic life, Dwight provided his readers with details about the theologian's wife, Sarah, their childrearing practices, and their household economy. Where Hopkins had merely outlined the circumstances surrounding Edwards's dismissal from his Northampton church, Dwight went on, page after densely packed page, examining the dispute and vindicating Edwards. Above all, Dwight's exhaustive volume enlarged upon Edwards's role as the "father" of the "great" colonial awakening.

A reverential, filiopietistic view of Edwards informed Dwight's voluminous memoir. Since the apostolic era, Dwight proclaimed, no individual had done more to unfold scriptural truth and advance evangelical Christianity.

> And when we remember, in addition to all this, that we can probably select no individual, of all who have lived in that long period, who has manifested a more ardent or elevated piety towards God, a warmer or more expended benevolence towards Man, or greater purity, or disinterestedness of character – one who gave the concentrated strength of all his powers, more absolutely, to the one end of glorifying God in the salvation of Man; – and then reflect, that at the age of *fifty-four*, in the highest vigor of all his faculties, in the fullness of his usefulness, when he was just entering on the most important station of his life, he yielded to the stroke of death, we look toward his grave, in mute astonishment, unable to penetrate those clouds and darkness, which hover around it.[8]

Dwight's extravagant historical assessment both reflected and contributed to what one might call the Second Great Awakening's "reinvention" of Edwards: the elevation of the theologian to the status of major cultural authority, the canonization of his works, and the creation of an Edwardsian religious tradition. Dwight's memoir was frequently reprinted, and almost every evangelical who wrote about Edwards relied on it for the first and last word on the theologian's life and career.[9] In short, Dwight, the family curator of both Edwards's image and of his unpublished papers, superseded Hopkins as the historical authority on New England's most illustrious religious luminary.

Edwards's profound personal piety, rather than his intellectual brilliance, emerged as the central motif of Dwight's memoir and of the numerous depictions of the theologian that it influenced. His personal piety
and the works of practical divinity that grew out of his commitment to experimental religion established the basis for Edwards's broad appeal to
both Calvinist and non-Calvinist evangelicals during the Second Great
Awakening. Despite the distinctly doctrinal cast of Edwards's major theological works, "no denomination has ever yet been able to appropriate his
name to themselves," the *Christian Spectator* observed in 1821. "In this respect he has attained higher honor than Calvin, or Luther, or Zwingle
[*sic*]. As no sect of christians has ever been able to appropriate the name
Christian exclusively to themselves, so no sect will ever be denominated
Edwardean." [10]

During the course of the Second Great Awakening, Edwards's deep
piety, private writings, and works of practical divinity enabled moderate
Congregationalists, Old and New Side Presbyterians, and even Methodists
to bypass the metaphysical Edwards and to co-opt the New Divinity's exclusive claim to Edwardsian tradition. [11] Ordinary evangelicals came to
know Edwards through his private writings and works of practical divinity, which were extensively republished and widely disseminated, rather
than through his powerful theological treatises. In particular, Edwards's
Personal Narrative, his brief spiritual autobiography/conversion narrative,
and his private "Resolutions" for spiritual and moral improvement appealed to a diverse evangelical audience and established the literary foundation for Edwards's image as a man of saintly piety. [12] The *Personal Narrative* was reprinted in pamphlet form by, among others, the American
Tract Society and the Congregational Board of Publication. The former
edition, titled the *Conversion of President Edwards*, was first issued in 1827,
and by 1875, 124,000 copies had been distributed. [13] Edwards's "Resolutions" were also printed separately and distributed widely. Joseph Emerson, the Edwardsian minister of the Third Congregational Church in
Beverly, Massachusetts, published the first separate edition of the "Resolutions" in 1807. He combined Edwards's work with the articles of Faith and
Covenant of the Third Church as a devotional manual for members.
Emerson's effort proved so successful that he prepared a new edition of his
work, which was adopted by churches in Massachusetts, Vermont, and
New Hampshire. [14] The publishing history of the *Personal Narrative* and
the "Resolutions" suggests how local, denominational, and interdenomi-

national religious institutions all made contributions to the cultural revival of Edwards.

Evangelical commentary on Edwards's private writings focused on the saintly spirituality embodied in these works and urged Christians to aspire to an Edwardsian level of piety. Edwards's humility came to be seen as a dominant theme of his life and as the foundation of his piety, enabling moderate evangelicals to fashion a tradition that could be invoked against the perceived spiritual excesses of Finneyites and Methodists. In the *Religious Affections*, a newly canonical text for Second Great Awakeners, moderates found a useful expression of the "evangelical humiliation" that, it was argued, shaped Edwards's spiritual life and private writings. Edwards defined evangelical humility as "a sense a Christian has of his own utter insufficiency, despicableness, and odiousness with an answerable frame of heart."[15] Such an understanding of genuine religious affections derived from the familiar Puritan view that the individual with the most reason for hope and comfort was the one who felt most lost and undeserving. In an age of new-measures revivalism and religious perfectionism, Edwards's figure and his brand of piety were employed as an antidote to spiritual pride and nascent antinomianism. "It has often appeared to me," the eminent divine wrote in the *Personal Narrative*, "that if God should mark iniquity against me, I should appear the very worst of all mankind; of all that have been, since the beginning of the world, to this time." Evangelical humiliation originated in the converted person's new sense of God's majesty. The true convert's humility intensified as an awareness of God increased. Thus Edwards couldn't "bear the thought of being no more humble than other Christians. It seems to me, that though their degrees of humility may be suitable for them, yet it would be a vile self-exaltation in me, not to be the lowest in humility of all mankind."[16]

Evangelical humiliation comprehended a denial not only of self-exaltation, but of worldly pleasure as well. Indeed, worldly self-denial was an important sign that spiritual pride and self-love, which were affections or inclinations of the heart, had been subdued. Edwards's "Resolutions" furnished evangelicals with a brief, readable work of practical piety that complemented the high-flown quest for evangelical humility described in the *Personal Narrative*. Composed by Edwards when he was nineteen years old, the seventy resolutions comprised the practical efforts he made to sanctify his heart and root his life in the denial of self-centeredness and worldliness. Some resolutions were directed at the regulation of daily life:

"Resolved, to maintain the strictest temperance in eating and drinking." Others expressed the lofty objective behind such self-denial: "*Resolved, never henceforth, till I die, to act as if I were any way my own, but entirely and altogether God's.*" Still others established daily, weekly, monthly, and yearly schedules of self-examination to monitor his faithfulness to the resolutions.[17]

Perhaps more than any other of his writings, the "Resolutions" shaped the nineteenth-century evangelical image of Edwards's piety. Biographers portrayed his life as a fulfillment of the "Resolutions," constructing a towering model of piety for all Christians to emulate. Youthful aspiration became adult reality, as Edwards was allowed to define his own character. One resolution summed up the personal attributes that, following Dwight's biographical interpretation, became the standard evangelical portrait of Edwards: "Resolved, To endeavor, to my utmost, to deny whatever is not most agreeable to a good and universally sweet and benevolent, quiet, peaceable, contented and easy, compassionate and generous, humble and meek, submissive and obliging, diligent and industrious, charitable and even, patient, moderate, forgiving and sincere temper."[18] Armed with Edwards's authority and saintly image, evangelical leaders set out on their mission of morally domesticating antebellum Americans.

Many evangelicals echoed the judgment of Sereno Dwight, who proclaimed that Edwards's "Resolutions" were "the best uninspired summary of christian duty, the best directory to high attainments in evangelical virtue, which the mind of man has hitherto been able to form."[19] The "Resolutions" invited favorable comparison with Benjamin Franklin's more famous quest for moral improvement. Franklin's effort, the author of the Sunday School Union's biography of Edwards noted, was admirable but limited to "mere moral precepts." To be a Christian, however, required more than morality; "and never has this applied with such fullness and beautiful symmetry as in the 'Seventy Resolutions,' which Edwards laid down for the guidance of his social and religious actions." Edwards's quest for sanctification was so superior to Franklin's that the "Resolutions" ought "to be written by every christian in letters of gold; or rather to be engraved on the tablets of his memory."[20]

Evangelicals often used the "Resolutions" to help them establish an Edwardsian moral regimen in their lives, as Basil Manly, Jr., a southern Baptist, demonstrated. Inspired by Edwards, Manly initiated a process of periodic intensive self-examination in 1841, though he felt spiritually inadequate in comparison to America's Augustine. "When I contrast the feeling of my heart with the exercises of that blessed man of God, Jon. Edwards," Manly recorded in his diary, "I am astonished at the coldness of my own heart." Using Edwards's work as a model, Manly drew up a list of one hundred resolutions to aid him in his pursuit of moral and spiritual sanctification.[21]

Such enthusiastic imitators and promoters of the private Edwards repeatedly commented on the "childlike piety" the eminent divine expressed in the "Resolutions" and the *Personal Narrative*. Evangelical leaders seized on the contrast between Edwards's humble, childlike piety and his "muscular," unrivaled intellect to support the reigning commonsense philosophy, which held that no matter how much people differed in mental ability and social standing, they were all created morally equal.[22] God bestowed on humankind a universal or common moral sense that helped establish a basic ethical order in the world. Through conversion and the cultivation of this moral sense, conscience, or intuitive affection, all individuals could strive for the kind of evangelical piety that Edwards had attained. Thus, however intimidating and original Edwards's intellect appeared, his equally profound, yet humble, childlike piety remained a realistic model for evangelical spiritual and moral aspirations. Edwards's piety and the commonsense philosophy enabled evangelicals to democratize the distinguished theologian. As one evangelical put it in a biographical sketch of Edwards: "It is peculiarly sweet to observe that in matters of spiritual concern the philosopher and the ploughman, if truly regenerated, have the same feelings, and speak the same language: They all 'eat of the same spiritual meat, and drink of the same spiritual rock, which follows them, and that rock is Christ.'"[23] In short, all converts – the renowned Edwards included – belonged to a spiritual family whose members bore a striking resemblance. Edwards's piety, then, differed only in degree, not in kind, from other family members.

·   ·   ·

Second Great Awakeners canonized Edwards's *Personal Narrative*, esteeming it as a classic – an American archetype of the conversion narrative, an established and familiar evangelical religious genre. Similarly, the *Faithful Narrative*, Edwards's account of the Northampton and Connecticut Valley revivals of 1734–35, was canonized as the prototype of a more recent evangelical religious genre – the revival narrative. As Michael Crawford has recently argued, Edwards's *Faithful Narrative* "was the first extended account and analysis of a season of religious awakening in a congregation, let alone in a full thirty communities." Edwards's *Faithful Narrative*, which was published in 1737, "established a new religious genre, creating a model of American revival narratives for a century to come."[24]

Yet the publishing history of the *Faithful Narrative* suggests that neither its archetypal importance and influence nor the revival narrative's development in America was fully realized until the Second Great Awakening. First published in England, the *Faithful Narrative* was not extensively reprinted in America during the era of the colonial revivals. The publication of the *Faithful Narrative* in London and Edinburgh in 1737 encouraged American editions in 1738, but not thereafter. Indeed, in the mid-eighteenth century, it was Scottish Presbyterians and English evangelicals who recognized the novelty of Edwards's account and who published seven editions by 1750. The *Faithful Narrative* was not widely reprinted in America until the Second Great Awakening. Nor, for that matter, was the revival narrative fully established in evangelical culture until publications such as the *Connecticut Evangelical Magazine* institutionalized such accounts as part of their religious and inspirational fare.[25] Second Great Awakeners' appropriation and canonization of the *Faithful Narrative* extended to other Edwardsian revivalistic works, whose republication was an integral part of the invention of the "great" colonial awakening and of Edwards's elevation to the status of founding father of the American revivalistic tradition.

The century preceding the outburst of revivalism in the 1730s, evangelicals argued, witnessed an uninterrupted erosion of American piety, culminating in a religiously deplorable state of affairs. Uncritically accepting the formulaic history of declension that became a convention of the revival narrative beginning with Edwards, nineteenth-century evangelicals often pointed to the Halfway Covenant, uninspired preaching, and creeping moralism as signs of the grievous condition of American church life. "The clergy were, for the most part, grave men," Lyman Beecher claimed in the *Spirit of the Pilgrims* in 1829, "but in some instances, had . . . lost the spirit of religion, and in others, it may be feared, had never felt it."[26] Edwards became "God's chief instrument of all born in this land for . . . restoring prosperity to our American Sion," the *Congregational Quarterly* boasted. "One such man . . . is sufficient alone to redeem the nation, the church, the age to which he belonged."[27] In this dominant evangelical view, Edwards single-handedly ignited the colonial awakening, fanned its flames with the assistance of the likes of George Whitefield and Gilbert Tennent, and labored – though not always successfully – to prevent it from raging out of control. "He was," evangelicals concluded, "the father of the Great Awakening."[28]

But Edwards's authority on revivalism did not derive simply from the evangelical belief that he had sired the Great Awakening. Rather, as the Presbyterian minister Charles Spaulding emphasized in 1832, Edwards also gave birth to the "science of revivals."[29] His deep personal piety and profound intellect, evangelicals noted repeatedly, combined to make Edwards an expert on experimental religion. Edwards's rich devotional life and his quest for holiness established an unrivaled personal understanding of religious affections. Such piety sanctified his powerful intellect and enabled him to become an "eminently discriminating" observer of both individual and mass conversions.[30] Furthermore, the father of the Great Awakening was afforded unequaled opportunities to study the operation of the Holy Spirit in individuals, families, churches, and entire communities over a number of years.

Understandably, then, nineteenth-century evangelicals invested Edwards's revivalistic writings with an authority that far exceeded their eighteenth-century reception and reputation. When, in the midst of the fervor and controversy over Finney's new measures, a publisher approached Charles Spaulding to write a work on revivalism, the Presbyterian minister concluded that, since he could not equal, let alone surpass, Edwards, it made more sense to republish the master. In 1832, he published *Edwards on Revivals*, which contained selections from the theologian's works on the colonial awakening.[31] These works – *A Faithful Narrative of the Surprising Works of God* (1737), *The Distinguishing Marks of a Work of the Spirit of God* (1741), *Some Thoughts Concerning the Present Revival of Religion in New England* (1742), and *A Treatise Concerning Religious Affections* (1746) – were among the most popular and frequently reprinted Edwardsian volumes in the nineteenth century. They were also the kind of Edwardsian works that John Wesley, Bishop Francis Asbury, and other Methodist leaders deeply admired, regularly reissued, and enthusiastically recommended to their clergy and laity.[32] Edwards's revivalistic works were equally popular with the American Tract Society. Between 1833 and 1875, to cite just one example, the Society distributed 171,000 copies of Edwards's concluding remarks to *Some Thoughts Concerning the Present Revival of*

Religion in New England. Edwards's writings on the colonial awakening, the Reverend William B. Sprague, the influential Presbyterian historian of the American clergy, proclaimed in 1833, "have done more than any other uninspired productions to maintain the purity of revivals, from the period in which they were written to the present." Even if Edwards "had rendered the church no other service," Sprague maintained, "for this alone she would have embalmed his memory."[33]

Edwards's *Religious Affections* came to be appreciated as a contribution to the "science of revivalism," though creative editing, as we have seen, was required to transform it into an accessible religious classic. Recoiling from the emotional excesses of the colonial revivals, Edwards offered a tempered interpretation of genuine spirituality in the *Religious Affections.* By sorting through Edwards's signs of genuine spirituality and by distilling his swollen rhetoric, antebellum evangelicals offered the public a work of practical divinity, which – like Edwards's "Resolutions" and *Personal Narrative* – supported evangelical humility and self-denying, sanctified behavior, not self-exalting antinomianism and prideful enthusiasm. The *Religious Affections* helped make the examination of a prospective church member "a rational ordeal," a writer in the *Christian Review* commented in 1841. "This book ought to be labelled the 'Pastor's Manual for the Inquirer's Room' ... [,] the only work ... in the English language in any degree entitled to such designation." Another evangelical writing in the *New Englander* agreed that the *Religious Affections* had become "the text-book of christendom on experimental religion." Even religious rationalists acknowledged, at the same time they lamented, the authority that Edwards's treatise carried during the Second Great Awakening. The Unitarian John Brazer, for instance, described the *Religious Affections* in the *Christian Examiner* in 1835 as "a book which is now in unquestioned repute, and which ... has been referred to and quoted, reprinted and circulated by the predominant class of Christians in this country, with a deference only less than that which is paid to the Bible itself."[34]

Edwards's *History of the Work of Redemption* went through a similar process of canonization during the Second Great Awakening and added to his stature as the preeminent authority on revivalism. Based on sermons he delivered in Northampton during 1739, Edwards's *History of Redemption* drew on scriptural evidence and Christian history to place revivals at the center of the providential plan for human redemption. Edwards offered not a new departure in eschatology, but an original contribution to evangelical historiography. As the most comprehensive recent history of colonial revivalism documents clearly, Edwards "made the phenomenon of the revival the key element in the drama of redemption. He conceived of revivals as the engine that drives redemption history."[35]

Yet, neither Edwards's *History of Redemption*, nor his millennial perspective on revivals, appears to have found a secure place in American evangelical culture until the Second Great Awakening. In fact, Edwards's *History of Redemption* was one of his posthumous works that his New Divinity disciples were unable to place with an American publisher. Jonathan Edwards, Jr., shipped this work to Scotland, where it was first issued in 1774. The publisher included an advertisement with an appeal to the evangelical community for support: "Whether the publisher shall favor the world with any more of these valuable remains, will probably in a good measure depend on the encouragement this work meets with."[36] Scottish evangelicals proved to be more receptive to Edwardsian works than their mid-eighteenth-century American counterparts. The *History of Redemption* was not published in America until 1782 (a reprint of the Scottish edition) and not regularly reissued and extensively distributed until the Second Great Awakening. Perhaps the most influential American edition of this work was first issued in 1838 as part of the Tract Society's "Evangelical Family Library." More than 60,000 copies of this edition were circulated at midcentury.[37] By then revivalism had become an enduring, widespread, and even institutionalized rite within evangelical Protestantism, and not the short-lived, geographically limited outbursts of the colonial period, including the era of the "great" awakening. Edwards's *History of Redemption* contributed the drama of redemption to the powerful revivalistic religious culture that emerged during the Second Great Awakening. The work encouraged antebellum evangelicals to link America's two great awakenings and to invoke Edwards's authority in the service of nineteenth-century millennialism.

One evangelical described the *History of Redemption* in 1827 as "one of the most popular manuals of Calvinistic theology."[38] The work proved to be popular both with lay readers and revivalistic preachers. Edwards's account offered antebellum evangelicals an understanding of history as a grand narrative propelled by a divine "design and a covenant of redemption" that God "carries on from the fall of man to the end of the world."[39] Edwards presented biblical and doctrinal explanations of the historical drama in accessible sermonic form that encouraged human contributions to the work of redemption through individual conversion and revivalism. Indeed, the *History of Redemption* served to "universalize" the revivals of the Second Great Awakening, situating them in a cosmic scheme of redemption and exciting interest in such evangelical causes as missionary work at home and abroad.[40]

Thus, nineteenth-century evangelicals added the *History of Redemption* to the canon of Edwardsian works on revivalism. Edwards emerged as an authority not only on personal piety and individual conversion, but also on the "morphology" of revivals and their millennial significance. As the father of the great colonial revival, Edwards had laid the groundwork for the Second Great Awakening, one nineteenth-century evangelical concluded, by persuading "a generation that feared more than they knew about revivals of their utility and benefit."[41]

· · ·

Of course the Edwards who was presented to the evangelical public in the 1820s, 1830s, and 1840s by architects of the benevolent empire was different from the Edwards who had been resurrected by the New Divinity men in the early stages of the Second Great Awakening. New Divinity men were theological improvers and not simply advocates of Edwardsian piety and revivalism. They sought to create and extend theological, as well as pietistic and revivalistic, traditions derived from the era of the colonial awakening and to resist the Methodization of orthodoxy on all fronts. As we shall see, "Edwards on the will," as Alan C. Guelzo has recently put it, continued to present moral, philosophical, and doctrinal problems that influenced religious discourse through the middle of the nineteenth century.[42] But Edwards's hyper-Calvinist works were not the texts that were canonized and propagated to a broad lay audience during the Second Great Awakening. The popular piety of the Awakening led evangelical leaders to foreground the "Methodistical" side of Edwards beginning in the 1820s – a process of cultural reinterpretation that enabled moderate Calvinists, such as Lyman Beecher and Charles G. Finney, to challenge the New Divinity's exclusive claim to Edwardsian religious tradition. Edwards's newly established authority on personal piety, conversion, and revivalism also encouraged Old School Presbyterians to downplay the metaphysical Edwards of *Freedom of the Will* and *Original Sin*, to dismiss New Divinity doctrinal improvements, and to claim an orthodox Calvinist Edwards as their own. While Princeton's Archibald Alexander boasted of

Edwards in 1844, "few men ever attained, as we think, higher degrees of holiness, or made more accurate observations on the exercises of others," his fellow Old School Presbyterians resisted both the New School Methodization of Edwards and the New Divinity theological appropriation of his legacy.[43]

As the multidenominational authority of a Methodized Edwards became institutionalized in antebellum evangelical culture, the metaphysical, Calvinist Edwards – and theology in general – became increasingly relegated to seminaries, specialized religious journals, and a professionalized ministry. With Congregationalists and Presbyterians in the forefront, fourteen seminaries were opened between 1808, when Andover was established as America's first postgraduate theological school, and 1836.[44] Some of these seminaries published their own journals, representing an academic phase of the antebellum religious print culture that was so central to the invention of the Great Awakening and to the cultural revival of Edwards. In 1828, for example, Lyman Beecher and Professor Chauncey Goodrich purchased the *Christian Spectator* as a quarterly for the theological faculty of Yale, as well as for the promotion of Nathaniel Taylor's New Haven theology.

Taylor and the *Christian Spectator* offered one strategy for acknowledging and employing the authority of Edwardsian tradition without accepting the hyper-Calvinism of the metaphysical Edwards: invoking Edwardsian rhetoric while justifying improvements on the master. Such a strategy made seminary journals the front line in the war of words over Edwards's theological legacy. "It is not the first, nor the thousandth time," Asahel Nettleton complained to Princeton's Samuel Miller in 1835, "that Edwards has been claimed as vindicating the measures and doctrines which everyman who is acquainted with his works knows he did most sadly deplore and publicly condemn."[45] A year earlier, Nettleton and other New Divinity men, claiming to be legitimate religious descendants of Edwards, deputized themselves as his official theological guardians and established their own seminary in Connecticut. The Theological Institute of Connecticut (later Hartford Seminary) was located in East Windsor, a short distance from Edwards's birthplace. In fact, the cornerstone of the new seminary was a step-stone from the Edwards homestead and signified, as the dedication address described it, the founders' determination to preserve the doctrines "of our Pilgrim Fathers – of Edwards, of Bellamy, of Smalley, of Dwight, – and a host of other distinguished divines of our country."[46]

Led by seminary journals, but overflowing into the broader religious periodical press, evangelicals' efforts to reconcile and appropriate the metaphysical and the Methodized Edwards produced a paper war whose volume surpassed the output of the mid-eighteenth-century pamphlet skirmishes that had marked the emergence of an Edwardsian New Divinity school of theology. The seminary paper war sent divinity students, among others, scurrying to consult Edwards's publications. In the 1830s, for example, Edwards's collected *Works* was withdrawn from the Yale library at almost twice the rate of the next most circulated volume.[47] As Samuel Miller accurately noted in 1837, "for the last half century no other American writer in the school of theology has been so frequently quoted, or had any thing like such deference manifested to his opinions as President Edwards."[48] Yet such deference to Edwards and acknowledgment of his cultural authority was discharged and appropriated in a variety of ways. Some evangelicals simply downplayed the metaphysical Edwards for the Methodized Edwards; others combined Edwardsian rhetoric and "improvements" to traditionalize their alterations of Edwards's thought; still others sought to neutralize the New Divinity by upholding an orthodox Calvinist Edwards, rather than the highly original metaphysician.

The emergence of Edwards as a kind of American cultural icon undergirded each of these appropriations.[49] Moreover, the theologian as cultural icon helped reduce the distance between the metaphysical Edwards and the Methodized Edwards, between the seminary Edwards and the Tract Society Edwards. In addition, the transformation of the theologian into a cultural icon enabled a spectrum of evangelicals to affirm Edwards's intellectual brilliance without necessarily accepting his specific doctrinal stands.

Foreign respect and admiration for Edwards's mind and writings reinforced his intellectual authority and helped shape his cultural image in America. Nineteenth-century evangelicals rediscovered and publicized European, particularly Scottish, esteem for America's preeminent theologian. Edwards became a kind of religious Hawthorne, his cultural figure and body of work repeatedly invoked to counter European intellectual condescension toward America.[50] Edwards was the one American religious thinker whose works included impressive private spiritual writings, penetrating analyses of revivalistic religion, and powerful theological dissertations. Evangelicals proudly cited the judgment of the *North British Review* that Edwards's works constituted "the only considerable literary monument of American Puritanism." Edwards was not simply the "first American to command by his arguments and opinions the attention of Protestant Christendom," a writer argued in the *Congregational Quarterly*, but he was the first and only American religious thinker to achieve a lofty international reputation. "He gave America that rank in the religious world that Washington gave it in patriotic statesmanship and Franklin in philosophy." [51]

In a monotonous biographical refrain, evangelicals repeated the praises of Edwards sung by Dugald Stewart, the respected commonsense philosopher at the University of Edinburgh. Edwards, Stewart remarked, is the "one metaphysician whom America has to boast, who, in logical acuteness and subtlety, does not yield to any disputant in the universities of Europe." [52] Evangelicals seized on statements that supported Stewart's glowing assessment of Edwards, such as the views of Thomas Chalmers, professor of moral philosophy at St. Andrew's in Scotland. "There is no European Divine to whom I make such frequent appeals in my class rooms as I do to Edwards," Chalmers asserted, "no book of human composition which I more strenuously recommend than his Treatise on the Will." Edwards's famous volume, Chalmers claimed, "helped me more than any uninspired book to find my way through all that might otherwise have proved baffling and transcendental and mysterious in the peculiarities of Calvinism." [53]

Evangelicals fashioned a heroic account of a frontier philosopher who rose from the wild forest of America to reach a sophisticated university audience in Europe. Edwards's intellectual ascent betokened a kind of New World originality and sheer mental muscularity that evangelicals played off against popular nineteenth-century perceptions of European corruption and effeteness. As a reviewer of a new edition of Edwards's works conceded in the *Christian Spectator* in 1821, Europe held significant cultural advantages over America. Unlike England, America's abundant economic opportunity, short history, and modest libraries and colleges presented "obstacles" to cultural achievement. Yet, "in every branch of knowledge which there are motives and means to cultivate," Americans had demonstrated that they measured up to or exceeded the intellectual accomplishments of England. "In proof of this we refer to Edwards as an author. He has commanded the admiration of Europeans, even his enemies; among who [*sic*] have been opposed to his conclusions, have done ample justice to the strength of his reasoning powers." [54]

For other evangelicals, such as the Reverend Increase Tarbox, secretary for the American Education Society, Edwards's intellectual attainments demonstrated that America offered important compensations that offset the cultural advantages of Europe. While it was certainly true, Tarbox argued on the pages of the Andover's *Bibliotheca Sacra*, that America could not match Europe "in refinement, general culture, and all the dainty delicacies of learning," American thinkers like Edwards were not weighed down by history, custom, and established cultural institutions. Edwards possessed a mind "more profoundly new, fresh, original . . . than any which the old world could boast." From the "shadows of a wilderness well-nigh unbroken," Tarbox rhapsodized, Edwards offered "a glimpse at least of the primeval man before the fall" that was imposing "for the beauty of his face and person, lordly in the easy sweep and grasp of his intellect, wonderful in his purity of soul and simple devotion to truth." Edwards's vigorous, original intellect thrived in the American wilderness, where it was free to develop "by an inward force rather than by outward formative power." Had Edwards been born and bred in Europe, his mind would have been "cramped," "confined," and "impeded" by supposed cultural advantages.[55]

In the process of transforming Edwards into a cultural icon, biographers apotheosized the mind that produced such formidable and internationally renowned works as *Freedom of the Will*. Just as Edwards displayed an advanced piety in boyhood, constructing a prayer hut in the woods near his Connecticut home that nineteenth-century travelers pointed out as "a hallowed location,"[56] so too, biographers stressed, the youthful Edwards showed an intellectual precocity that foreshadowed the adult genius. Edwards's juvenile writings revealed an impressive "mature and manly mind" which complemented the more "feminine" affective side of the evangelical boy wonder that the private works of his youth reflected. Edwards's account of the movement of the wood spider through the New England forest, which he wrote at the age of eleven, was consistently cited as evidence of his precocious powers of observation and analysis. "Here was a young philosopher of the Baconian stamp and spirit," one evangelical enthused, "who probably hardly knew as yet that such a man as Bacon ever lived."[57]

Edwards's supposed mastery of Locke at the age of thirteen, "when most boys would scarcely have betaken themselves to any thing more profound than 'Robinson Crusoe,'" followed by the composition of notes on

"The Mind," furnished additional evidence for evangelical awe of the youthful Edwards's intellectual ability.[58] While religious liberals and secular commentators regretted that Edwards had squandered his genius by using it to defend Calvinism, evangelicals were grateful that from an early age Edwards's piety served "to enlarge, as well as purify," his mind.[59] "But for his piety," Lyman Beecher wrote to his son George recommending the close study of Edwards's life and writings, "he might have been a skeptic more dangerous than Hume or Voltaire; but for the command of religion over all his powers he might have been one of the more dangerous, as he certainly was one of the most original and fearless of speculators."[60]

Of course, as the founders of both Andover Seminary and the Theological Institute of Connecticut asserted, New England Congregationalists could lay special claim to their "moral Newton," as Timothy Dwight described his grandfather.[61] Even Harriet Beecher Stowe, who once glibly dismissed Edwards's theology as "the refined poetry of torture,"[62] claimed, along with other lapsed Calvinists, that it was neither possible, nor desirable, to uproot an intellectual tradition so firmly attached to New England soil. While Stowe regretted that Edwards had opened the floodgates of Calvinist discussion in New England, she nevertheless conceded that there was something noble in the regional and American intellectual tradition that flowed from his thought. In many respects, she made clear in an essay on Calvinism, she admired Edwards and his New Divinity disciples, "who, leviathan-like have made the theological deep of New England boil like a pot, and the agitation of whose course remains to this day." Only a "shallow mind," Stowe insisted, would fail to recognize something "sublime" in the intricate intellectual maneuvers of Edwardsian thinkers, who "have constituted in New England the strong mental discipline needed by a people who were an absolute democracy."[63]

While rationalist descendants of the Puritans belittled Edwardsianism as a provincial, and therefore embarrassing, intellectual expression, New England's Calvinist evangelicals concurred with Stowe's assessment. Samuel Hopkins, Joseph Bellamy, and other New Divinity theologians possessed a kind of raw Edwardsian mental power, one writer suggested in an essay entitled "Jonathan Edwards and the Old Clergy," which appeared in the *Continental Monthly* at midcentury. "I doubt," the author argued, "if Britain and Germany, with their combined universities could have equaled during the last century the New England pulpit in mental acuteness or philosophical discrimination."[64] As we shall see, the mid-nineteenth-century effort, spearheaded by Edwards A. Park at Andover and the Doctrinal Tract and Book Society in Boston, to publish the collected works and filiopietistic memoirs of Edwards's eighteenth-century New Divinity disciples was part of a successful and influential endeavor to codify, celebrate, and perpetuate one hundred years of Edwardsian theological tradition. To supporters of Park's work of historical reconstruction, there seemed to be little doubt that Edwards and his theological disciples both reflected and contributed to the shaping of the New England and American mind. Perhaps Edwardsian preaching cultivated Yankee ingenuity, one evangelical speculated: "Those who listened to the preaching of such men could not avoid becoming thinkers. . . . A man who could think out the most subtle theories of the pulpit could think out the most elaborate machinery."[65]

Clearly, the mental power that Edwards and his "Farmer-Metaphysician" votaries displayed in their backwoods pulpits and that placed New England and America on the theological map remained, contemporaries were reassured, part of the region's and the nation's lifeblood. Edwardsian ministers in general, and their teacher's "pen" in particular, the Reverend John Todd of Northampton argued in two addresses delivered in 1833 and 1834, shaped "the moral character of New England (and of consequence, that of the rest of this country)." New England's "strong, energetic, untiring" character was merely Edwards's writ large and could be "read" across the American landscape: "in the forests that melt before it, in the sails that whiten the seas, – in the canals and rail-roads, in the factories – on the brow of the whale ship, – in the Temperance Reformation and throughout the world, wherever noble enterprise is to be found."[66]

Edwards's cultural figure was assimilated to what now appears as familiar and contrived rhetoric about Yankee ingenuity, character, and moral energy. But the Yankee cultural identity was still in the process of emerging during the era of the Second Great Awakening, and evangelical writers contributed significantly to its formation. One sees the Yankee identity emergent in the poetry of Timothy Dwight, the moralistic geography of Jedidiah Morse, and the fiction of Harriet Beecher Stowe. More secular sources, such as visual representations of America's "Jonathans," also shaped the creation of the Yankee character.[67] As a cultural icon, Edwards became a "Brother Jonathan" of his own in the nineteenth century.

.   .   .

Esteemed cultural icon, father of the Great Awakening and of American revivalism, and embodiment of a lofty standard of evangelical piety, Edwards was exhibited as the leading luminary in a heroic generation that laid the foundation for the developing nineteenth-century righteous empire. Presbygationalists, in particular, regularly associated Edwards with the revered Founding Fathers of the nation. Such extravagant filiopietism led some evangelicals to caution against the tendency of their contemporaries to derogate from nineteenth-century religiosity because "they judge of the piety of the past from a few picked specimens as Baxter, Bunyan, Henry, Edwards, Brainard [sic], and others whose lives or writings form part of our current literature." [68] Of course, in the process of transforming Edwards into an eighteenth-century founding father of America's righteous empire, nineteenth-century factotums of filiopietism performed a kind of historical face-lift to remove the major blemish on Edwards's image. After all, in what Sereno Dwight described as "one of the most painful and most surprising events recorded in the Ecclesiastical history of New England," [69] Edwards was dismissed in 1750 from the Northampton church that he had served for twenty-three years and that had been the "birthplace" of the colonial awakening. How could this church, which seemingly had been spiritually regenerated by impressive outbursts of revival religion, turn its back on a man of such piety, intellect, and evangelical skill, branding him at middle age with the stigma of dismissal?

Samuel Hopkins had offered an explanation of the controversy, but his brief account was not an adequate defense of Edwards. It remained for Sereno Dwight to furnish evangelical America with a detailed historical apologia for Edwards. The sizable portion of his biography of Edwards that Dwight devoted to the dismissal testified to the personal and historical importance of his coming to terms with the unfortunate event. One-quarter of the *Life of Edwards* (150 pages, not counting Dwight's reprinting of Edwards's entire *Farewell Sermon*) dealt with the dismissal; and this account, like the biography as a whole, became the authoritative evangelical interpretation of the controversy upon which subsequent writers drew.

The intrusion of Unitarians into the cultural debate over Finney's new measures and the legacy of colonial revivalism lent special urgency to Dwight's historical apologetic. From the late 1820s through the 1830s, the *Christian Examiner and Theological Review* and other Unitarian journals sustained a running critical commentary on both specific evangelical excesses and the "revival system" in general. James Walker, minister in

Charlestown, editor of the *Christian Examiner* between 1831 and 1839, and subsequently professor of moral philosophy at Harvard as well as president of the university, emerged as the most intelligent and combative Unitarian antagonist of the evangelicals. Indeed, Walker adopted the strategies and the persona of Charles Chauncy, Edwards's major eighteenth-century rationalist foe. As evangelicals quoted chapter and verse from Edwards and republished the great revivalist's writings with commentaries designed either to legitimate or repudiate new measures, so, too, Walker appealed to Chauncy and strove to undermine evangelical invocation of Edwards's cultural authority.[70]

Of particular importance to Dwight's elaborate defense of Edwards in the church dismissal controversy was a lengthy article, entitled "The Revival under Whitefield," that Walker published in the *Christian Examiner* in 1827. The history of the colonial awakening, Walker claimed, provided a forum for a rational, "less prejudice[d]" examination of the emotionally charged, divisive issues that the revivalism of the 1820s aroused. In his own way, Walker invested the "great" colonial awakening with enormous historical significance, though his reconstruction of that seminal event diverged from the evangelicals' historical scripts. Walker's analysis, for example, suggested that the Second Great Awakening was in the process of unfolding as a historical rerun of the First, with the same contrived origins, the same failed promise, and the same opportunities for proponents of rational religion on the one hand and for "nothingarians" on the other. Far from being "naturally inspired by the circumstances or the subject," Walker argued, revivalism was aroused "by artificial means, and so directed and controlled, by its contrivers and managers, that it might answer their purposes." Yet, once passions became "excited inordinately," it was as difficult to manage them "as to control the storms when they are wildest." Walker recalled the fate of the distinguished Edwards to show the destructive consequences of religious enthusiasm, even to those who had "gotten up" a revival and who had labored to control it.[71]

Walker conceded the evangelical view that Edwards was an impressive historical figure – a man of "great piety" who displayed a "strong natural turn for metaphysical investigation" and who "was as remarkable for his abilities in managing a revival, as in getting it up in the first instance." Perhaps no other minister, Walker concluded, "ever possessed so much influence over his people in time of a revival, and . . . none on the whole, ever exerted it with more judgment and discretion" than Edwards. And yet the revivalistic message, even in the hands of such a saintly, skilled preacher as Edwards, excited enthusiasm and false expressions of piety that the father of the colonial awakening could not control.[72]

Consider, Walker stressed, how the history of Northampton after the colonial awakening established the wisdom of Chauncy's courageous dissent from the popular enthusiasm of revivalistic religion. More than any other community in eighteenth-century America, Northampton had been supposedly purified by the recurring fires of revivalism ignited by the "most reknowned" preacher of the era. One might expect, then, that the town "long continued the abode of peace and virtue, so that in all after time, if any durst lisp a syllable against revivals, men might say 'look at Northampton.'" Instead, within months of the decline of the revival, the town was embarrassed by an obscene book episode involving children of some of the most prominent families in the First Church. Edwards's handling of the incident became the first in a series of divisive issues that pitted the membership against the distinguished revivalist and "that were a scandal to the whole country."[73] The church that had witnessed the birth of the colonial awakening dismissed the "father" of American revivalism in 1750. To Walker, the historical lesson for Second Great Awakeners was clear: if such a distinguished revivalist and student of religious affections as Edwards could not prevent false piety and religious enthusiasm from corrupting his own church, could lesser men a century later contain the destructive consequences of the new generation of James Davenports who had invaded America's churches?

Sereno Dwight prepared what amounted to a bulging legal brief in his *Life of Edwards* that directly responded to Walker's incisive, and often sarcastic, interpretation of Edwards's dismissal and that endeavored to erase this blot from the historical record by transforming it into a morally sublime and providentially inspired episode. Dwight overwhelmed his readers with detailed discussions of the background to the dispute, the political maneuvering that led to the calling of an ecclesiastical council, the politics of that council, and the "uncharitable" treatment of Edwards after the dismissal decision was rendered. He portrayed Edwards as a hero, as a martyr who embodied "*evangelical integrity* – a settled unbending resolution to do what he thought right, whatever self-denial or sacrifices it might cost him." Dwight emphasized that his exhaustive review of the dismissal uncovered no evidence that Edwards was ever accused of neglecting his pastoral duties or of private misconduct. "The only charges brought against him, were, – that he had changed his opinion, with regard to the Scriptural Qualification for admission to the Church; that he was very pertinacious in adhering to his new opinions; and that, in this way, he gave his people a great deal of trouble."[74]

Dwight defended Edwards on each score, transforming him into a spiritual brother of the notable martyrs of Anglo-American Protestantism. Certainly Edwards had reversed himself on Solomon Stoddard's practice of opening church membership, and therefore communion, to all individuals who led moral lives, not just to those who had experienced conversion. But, Dwight argued, when Edwards first arrived in Northampton to assist his grandfather, the initial controversy over open communion had subsided and the practice had become well established in the Connecticut River Valley. In light of local popular and clerical opinion, and with the authority of his venerated grandfather behind open communion, "it is not surprising that a young man of *Twenty-three* should conclude, that the practice was probably right, and adopt it of course."[75]

After extensive study, Edwards determined that neither scripture, nor New England ecclesiastical history, supported open communion. Though he was in middle age, had eight children, and benefited from "the largest salary paid by any country congregation in New England," he decided to challenge the entrenched practice, recognizing that he would alienate not only his own church, but also local ministers, who would most likely recommend his dismissal. "Rare indeed is the instance," Dwight observed, "in which any individual has entered on the investigation of a difficult point in casuistry, with so many motives to bias his judgment."[76] Edwards's heroic stand against popular opinion was a testimony to his character and a fulfillment of the self-denying piety of the "Resolutions." Moreover, for Dwight and for other evangelicals writing in the age of Andrew Jackson and Charles G. Finney, Edwards's dismissal became a kind of parable on the excesses of democracy, an "example," in the words of one prominent Presbyterian who adopted Dwight's interpretation, "of the blindness and violence of popular feeling, even in a population of the most enlightened, sober, and reflecting character."[77]

In the end, Dwight skillfully exonerated revivalism and arraigned Stoddardeanism for subverting genuine evangelical religion in Northampton and for pitting against Edwards a corrupt church erected through lax admission standards. Because of long-standing Stoddardean practice, Edwards was unable to use ecclesiastical "safeguards" that were critical to

protecting the spiritual purity of the church, especially in periods of revivalism. Thus, his church "must have embodied within its pale, an un-
happy proportion of hypocrisy, worldly-mindedness and irreligion"; and
these elements, "on the first plausible occasion," rose in opposition to "the
prevalence of truth, and the welfare of real religion." Even after his dismissal, Edwards displayed humble disinterested benevolence toward
church members, who descended to even deeper depths of disgrace. Since
the church had no minister, Edwards, still concerned for his former flock's
spiritual well-being, offered to supply the vacant pulpit until a minister
was settled. In response, the church voted to prohibit Edwards from
preaching to anyone from his old pulpit.[78]

From a nineteenth-century historical perspective, it became clear to
Dwight that Edwards's dismissal actually served the designs of "an All-
wise Providence." The Stockbridge years, despite their poverty and hardship, gave Edwards the time to pursue theological studies and to make
major contributions to the advancement of religious truth. If he had continued in Northampton, where his pastoral responsibilities were "so numerous and engrossing," Edwards would not have been able to fulfill his
providential role. Instead, "at the best time of life, when his powers had
gained their greatest energy," he settled in Stockbridge and produced
"four of the ablest and most valuable works, which the church of Christ
has in its possession."[79]

By marshaling a carefully selected, but still impressive, array of evidence
favorable to Edwards, Dwight transformed defeat into a heroic stand
against and providential victory over popular sentiment run amok.
Dwight's ex cathedra interpretation, based in part on family documents to
which only he – as the curator of a major portion of Edwards's manuscripts – had access, decidedly influenced subsequent biographers and
contributors to religious journals, who often described the grandeur of
Edwards's stand and the moral lessons that the dismissal episode offered.
"With the single exception of the history of Christ," Noah Porter, professor of moral philosophy and metaphysics at Yale, wrote in the *Christian
Spectator* in 1831, two years after the publication of Dwight's biography of
Edwards, "it would be difficult to find a more wonderful example than is
here presented, of wisdom, patience, meekness, condescension, and firm-
ness, on the one hand, or of infatuation, and violent inflexible resistance
of truth, kindness and obligation on the other."[80]

In the midst of evangelical America's "rediscovery" of Edwards's heroic stand – which, of course, was only one aspect of the larger Edwards cultural revival – Northamptonites found an opportunity to expiate the historical sins of their community. By the early 1830s, the First Church of Northampton had outgrown its meetinghouse. In a peaceful settlement, a separation was effected in the church and a new society organized. By a unanimous vote, the members of the new church agreed to name it after Edwards. "How little did Edwards think," the Reverend John Todd remarked in the address delivered when the cornerstone of the new meetinghouse was laid on, appropriately, July 4, 1833, "that a church would ever arise here, cherishing as her heart's blood the doctrines which he taught, and calling herself and her Temples by his name because his dear memory lingers on earth."[81] The process of "reinventing" Jonathan Edwards involved not only the canonization of texts, but also the consecration of sacred shrines and relics – the Edwards church, the step-stone from the Edwards family homestead, the site of the youthful Edwards's prayer hut. The creation of such Edwards "antiquities" offers compelling evidence that the eminent divine's religious relevance was not simply rediscovered in the nineteenth century; it was a product of the cultural work of the Second Great Awakening.

3

• • •

DAVID BRAINERD AND DISINTERESTED
BENEVOLENCE IN ANTEBELLUM EVANGELICAL
CULTURE

The Connecticut River Valley offered mid-nineteenth-century Americans an appealing national landscape and a cultural heritage that made the region a major tourist destination. The Valley's rolling hills, loamy plains, and bustling white republican villages, celebrated in prose and poetry by Timothy Dwight and others, reassured Americans that the new nation was advancing in virtue and culture.[1] Historical associations from the Valley's Puritan past, such as the Deerfield Massacre and the colonial awakening, imbued the region's natural beauty and republican townscapes with an American antiquity. For evangelical travelers in the Connecticut Valley, Edwardsian relics were part of the region's sacred past; and so was the Northampton grave of Edwards's most famous disciple – David Brainerd.

William B. Sprague reported at midcentury that Brainerd's grave was a site "hallowed to the hearts of thousands," and an evangelical shrine visited by pilgrims from both sides of the Atlantic.[2] One pilgrim recalled in the late nineteenth century the emotional intensity of his first visit to Brainerd's grave. "Does it savor of saint-worship or superstition," Baptist minister Adoniram Judson Gordon asked, "to be thus exploring old grave yards, wading through snowdrifts, and deciphering ancient headstones on a cold day in mid-winter?" This zeal, Gordon explained, resulted from the fact that he had "never received such spiritual impulse from any other human being as from him whose body has lain now for nearly a century and a half under that Northampton slab."[3]

Gordon was far from alone in his emotions. Between the late eighteenth and mid-nineteenth centuries, prominent evangelicals, from Francis Asbury, the first Methodist bishop in America, to Samuel J. Mills, "the father of Congregational missions," and Francis Wayland, the Baptist president of Brown University, to cite only a few examples, all enthusiastically testified to the influence Brainerd exerted on their lives, and they described the importance of his heroic Edwardsian figure for the American evangelical community in general.[4] Such testimony enhances the historical credibility of Sereno Dwight, who observed in 1822 that "the veneration felt for his [Brainerd's] memory, by the church, approaches that with which they regard the early evangelists and Apostles." When the General Association of Massachusetts met at Northampton in the middle of the nineteenth century, the clergymen marched en masse to Brainerd's grave and paid their respects to the Edwardsian apostle who had attained an exalted place in evangelical hagiography.[5]

Edwards initiated the historical process that resulted, by the early nineteenth century, in widespread reverence for his distinguished disciple. In the mid-1740s, Brainerd became an intimate of the theologian and his family. It was in Edwards's Northampton parsonage in 1747 that the young missionary died from tuberculosis, which for years had caused him to cough up blood. Closely tied to Edwards in life and death, Brainerd became even more securely attached to his teacher in nineteenth-century evangelical collective memory and filiopietism. Not surprisingly, the volume of Jared Sparks's *Library of American Biography* that contained Samuel Miller's *Life of Edwards* also offered the public a companion biography of Brainerd.[6]

Before his death, Brainerd consented to the publication of his private diary, which contained a detailed account of his spiritual life, his devotional exercises, his physical afflictions, his psychological difficulties, and his quest for Indian souls during the four years he spent as a missionary. Brainerd devoted the last weeks of his life to preparing the work for publication; upon his death Edwards inherited the uncompleted task. Through careful editing, which included omissions and alterations of as well as additions to Brainerd's words, Edwards fashioned the diary into a heroic memoir and inspirational guidebook which he published in 1749 as *An Account of the Life of the Late Reverend Mr. David Brainerd. . . .*[7] The volume became the most popular and most frequently reprinted of all Edwards's works. Nineteenth-century evangelicals elevated what had been a largely neglected post-awakening text into a religious classic. They also transformed an obscure, sickly, generally ineffectual young missionary into a saintly figure who embodied authentic spirituality, not simply ephemeral revivalistic enthusiasm, and who sacrificed his life for Christianity. As a result, William Warren Sweet observed decades ago in *The Story of Religion in America,* "David Brainerd dead was a more potent influence for Indian missions and the missionary cause in general than was David Brainerd alive." More significantly, in a review of an expanded edition of the *Life of Brainerd* published in 1950, Perry Miller pointed out that the work "has had an immense sub-literary and – if one will – sub-intellectual currency, and its part in influencing the American character has been considerable – far vaster, in all probability, than anything else that Edwards wrote."[8]

Yet, in spite of both abundant evangelical encomiums to Brainerd's influence and the large claims for the importance of Edwards's *Life of Brainerd* by Sweet, Miller, and others, there has been little scholarly analysis of the missionary or of the biography itself, though the recent republication of the volume in the Yale edition of Edwards's works has begun to stimulate interest in Brainerd.[9] Still, both the *Life of Brainerd* and the missionary himself need to be restored to their central place in the history of evangelical America. By the early nineteenth century, Brainerd, like Edwards, had secured an august position in evangelical hagiography, and the *Life of Brainerd* had become an immensely influential devotional-inspirational work among evangelical clergy and laity. Indeed, the *Life of Brainerd,* like Edwards's *Personal Narrative* and "Resolutions," enabled leaders of the Second Great Awakening to shape and popularize an Edwardsian brand of piety that addressed the concerns and needs of evangelical Protestantism. The work played a crucial role in the transformation of Edwards's ethics into the ethics of antebellum evangelicalism. In particular, Brainerd personified, and the *Life of Brainerd* described, an interpretation of true holiness as radical disinterested benevolence that became a vital element in the theological rationale for religious reform, especially missionary work. Leaders of the missionary movement invested the *Life of Brainerd* with literary and religious authority; the work became the archetype for the missionary memoir, a major subgenre of religious biography that was enormously popular and influential in the nineteenth century. Antebellum evangelicals popularized and invoked Edwards's *Life of Brainerd,* and the lofty commitment to disinterested benevolence it embodied, in ways that challenged prospective missionaries, shaped an emerging missionary sensibility, and even hastened Brainerd's evangelical successors in their journeys toward the grave.

. . .

The nineteenth-century reverence Edwards's distinguished disciple evoked in evangelical circles and the authority he held for missionaries, in particular, were drastically out of proportion to the modest accomplishments of his brief life. Born in Haddam, Connecticut, in 1718, Brainerd was left an orphan at the age of fourteen when his mother died (his father, who had served as Speaker of the Connecticut House of Representatives and as a member of the Governor's Council, had died five years earlier). Brainerd went to live with relatives and seemed destined for life as a Connecticut farmer, tilling land that his father had left him and his brothers. In 1739, however, he experienced conversion, and, though well past the age of the typical Yale freshman, he enrolled at college with aspirations for the Congregational ministry. By his sophomore year, when the colonial awakening swept through Yale, Brainerd was recognized as one of the college's "New Light" student firebrands. In defiance of the college's social rules, he led groups of zealous students to every dormitory room, where they probed each occupant's spiritual state and stressed the need for regenerating grace. By the September 1741 commencement, Yale authorities were prepared to launch a counteroffensive against a looming student religious insurgency that had been inflamed by itinerant preachers such as Gilbert Tennent and James Davenport. On commencement day, the trustees took their first step to suppress New Light insubordination, voting "that if a student shall directly or indirectly say, that the Rector, either of the Trustees or Tutors are Hypocrites, carnall or unconverted Men, he shall for the First Offense make a public Confession in the Hall, and for the Second Offense be expelled." [10] Yet Brainerd and his fellow New Lights took heart from the commencement speaker. In a sermon that he would later publish as *Distinguishing Marks of a Work of the Spirit of God* (1741) and that anticipated the *Religious Affections*, Jonathan Edwards affirmed the authenticity of the revival. The inordinate emotionalism, unrestrained conduct, censorious attitudes, and other objections that critics raised to discredit the revival, Edwards argued, "are no evidence that the work is not of the Spirit of God." [11]

Edwards's address did not endear him to Yale authorities, who would soon turn a deaf ear to his efforts to intercede on Brainerd's behalf. Rector Thomas Clap expelled Brainerd in 1742 for remarking that tutor Chauncy Whittelsey had no more grace than a chair and for attending a meeting of Separate Congregationalists in defiance of college rules. Though Brainerd wrote a remorseful letter to the trustees, he refused to issue a public apology for his intemperate remark, the condition that Clap laid down for his readmission to Yale. His comment about Whittelsey had been made in private; moreover, Brainerd and his evangelical supporters within and outside of Yale saw the expulsion for exactly what it was: a calculated move by Clap to threaten and demoralize pro-revival students by humiliating one of their leaders. Neither the intercession of Edwards, nor that of other Congregational and Presbyterian ministers, won Brainerd's readmission to Yale.[12]

Brainerd's defiance became a cause célèbre for some New Lights, furnishing them with powerful confirmation of the perceived spiritual rot at the center of the Standing Order's institutions and leadership. His confrontation with representatives of this seemingly corrupt establishment only served to deepen Brainerd's melancholic personality and compel him to humble himself before God the way he was unable to submit before Yale authorities. In the less than six years that he lived after his expulsion from Yale, Brainerd found socially approved outlets for his religious fervor. He studied for the ministry, received a license to preach, and in November 1742 accepted an appointment as a missionary of the Society in Scotland for Propagating Christian Knowledge. The following spring he took up his first assignment among a small group of Mahican Indians at Kaunameek, New York, between Stockbridge, Massachusetts, and Albany. After a year filled with physical ailments, psychological depression, and struggles to learn the Mahican language, Brainerd had little to show for his missionary efforts, and he began to cast about for another Indian outpost. In June 1744, he was ordained by the Presbytery of New York at Newark, New Jersey, and he launched new Christianizing endeavors among the Delaware Indians near the forks of the Lehigh and Delaware Rivers in Pennsylvania and more than one hundred miles west of this location along the Susquehanna River. Again, a year of effort proved unproductive.[13]

Finally, at yet another Indian settlement, Crossweeksung, New Jersey (near Trenton), Brainerd experienced his only notable success as an Indian missionary. Between 1745 and 1746, he led a revival among small bands of Delawares, who had been stripped of most of their land and victimized by disease and alcohol. At the start of the revival, Brainerd remained cautious, even skeptical, because he "had pass'd thro' so considerable a Series of almost fruitless Labours and Fatigues." Thus, he was unable to "Believe and scarce ever found myself more suspended between Hope and Fear, in any affair, or at any time, than this."[14] The critical role that his Indian translator, Moses Tattamy, played in these conversions explains, at least in part, the self-doubt that Brainerd expressed over his sudden success, a reversal of his fortunes that he attributed to Divine Providence. Tattamy, who had served as an interpreter and emissary between Indian and white authorities, offered his services to Brainerd. Just as his patron, Edwards, was unable to preach to the Stockbridge Indians in their native language and relied on a translator, so too Brainerd could not preach to the Delawares in their own dialect and depended on his interpreter to translate his sermons and awaken his Indian audience. Indeed, Tattamy may have been more the instigator of these revivals than Brainerd. "My interpreter being absent," the bewildered missionary acknowledged in his diary at one point, "I knew not how to perform my work among the Indians."[15]

Tattamy and his wife were Brainerd's first converts. Almost immediately after their conversion, religious emotions were astir among the Delawares. Indians regularly attended Brainerd's religious services, and occasionally he found himself preaching to more than ninety worshipers. Brainerd took a conservative, watchful approach to the administration of baptism to apparent Indian converts, a practice that helps explain the meager accomplishments of Calvinist evangelical missionaries among Native Americans. Following Edwardsian church admission policies, Brainerd sought convincing evidence of authentic conversion as well as some reassurance of Indian understanding of the doctrines implied in his sermons. Brainerd baptized thirty-eight adults, who, he was persuaded, had experienced saving grace; he also formed a small church.[16] The missionary described his modest achievement in his *Journal,* which was published by the Society in Scotland for Propagating Christian Knowledge, the sponsor of his missionary efforts, in 1746.

Though in declining health, Brainerd left New Jersey in the spring of 1747 to visit family and friends in New England. Throughout the summer and early fall, the physical distress of Brainerd's tuberculosis worsened. He became bedridden in Edwards's Northampton parsonage, where the theologian's daughter Jerusha nursed him until he died on October 9, half a year short of his thirtieth birthday. According to Edwards, Brainerd continually "manifested much concern lest he should dishonor God by impatience under his extreme agony."[17] For Edwards, such a laudable attitude of resignation was only one of a number of moral and spiritual ideals that the missionary embodied. Nearly a year after Brainerd's death, Edwards wrote to the Reverend John Erskine in Scotland, explaining how his possession of the missionary's diary had changed his writing and publication plans: "I have for the present, been diverted from the design I hinted to you, of publishing something against some of the Arminian Tenets, by something else that Divine Providence unexpectedly laid in my way, and seemed to render unavoidable, viz. publishing Mr. Brainerd's Life, of which the enclosed papers of proposals gives some account."[18] Edwards carefully assayed the raw material Brainerd left behind, passed it through the sieve of his own religious experience, and cast off what he considered spiritual slag. Thus, from the literary remains and meager accomplishments of Brainerd's brief life, Edwards fashioned a didactic, romantic tale of a sickly, orphaned, young missionary who persevered against physical, spiritual, and emotional hardships, who finally experienced success, and who was guided by Providence back to family and friends, where his precious diary was preserved. In short, Edwards became Brainerd's Parson Weems.

The publishing history of the *Life of Brainerd* furnishes strong evidence of its popularity and establishes a framework for analyzing its influence. More editions and reprints of the *Life of Brainerd* have been issued than of any other Edwardsian work. As with other Edwardsian volumes, the initial appeal of this work was stronger abroad than in America. In the second half of the eighteenth century, both Edwards's *Life of Brainerd* and Brainerd's *Journal* were frequently reprinted in Scotland and promoted by the missionary's Presbyterian sponsors; several editions of the *Life of Brainerd* were also issued in England and Holland. In fact, Edwards's work became the first American biography to reach a large European audience. During the first half of the nineteenth century, the *Life of Brainerd* attained its widest popularity and influence both in America and abroad.[19]

John Wesley was among the first to see the value of the *Life of Brainerd* as a devotional-inspirational work, especially for evangelical ministers. "Find preachers of David Brainerd's spirit," he observed in 1767, "and nothing can stand before them."[20] Wesley prepared an abridgment of the *Life of Brainerd*, published in seven separate editions between 1768 and 1825, and urged the volume on his clerical disciples as a way of firing their evangelical commitment. "Let every preacher read carefully over *The Life of David Brainerd*," he wrote. "Let us be followers of him, as he was of Christ, in absolute self-devotion, in total deadness to the world, and in fervent love to God and man." Wesley even inserted his enthusiastic endorsement of the *Life of Brainerd* into the handbook of the Methodist ministry.[21] Though he rejected Edwards's high Calvinism, Wesley approved of Brainerd's Edwardsian piety, and thus he anticipated the reaction to the *Life of Brainerd* of nineteenth-century evangelicals of varying doctrinal persuasions. More important, as a result of Wesley's aggressive recommendation, the *Life of Brainerd* became a devotional-inspirational manual for Methodist circuit riders, while the figure of the sickly Brainerd traversing the American backcountry on horseback in search of souls for Christ became a model of selfless heroism.

Wesley was the most important, but not the only, zealous English promoter of the *Life of Brainerd*; John Styles, who prepared a popular edition of this work, first published in 1808, was another. Styles reduced the size and cost of the volume so that it would reach a large audience and "prove an acceptable addition to the devotional library of younger Christians and students for the ministry."[22] Styles's work was reprinted in England and America and became the standard early-nineteenth-century edition. Sereno Dwight, who published his own important edition of the *Life of Brainerd*, gave Styles credit for promoting Brainerd's name in America. For while this volume was reprinted in late-eighteenth-century America, it was not until Styles's edition appeared in the nineteenth century that Edwards's biography became widely popular and influential.[23]

Indeed, the canonization of Brainerd and the transformation of the *Life of Brainerd* into an American religious classic were yet additional aspects of the cultural work of the Second Great Awakening that included the revitalization of Edwards as a religious authority and the invention of the "great" colonial awakening. Through repeated reprintings of the *Life of Brainerd*, the missionary was once again called on to serve the evangelical cause. Edwards's biography of Brainerd provided evangelicals with an exemplary life of self-denying piety and with a historically rare example of a partially successful Indian missionary. Like Edwards, Brainerd was invoked as a cultural authority and inspirational model for evangelical religious crusades. In 1822, near the height of evangelical interest in revivalism, millennialism, and missionary work, Sereno Dwight published his enlarged edition of the *Life of Brainerd*, which incorporated Brainerd's public *Journal,* a work that also had been reprinted frequently in Europe and America. Dwight's volume was particularly popular with the Sunday School Union, which published abridged editions of it in 1826, 1827, and 1830.[24]

The American Tract Society issued still another edition of the *Life of Brainerd,* whose influence rivaled the redactions of Wesley, Styles, and Dwight. As one of the largest and most thoroughly interdenominational organizations in the "benevolent empire" of nineteenth-century Protestantism, the Tract Society attempted to Christianize America by publishing and distributing tracts that stressed common religious ground shared by the various denominations. Edwards was among the Society's most popular authors, and the *Life of Brainerd* was one of its most successful publications. First issued in 1833, the Society's edition of this work remained on its publication list until 1892. Between those dates, the Society frequently reprinted the missionary's biography and distributed thousands of copies.[25]

The American Education Society, which provided scholarships for indigent ministerial aspirants, served as another conduit for the distribution of the *Life of Brainerd.* Elias Cornelius, the Society's secretary, presented each scholarship student with a copy of the biography.[26] The popularity of the *Life of Brainerd* with the Education, Tract, and Sunday School Societies suggests how conversion of the heathen could be the kind of hoary and conventional religious reform around which an increasingly fragmented American evangelical community could rally. Brainerd's traditional form of benevolence attracted nineteenth-century Protestants from various points of the theological compass and provided them with opportunities to assert the superiority of white Anglo-Saxon evangelical culture. Moreover, the missionary cause and the kind of personal Edwardsian piety that the *Life of Brainerd,* the *Personal Narrative,* and the "Resolutions" portrayed appealed not only across evangelical doctrinal lines, but also across differences between northern and southern pietists and eastern and western revivalists.

The major redactions of the Tract Society and of Wesley, Styles, and Dwight were supplemented by numerous other editions of the *Life of Brainerd* that were published and republished in American, England, and Scotland during the first half of the nineteenth century.[27] At the same time, biographical accounts of Brainerd began to appear, particularly in the religious periodical press. These accounts reflected the extensive interest in the missionary; they also reinforced and propagated Edwards's heroic interpretation of Brainerd's missionary career and thereby document the influence of the *Life of Brainerd*. "Of the ministers of the Gospel in modern times," one writer panegyrized in the accustomed fashion, "there is no one whose history I remember, whose piety and success remind one more of apostolic times, than the missionary David Brainerd." [28]

The abundant published material about Brainerd won him a prominent place in evangelical oral tradition alongside Edwards. Ministers recounted his life from the pulpit, and parents in evangelical households described his self-denying exploits in inspirational stories that were passed down to children. Congregational missionary Samuel J. Mills, for example, recollected that he was first attracted to missionary work by stories of Brainerd and John Eliot that his mother told him in his youth. Evangelicals spoke of Brainerd as the successor to Eliot; ministers and parents held up Edwards and his missionary disciple as heroic models of piety to be emulated by Christians of all ages. Brainerd became a kind of evangelical folk hero and, like Edwards, the subject of a body of lore. Stories depicted him as a frontier saint who subsisted on bear meat and Indian corn meal. Often forced to sleep on the ground during his travels between Indian settlements, he supposedly encountered poisonous snakes that always refused to attack him. Frequently, the apocrypha related, he knelt with clenched hands and prayed for so long that he was unable to walk or flex his fingers.[29] Clearly, evangelicals were reminded, Brainerd challenged the human boundaries of his teacher's humble self-denying piety.

·   ·   ·

Evangelical diaries and memoirs are replete with references to Brainerd and to the influence of Edwards's *Life of Brainerd*, impressive testimony to the success of the cultural agents – religious publishers, reformers, and teachers – of the Edwardsian piety that the biography helped codify. Diaries and memoirs reveal a range of ways in which Edwards's most popular work aided the "practice of piety"[30] and influenced evangelical values and behavior. The work became a valuable guidebook for individuals experiencing the emotional throes that usually preceded conversion. Evangelicals used the *Life of Brainerd* precisely as Edwards had intended – as a companion volume to the *Religious Affections*. Edwards's elaborate study of authentic spirituality was not published until 1746, but his earlier works on the colonial awakening, such as the *Distinguishing Marks of the Work of the Spirit of God*, contained many of the arguments that were developed at length in the *Religious Affections*. By the time Brainerd read and enthusiastically endorsed the *Religious Affections*, Edwardsianism already pervaded his spiritual life, informing the penitential rhetoric of the diary and provoking him compulsively to use the text as a kind of substitute for sackcloth and ashes.[31] Not surprisingly, Brainerd's diary reads like the record of his efforts to discern in his interior life the presence of the distinguishing marks of conversion that Edwards analyzed in detail in the *Religious Affections*. As Norman Pettit has accurately observed, "Certain notions that appear in the diary could only have come from Edwards. More than that, one senses on Brainerd's part an attempt to parrot his mentor. He conformed, with certain exceptions, to Edwards's rules."[32]

When, after judicious editing, Edwards incorporated the diary into the *Life of Brainerd*, he created a nearly perfect extended case study of genuine religious affections – a case study similar to the brief life histories he had employed in such popular nineteenth-century works as *A Faithful Narrative of the Surprising Work of God*. In his concluding "Reflections and Observations," Edwards applied the signs of true spirituality to Brainerd and penned a vignette of his disciple's religious life that was sharper than the broad portrait of authentic sainthood contained in the *Religious Affections*. In succinct, rapid-fire fashion Edwards described how Brainerd exemplified such marks of holiness as "uncommon resignation to the will of God," "great and universal benevolence to mankind," "sweetness of speech and behavior," "decent deportment among superiors, inferiors, and equals," "great watchfulness against all sorts of sin, of heart, speech, and action," "extraordinary humility," and "unmovable stability, calmness, and resignation, in the sensible approaches of death."[33] By casting the *Life of Brainerd* in the form of a case study of true holiness, Edwards made his interpretation of genuine spirituality accessible to ordinary evangelicals. Thus, along with the *Personal Narrative*, ministers, missionaries, and teachers recommended the *Life of Brainerd* to awakened sinners as a supplementary or alternative spiritual guidebook to the *Religious Affections*.[34]

The *Life of Brainerd* was also a popular devotional work for evangelicals who were already converted. Brainerd displayed what came to be viewed as typically Edwardsian self-denial and self-abasement, culminating in a desire "to burn out in one continued flame for God."[35] The intensity of his religious affections, rather than their character, made him unique among Edwards's disciples. Moreover, Brainerd engaged in elaborate and

continuous exercises of fasting and prayer as rituals of religious purifi-
cation. Like Edwards's "Resolutions," then, the *Life of Brainerd* described a
lofty standard of piety and practice to which converted Christians could
aspire. As Edwards pointed out, Brainerd's life after conversion was a process of "progressive sanctification" and deepening "evangelical humiliation."[36] The missionary demonstrated how conversion marked only the
start of a lifelong quest for true holiness.

In editing the diary, Edwards was determined to use the accounts of
Brainerd's self-abasing exercises, quest for sanctification, and missionary
activities as a corrective to the antinomianism – the spiritual pride and
moral complacency – that the colonial awakening fostered. To achieve his
goal, Edwards deleted passages, such as the following, which contained expressions of religious enthusiasm that had encouraged challenges to social
authority during the revival:

> I used now (as well as when under conviction) to marvel at the conduct
> of most (both ministers and people) that called themselves Christians,
> that when they met together they could talk of all the world, and spend
> their time in jesting and the like and never say a word of spiritual con-
> cerns or anything of that dreadful wilderness that I have been led along
> through. I used sometimes to leave the company and society of such
> and get alone in the woods, or any other place of retirement in order to
> pray. Sometimes I used to think such persons were not nor could be
> Christians, and sometimes I thought there were two sorts of Christians,
> but I desired not be of that sort, for I thought they felt nothing of the
> sweetness of religion. At other times I thought I was a creature alone
> and by myself and knew not of any that felt as I did, though I thought
> some certain persons did, by their actions and discourse that I had for-
> merly observed: but being now at a distance from them I had no oppor-
> tunity to converse with them.[37]

By omitting overly enthusiastic, potentially antinomian passages, Edwards
deradicalized Brainerd and brought his piety even closer to the humble,
self-effacing, and socially safe religiosity of the *Personal Narrative* and the
"Resolutions." In the process, he gave nineteenth-century evangelicals another sacred text that could be used to combat the antinomianism and
moral complacency of their own revivalistic era. Unlike such Edwardsian
works as the *Religious Affections*, the *Life of Brainerd* did not have to be
heavily edited and recast before making its way to the evangelical public as

a religious classic. Edwards had already shaped Brainerd's short life and edited his diary for didactic ends, though an occasional Calvinist outcropping and the bedrock melancholy of the missionary's temperament, evidence of which Edwards was unable to eliminate completely, sometimes unsettled nineteenth-century promoters and readers of the text. Methodists especially preferred to expunge from the *Life of Brainerd* Calvinist elements and passages of brooding dejection before publishing and promoting the text as a classic.[38]

Evangelical diaries and memoirs document the popularity of the *Life* as a devotional aid to sanctification and moral activism. "For many years," one New Englander recalled, "an old and worn volume of his [Brainerd's] life and journals has lain upon my study table, and no season has passed without a renewed pondering of its precious contents."[39] The *Life of Brainerd* was often read as part of private spiritual practices. Missionaries regularly took the work into the field, where it became part of their devotional exercises. In Egypt in 1823, for example, Congregational missionary Pliny Fisk noted in his diary one sabbath that, while reading the *Life of Brainerd*, he was led "to contrast this monument of Brainerd and his character" with the character and accomplishments of the Pharaohs. "All their cities, mausoleums, temples and pyramids," Fisk concluded, "seemed insignificant compared to the crown of glory which Brainerd won."[40] Fisk was not simply commenting on the worldly values of ancient Egypt. Rather, like other young men who were converted in the local revivals of the Second Great Awakening and who aspired to the missionary ministry, Fisk drew on Brainerd's life for the inspiration that enabled him to reject the secular values of his contemporaries who were pursuing the impressive worldly opportunities that antebellum America offered.[41]

As Fisk's case suggests, the *Life of Brainerd* had its greatest impact on American missionaries. Edwards stressed that Brainerd's "example of laboring, praying, denying himself, and enduring hardness with unfainting resolution and patience, . . . may afford instruction to missionaries in particular."[42] At Andover Seminary, the institutional center of the missionary movement in nineteenth-century America, Leonard Woods, professor of theology, reported that the *Life of Brainerd* was among "the most sound and searching books on experimental and practical religion"[43] that the faculty recommended to students. Seminarians drew from Brainerd the kind of inspiration that Levi Parsons, the first American missionary to Palestine, described in his diary in 1815 while he was a student at Andover:

"Much refreshed this day by perusing the life of Brainerd. How completely devoted to God, how ardent his affections. What thirst after holiness, what love for souls. His life was short but brilliant and useful. He ushered in a glorious day to the church. Counting pain and distress and every bodily infirmity as dross, he patiently encountered difficulties and dangers, and at last sweetly resigned his all to his savior. Multitudes have reason to call him blessed."[44] For Parsons, Fisk, and other Andover graduates, Brainerd stood first in missionary hagiography. They spoke of him as continuing to inspire the missionary movement from heaven and as escorting the souls of deceased missionaries into the Divine presence. Perhaps Brainerd's lofty status in evangelical hagiography and the popularity of the *Life of Brainerd* among nineteenth-century missionaries are summed up by the fact that when the American Board of Commissioners for Foreign Missions established its first Indian post, among the Cherokees in 1817, the missionaries named it Brainerd.[45]

Memoirs of Andover graduates who enlisted in missionary service not only contain direct testimony to the influence of the *Life of Brainerd*, but they also disclose an Edwardsian approach to spirituality that clearly bears Brainerd's imprint. At the center of the complex of missionary ideas that Andover transmitted to students lay an Edwardsian conception of disinterested benevolence that Brainerd was perceived as embodying to the highest degree humanly possible. In *The Nature of True Virtue*, written in 1755 and published posthumously ten years later, Edwards defined authentic holiness as benevolence to "Being in general," that is, "the great system of universal existence." Through regeneration, Edwards argued, a genuine Christian had a benevolent affection implanted in the heart that motivated the convert to love and seek the good of Being in general.[46] Such true virtue was disinterested in the sense that the regenerate person desired no individual good separate and distinct from the benevolence of Being in general. In *The Nature of True Holiness* (1773) and in subsequent works, Samuel Hopkins helped secure his reputation as Edwards's leading theological disciple by extending the Edwardsian doctrine of disinterested benevolence and advancing an even more radically self-denying interpretation than his teacher. Hopkins established a *willingness* to die and be damned, if necessary, for the good of Being in general as the ultimate test of true holiness. For both Edwards and Hopkins, David Brainerd was the "phantom figure in the text";[47] and the *Life of Brainerd* was the subtext – the text within the text – of *True Virtue* and *True Holiness*. While Edwards's writings had shaped Brainerd's self-abasing exercises and the religious idiom in which he recorded them, the missionary's diary informed subsequent Edwardsian theological formulations of true virtue and authentic sainthood.

Edwardsian and neo-Edwardsian interpretations of true holiness and disinterested benevolence furnished dynamic theological arguments for religious reform, in general, and the missionary cause, in particular. Hopkins's doctrine of disinterested benevolence, for instance, was as popular among Andover missionaries as Edwards's *Life of Brainerd*.[48] In fact, Hopkins incorporated Brainerd's experiential religion into his doctrine of disinterested benevolence. Not surprisingly, then, Brainerd came to be seen as a personification of radical disinterested benevolence; his self-immolating piety was construed as a practical demonstration of the powerful theological argument that Hopkins had developed.

The *Life of Brainerd* thus became a spiritual touchstone for missionaries, who used it to test the genuineness of their commitment to disinterested benevolence. Enduring the physical and emotional hardships of missionary work, as Brainerd had, was one element in this test; facing the prospect of death, especially from disease, was another. The risks of foreign missionary work are borne out by the number of Andover graduates who, like Brainerd, died at a young age after a relatively brief period in the field.[49] With Brainerd's example instilled in them, missionaries left Andover prepared to risk death. Before sailing from Andover to Bombay, missionary Gordon Hall wrote to his parents: "It will be trying to your parental tenderness to see your son leaving you to live and die in a foreign land. But have you not given me away in covenant to God?" Hall went on the remind his parents "That *death* will separate us whether we consent or not." Likewise, before departing for Palestine, Levi Parsons observed in his farewell address, after citing Brainerd's example: "Better, my brethren, wear out and die within three years than live forty in slothfulness." [50]

Such self-denying affections became so common among nineteenth-century foreign missionaries that Joseph Tracy, who was also a historian of the missionary movement as well as of colonial revivalism, issued a warning to young men burning with zeal to spread the gospel. In *The Great Awakening*, Tracy cautioned prospective missionaries against a close emulation of Brainerd's self-effacing piety, which "hurried him to his grave." He went on to observe that too many foreign missionaries had already experienced a "failure of health . . . in about the same length of time" as Brainerd and from the same kind of religious enthusiasm.[51]

The *Life of Brainerd* and the conception of disinterested benevolence that served as its theological cornerstone cultivated another predilection among nineteenth-century missionaries that may have undermined their proselytizing efforts, or at least helped these zealous young men endure failure. Historians have frequently noted how ambitious designs to Christianize American Indians or convert foreigners produced only meager tangible results at best. The cultural norms of American missionaries – their ethnocentrism – worked against the success of Christianizing endeavors. Brainerd's view of the Indians was all too typical of the cultural bias of his missionary successors: "They are in general unspeakably indolent and slothful, – have been bred up in Idleness – and know little about cultivating land, or indeed of engaging vigorously in any other Business. . . . They have little or no Ambition or Resolution. – Not one in a thousand of them has the Spirit of Man. And it is next to impossible to make them sensible of the Duty and Importance of being active, diligent, and industrious in the Management of their worldly Business; and to excite in them any Spirit and Promptitude of that Nature in them."[52] Hence, conversion was only one aspect of a larger process of anglicizing native people – or "reducing the Indians to civility."[53] The Edwardsian conception of disinterested benevolence added a theological element to this evangelical cultural perspective that may have contributed to the failure of Brainerd and the missionaries who followed in his train.

Especially when Indians were not only indifferent, but also outwardly hostile, Brainerd viewed his missionary work as a test of his commitment to disinterested benevolence. Indeed, in his *Journal* he stressed the numerous obstacles to converting Indians, from the problems of learning native languages to the bad examples that nominally Christian whites set for the Indians.[54] When these and other realities conspired to hinder his ministry, Brainerd turned inward, torn by doubts that he did not possess the spiritual resources – the saving grace and self-denying disinterested benevolence – to endure seeming failure. At times he expressed guilt for being too concerned with his own salvation rather than that of the Indians. Arriving at the forks of the Delaware and Lehigh Rivers in the summer of 1744, he noted his renewed hope "for the conversion of the heathen. . . . And when I long for holiness now, it is not so much for myself as formerly." Yet faced with hostile Indians, he resumed his quest for personal holiness. "Such fatigues and hardships as these," he recorded, "serve to wean me more from the earth; and, I trust, will make heaven the sweeter."[55] In early 1745, Brainerd confronted the prospect of yet another missionary failure and again began to recast it into a personal spiritual victory. "But God was pleased to hear my cries, and to afford me great assistance; so that I felt peace in my own soul; and was satisfied that if not one of the Indians should be profited by my preaching, but should all be damned, yet I should be accepted and rewarded as faithful; for I am persuaded God enabled me to be so."[56] Clearly, Brainerd was on a twofold mission in the American backwoods: to gather souls for God and to convince himself of his own holiness by demonstrating his commitment to disinterested benevolence. As, inevitably, the first part of his mission went poorly, the second increased in importance.

For young men influenced not simply by the ethical thought of Edwards and Hopkins but by a nineteenth-century revivalistic culture of self-denial that derived from popular texts, oral tradition, and heroic figures (all exemplified by Brainerd), missionary work came to be viewed as a spiritual trial – a test of their holiness, of their commitment to disinterested benevolence. Thus, like Brainerd, nineteenth-century Edwardsian missionaries often seemed disproportionately concerned with their own spiritual lives and quests for true holiness and only secondarily with the salvation of non-Christians. While their idealism or millennial outlook cannot be denied, Edwardsian missionaries apparently often saw the missionary crucible as a way of affirming a personal commitment to disinterested benevolence and of practicing the self-renunciation and moral activism that would bring them closer to the saintly spirituality they saw embodied in Brainerd.[57] In one sense, then, success at converting non-Christians was irrelevant; failure in the field became another part of the test of the missionary's spiritual endurance. Edwards's *Life of Brainerd* provided missionaries and other religious reformers with more than ample inspiration and instruction for enduring failure and for transforming it into a personal spiritual triumph.

. . .

As a model of Edwardsian piety, the *Life of Brainerd* not only gave missionaries and religious reformers an inspirational heroic figure and helped shape a self-denying spiritual sensibility, but also became the archetype of an important subgenre of nineteenth-century religious biography – the missionary memoir. The first generation of missionaries sponsored by the American Board of Commissioners for Foreign Missions, which was founded in 1810, became heroic Christians in their own right. These pioneering American missionaries were the subjects of inspirational nineteenth-century memoirs that were patterned after the *Life of Brainerd*. From the perspective of literary history, the *Life of Brainerd* links such earlier Puritan works as Cotton Mather's biography of John Eliot (and, indeed, all of Mather's efforts in *Magnalia Christi Americana* to use biography to stimulate piety) and the formulaic popular missionary memoirs of the nineteenth century.

As a case study of genuine religious affections and true virtue, Edwards recommended the *Life of Brainerd* to "*Christians in General.*" But he had a more specific audience in mind: critics of the experimental religion of the colonial awakening; enthusiasts, converts who displayed "strong fancies" and antinomianism; and missionaries and their supporters. Consequently, the *Life of Brainerd* served a range of nineteenth-century evangelical objectives, from demonstrating and promoting genuine revivalistic piety and benevolent Christian activism to arousing interest in, as well as moral and financial support for, missionary work.[58] The memoir incorporated elements of several genres of popular religious literature that contributed to its appeal and to its usefulness in evangelical jihads against the moral and spiritual frailties of antebellum Americans. The *Life of Brainerd* was many things to many people: spiritual journal, case study of conversion, spiritual guidebook, inspirational-devotional manual, and heroic memoir.

The *Life of Brainerd*, moreover, was in part a travelogue. Though Brainerd focused on his spiritual experiences, he described his feverish physical movement through the eighteenth-century landscape as he searched for prospective converts, and he introduced his readers to backcountry corners of colonial America. Such travelogue elements increased in importance as the missionary memoir evolved. The genre changed to accommodate the new experiences and needs of Brainerd's successors. As missionaries journeyed farther from home, the travelogue aspects of their memoirs became more pronounced and developed than they had been for Brainerd. Missionaries gave their readers detailed accounts of foreign cultures and exotic lands that contributed significantly to the popularity of their memoirs. In contrast, the *Life of Brainerd* reveals a man who was preoccupied with the landscape of his soul. Yet the travelogue was an important structural link between the *Life of Brainerd* and the nineteenth-century missionary memoir.[59]

The pilgrim's journey and captivity motifs of the *Life of Brainerd* establish even more significant structural connections to the emergent missionary memoir of the antebellum decades. Indeed, the pilgrim, captivity, and travelogue elements of this work helped inspire and frame the epic Christian journey that informed most nineteenth-century missionary memoirs.

The *Life of Brainerd* described a circular itinerary not unlike the travels of the Methodist circuit riders to whom John Wesley and Bishop Francis Asbury strongly recommended Edwards's work. Brainerd left white civilization for the wilderness, rode on horseback between Indian settlements in New York, Pennsylvania, and New Jersey, and, from time to time, returned to white society. Brainerd used the language and the imagery of the Christian pilgrimage – one of the most popular motifs of Puritan devotional literature – to allegorize his travels. The alien American wilderness became the spiritually barren wilderness-desert of this world. "My soul longs to feel itself more of a 'pilgrim' and 'stranger' here below," Brainerd wrote, "that nothing may divert me from pressing through the lonely desert, till I arrive at my Father's house."[60] The perilous journey through the wilderness-desert of the American backcountry brought hardships that were depicted as spiritual tests of pilgrim Brainerd. On one missionary trip, he encountered particularly hazardous terrain: "we had scarce anything else but lofty mountains, deep valleys, and hideous rocks to make our way through." Brainerd's difficulties multiplied when his horse stumbled on a rock, broke its leg, and had to be destroyed. Badly scraped and bruised himself, Brainerd reacted like a devout Puritan pilgrim to this test of his physical and spiritual endurance: "This accident made me admire the divine goodness to me, that my bones were not broken, and the multitude of 'em filled with strong pain."[61]

In many respects, Brainerd's account of his wilderness travels and his experiences with the Indians reveals the influence of Puritan Indian captivity narratives, allegories of conversion that were enormously popular during the eighteenth century. Brainerd was never actually held captive by the Indians, though he lived on the frontier when Indian-white hostilities were intense and the prospect of capture was real. Like the authors of captivity narratives, Brainerd was forced to reside with the Indians and even to adopt some of their customs. Survival in the wilderness thus became a religious and cultural test, as it had been for the captives. The structure of

Brainerd's account of the test is strikingly similar to such orthodox Puritan captivity narratives as Mary Rowlandson's *The Sovereignty and Goodness of God* . . . , narratives that hardly offered a sympathetic view of Indians as promising subjects for conversion. After his departure from white society, Brainerd encountered indifferent, even hostile Indians. He underwent a series of physical and spiritual trials resulting from the difficulties of adapting to the wilderness and from his lack of success among the Indians. At this point Brainerd expressed the kind of utter despair of the awakened sinner facing eternal damnation and of the captive confronting endless days with the Indians. While in the "depths of distress," he crawled "into a kind of hovel, and there groaned out my complaint to God." [62]

In this emotional state, Brainerd developed a new awareness of the sinfulness of his previous life that was typical of both the awakened sinner and the Indian captive. He passed the test of despair by surrendering to God's will, even if it included capture by the Indians: "Was now much resigned under God's dispensations towards me, though my trials had been very great. But thought whether I could be resigned if God should let the 'French Indians' come upon me and deprive me of my life, or carry me away captive . . . ; and my soul seemed so far to rest and acquiesce in God that the sting and terror of these things seemed in great measure gone." Deliverance (that is, symbolic salvation) followed the appropriate attitude of resignation to the divine will. Brainerd's salvation was a variation on the restoration theme of the captivity narrative. He was delivered from his spiritual despair by leading a revival among the Indians. Moreover, as Edwards stressed, by "remarkable providences" Brainerd was restored to white society before his death, and his inspirational diary was delivered into the hands of his friends. [63]

Edwards followed the practice of ministers who had recognized the didactic and inspirational potential of the captivity narrative and had shaped its conventions. Undoubtedly, he recognized how Brainerd's interpretation of his experience drew on popular Puritan devotional literature. Clearly, Edwards added to, altered, and omitted the missionary's words as he transformed the diary into a biography that exemplified Edwardsian practical piety. During the Second Great Awakening, as part of the cultural revival of Edwards's authority and the canonization of his works, the *Life of Brainerd* emerged as the literary and religious model of the missionary memoir.

Authors of these memoirs created graphic case studies of disinterested benevolence that, like the *Life of Brainerd*, furnished young people and adults with heroic Christian tales, demonstrated and promoted the piety of the Second Great Awakening, and encouraged interest in, and support for, the missionary movement. One editor-biographer described the purpose of his work as follows: "If by the perusal of this volume some Christians should be comforted; if some sinner should be raised from his fatal slumber, if there would be excited in any bosom a truly apostolic zeal in the course of missions, the writer will have lasting occasion to rejoice that he has had an agency, however feeble, in giving this work to the public."[64] Missionary memoirs usually begin with conventional accounts of their subjects' pious childhoods in deeply Christian homes to impress upon readers the importance of early religious training. These childhood experiences laid the religious foundations for the missionaries' conversions, which most commonly occurred during early adulthood and which elicited a desire to bring the gospel to non-Christians. In farewell addresses, missionaries testified to their commitment to disinterested benevolence by describing their willingness to face the prospect of death while serving Christ.[65]

Authors concentrated on the private experiences of their subjects in the field, in part because missionaries recorded such meager success in their public work. Extensive quotation, even reproduction, of the private writings of missionaries formed the body of the memoirs. Here, showing the influence of Brainerd, the young men described the physical and emotional hardships that challenged their commitment to disinterested benevolence. Frequently, they turned to Edwards's memoir and Brainerd's heroic figure for the inspiration to persevere. "What must not Brainerd have suffered, when sick among the Indians?" Pliny Fisk noted in his diary in 1823 when he was seriously ill in Egypt.[66] References to Brainerd in widely read nineteenth-century missionary memoirs reinforced and further disseminated the saintly image that Edwards had cultivated in his biography.

In no small measure, the popularity of missionary memoirs derived from a literary formula that had evolved from the pilgrim, captivity, and travelogue motifs of the *Life of Brainerd*. A kind of epic Christian journey – a quest for spiritual knowledge and experience as well as for converts – underlay Edwards's work and informed the accounts of Brainerd's successors. This religious quest required a separation from family, friends, and home. After ritualistic and emotional farewells, in which kin, friends, and supporters formed a procession that ushered the missionary to the dock, the young man began his epic journey and was soon initiated into another side of life. He repeatedly confronted and surmounted physical, emotional and spiritual tests, as Brainerd had, which deepened his understanding of himself and of life. In the process, the missionary experienced a rite of passage into evangelical adulthood, and the certainty of salvation increased as the prospect of death was blissfully accepted. Having measured up to the saintly standard established by Brainerd, the new Christian hero was assigned a place in evangelical hagiography.

·   ·   ·

A special centennial edition of the *Life of Brainerd* was published in 1849, and the biography continued to be regularly reissued through the 1850s and beyond.[67] Historical details about the colonial revival in New England became widely known because of the popularity of Brainerd's biography, which contributed to the invention of the "great" awakening. As one evangelical leader observed in 1839, poor Chauncy Whittelsey was now "known to thousands in both hemispheres as the man of whom David Brainerd declared: 'He has no more grace than this chair.'"[68]

Leaders and supporters of the benevolent empire employed the *Life of Brainerd* to address major concerns of nineteenth-century evangelical America, from disinterested benevolence and religious reform to revivalism and conversion of the "heathen." American religious historians, however, have more often than not restricted Brainerd's significance, when they have recognized it all, to the colonial awakening. His difficulties at Yale which led to his dismissal, for instance, are usually cited as an example of the anti-institutional behavior that religious enthusiasm encouraged. Consequently, Brainerd has been frequently viewed as the spiritual brother of radical eighteenth-century evangelicals such as James Davenport and Gilbert Tennent. But the publishing record and cultural history of Edwards's *Life of Brainerd* suggest that Brainerd should be recalled, more accurately, as a spiritual forefather of nineteenth-century evangelicalism, which is precisely how antebellum evangelicals viewed him. In his *Biographical Sketches of the Founders and Principal Alumni of the Log College* (1851), for example, Archibald Alexander, president of Hampden-Sydney College in Virginia and former professor at Princeton, argued that esteem for Brainerd, combined with Yale's heavy-handed treatment of him, helped to inspire the founding of the first Presbyterian college. Re-

spect for Brainerd and outrage at Yale "quickened the zeal" of Jonathan
Dickinson, Aaron Burr, and other members of the New York Synod to establish the College of New Jersey.[69] Thus, having ordained, sponsored, and
drawn inspiration from the Edwardsian missionary in the eighteenth century, Presbyterians – like Andover missionaries – staked out a special claim
to Brainerd and his legacy in the nineteenth century.

What seems clear from the nineteenth-century canonization of the *Life
of Brainerd* and from its influence on the missionary memoir is that Edwards contributed to a popular nineteenth-century evangelical American
literature that paralleled the more famous and enduring work that established American cultural and literary independence during the antebellum
decades. Denominational, interdenominational, and commercial presses,
benefiting from rising literacy and drawing on improvements in the tech-
nology of printing, responded to and helped expand an evangelical audience that the Second Great Awakening created.[70] Religious biographies,
autobiographies, *and* fiction were not simply literary weapons in the evangelical arsenal that would conquer and Christianize America; they also
competed with a popular and rapidly developing secular American literature: tales of travel and adventure, as well as sentimental and sensational
fiction. Perhaps this competition helps explain important shifts in antebellum evangelical culture that the popularity of the *Life of Brainerd* and of
the missionary memoir signaled: the movement away from biblical and
classical to historical and contemporary heroic models of inspiration; the
rise of appeals to affecting examples of practical piety rather than to theological authority; the decline of doctrinal sermonizing in favor of pulpit
story telling; and the emergence of literary expressions of sentimental piety in the evangelical novel.[71] In any case, Edwards's newly established authority for an evangelical American literature went well beyond the influence of the *Life of Brainerd*. The popularity of such works as the *Personal
Narrative* and the "Resolutions," as noted earlier, influenced evangelical
literary expressions of private piety; and Edwards's revival narratives contributed to the development of that evangelical literary form which became firmly established and widely popular during the Second Great
Awakening.

Whatever the literary merits of evangelical American literature, it is
clearly a significant body of work for nineteenth-century religious and cultural history, as the *Life of Brainerd* and the missionary memoir attest. The

Life of Brainerd and its literary successors helped embed elements of an Edwardsian sensibility in antebellum evangelical culture. The work's most significant contribution to evangelical America was a high-flown definition of true virtue as consisting of radical disinterested benevolence, a doctrine that upheld the importance of personal self-denial and of Christian activism. Closely related to this challenging interpretation of disinterested benevolence was the Edwardsian commitment to progressive sanctification that Brainerd displayed. The quest for true holiness included a process of continual spiritual renewal and growth; disinterested benevolence, and the "evangelical humility" that revealed its presence, increased by degrees. Moreover, a rich spiritual life of devotional and meditative exercises was essential to progressive sanctification.

Of course the Edwardsian approach to disinterested benevolence did not hold out the prospect of spiritual perfection in this world; supreme selflessness, as Brainerd and his missionary successors demonstrated, could not be attained short of self-immolation. And yet, nineteenth-century evangelicals were not always restrained by the *Life of Brainerd* and other popular Edwardsian works from advocating doctrines of moral perfection in this world. Methodists, for instance, by ignoring (as John Wesley had) "the small vein of Calvinism"[72] running through popular works of Edwards such as the *Life of Brainerd*, enlisted Edwardsian piety in the service of an evangelical doctrine of moral perfection.

Finally, the influence of the *Life of Brainerd* – and the conception of disinterested benevolence which undergirded it – on missionaries, circuit riders, and other nineteenth-century evangelicals indicates that Edwards's legacy included a significant contribution to the reformist religious impulse that animated the benevolent empire, whose architects found the theologian's most popular work so useful. The *Life of Brainerd* added to an ongoing Methodization of Edwardsianism. Drawing on the sainted figures and pietistic texts of Edwards and Brainerd, nineteenth-century evangelicals of assorted doctrinal stripes contributed to the notion of a "mission for life" that challenged Christians to emulate the heroic disinterested benevolence of missionaries and to witness their faith constantly in the world. As Adoniram Judson, who was known as the "Baptists' Brainerd," put it in 1833, "The motto of every missionary, whether preacher, printer or schoolmaster, ought to be 'Devoted for Life.'"[73] For the equally famous former Andover student Theodore Dwight Weld, antislavery, rather than spreading the gospel in foreign lands, became the mission for life. Weld never forgot or freed himself from the influence of the heroic missionary stories that his pious mother read to him at an early age.[74]

It would be simplistic, however, to establish an airtight relationship between the Edwardsian doctrine of disinterested benevolence and antebellum *social* reform. As the impact of the *Life of Brainerd* on missionaries suggests, nineteenth-century Edwardsianism was not free of ambiguities, tensions, and contradictions. How, for example, can benevolence be characterized as disinterested when it was so frequently tied to quests for personal sanctification? Like Brainerd, Edwardsian missionaries often seemed as concerned with establishing their spiritual manhood through moral activism and self-annihilation as with serving others. All of which is to say that the Edwardsian doctrine of disinterested benevolence, as morally compelling and theologically original as it was, did not completely resolve the tension in revivalism and evangelical culture between personal holiness and social reform. Rather than assume an isomorphic relationship between disinterested benevolence and social reform, it is more accurate to say that Edwardsian Christian ethics and the heroes of the missionary movement were summoned by nineteenth-century evangelical leaders to help construct a religious culture of self-sacrifice and self-renunciation. The moral power and reformist impulse of this evangelical culture of disinterested benevolence served a variety of religious agendas, from the antislavery cause, to socially safer religious reforms such as the missionary and temperance movements, to comparatively privatized assaults on worldly pleasure and self-exaltation.

4

. . .

MARY LYON, MOUNT HOLYOKE SEMINARY,
AND FEMALE PIETY, 1830-1850

The religious culture of self-sacrifice codified around the doctrine of disinterested benevolence and powerfully dramatized in the *Life of Brainerd* and in Edwards's *Personal Narrative* and "Resolutions" became institutionalized at Mount Holyoke Seminary. Under the leadership of its founder, Mary Lyon (1797–1849), Mount Holyoke developed as a kind of New England "nunnery" whose female religious reformers were steeped in the resurgent Edwardsianism of the Second Great Awakening. Since Edwardsian tradition has been usually defined in narrow theological terms, women have been excluded as *active* participants in and contributors to it. Mary Lyon's engagement in the revitalized Edwardsianism of the Second Great Awakening, however, offers a different perspective on that religious tradition.

Recent studies of the Second Great Awakening have stressed the strong appeal of evangelical religion to female worshipers. The revival has been portrayed as a "women's awakening" that nurtured "bonds of womanhood," promoted female benevolence, and shaped antebellum canons of domesticity. Mary Lyon and the founding of Mount Holyoke Seminary, which opened in 1837, have not gone unnoticed by historians of a women's awakening. In a follow-up essay to her important study of Catharine Beecher, for example, Kathryn Kish Sklar established the educational significance of Mount Holyoke and situated Lyon's efforts in the context of the Second Great Awakening. Mount Holyoke's innovations included secure financial support funded by the evangelical community at large, a resultant low cost that enabled students from modest and even poor backgrounds to enroll, and an intellectually rigorous curriculum that eschewed "ornamentations," such as dancing and the cultivation of gentility. Lyon's innovative educational efforts for women, Sklar argued, were a consequence of the crusading moralism and organized female benevolence of the Second Great Awakening.[1]

However, Sklar did not probe beneath the surface of Lyon's evangelical religion to explore its doctrinal underpinnings, and the same may be said for social historians who have discovered the women's awakening. Lyon, in fact, was both a devoted disciple and an enthusiastic promoter of Jonathan Edwards. Such a religious commitment does not seem consistent with dominant interpretations of American religious and cultural development that have stressed a nineteenth-century transition from piety to moralism and from Calvinism to religious liberalism. Thus, Lyon's Edwardsianism has been ignored or downplayed not only by Sklar, but by other major interpreters of Mount Holyoke and of its founder's life.

Lyon's most recent biographer, for instance, grudgingly acknowledges that she was an "admirer" of Edwards but, in a caricature of what this might mean, quickly adds that "she talked to students much less about the pain of hellfire than the sadness of being left out of heaven and the exhilaration of life animated by faith."[2] Similarly, Arthur C. Cole, chronicler of the educational history of Mount Holyoke, suggests that Lyon was little more than a closet Calvinist who publicly "proclaim[ed] a 'covenant-keeping' God in terms that apparently caused little offense to the secure occasional Unitarian, Episcopalian or potential Roman Catholic that entered her student body."[3] Clearly, while Lyon's significance as an educator has been recovered, the Edwardsian Calvinist mainsprings of her religion, which informed her life and educational efforts, remain obscure.

Lyon's seemingly anachronistic doctrinal tastes and her influential career as an educator may be approached as yet another major episode in the cultural revival of Jonathan Edwards that was stimulated by the Second Great Awakening. In a reversal of what we have come to accept as a much more common historical pattern, Lyon converted from the Baptist church to Edwardsian Congregationalism in 1822. She acquired from Edwards's works and doctrines (particularly the doctrine of disinterested benevolence) and from a network of New Divinity ministers the inspiration and legitimation for "manly" self-assertion and self-expression in support of the evangelical cause. Lyon found in the New Divinity's renewed Edwardsianism a Calvinist theological framework, a self-denying social ethics, and a revivalistic tradition that shaped her religious and educational efforts.

Teacher, preacher, and proselytizer at Mount Holyoke, Lyon became a highly successful, if unordained, Congregational revivalist. Moreover, as a result of her Edwardsian loyalties, Mount Holyoke emerged as an orthodox bastion, a "sister" school not only to such orthodox provincial male colleges as Amherst, Williams, and Dartmouth, but also to Andover Seminary, whose missionary graduates readily found pious wives in Lyon's student body.

.   .   .

Born in the western Massachusetts town of Buckland, Lyon's life and career as an educator paralleled the rise and development of the Second Great Awakening and its attendant cultural revival of Edwards's writings and authority. Though raised as a Baptist, Lyon was a descendant of a family with long-standing Edwardsian loyalties. Indeed, in a dispute with the Congregational Church in South Hadley over its abandonment of Edwardsian pure church policies, Lyon's great-grandfather renounced his church membership, migrated deeper into the hill country of western Massachusetts, and helped establish a Baptist church more to his liking in Ashfield.[4] In the second half of the eighteenth century, orthodox congregations comprised of Connecticut River Valley migrants beckoned clerical disciples of Edwards to western Massachusetts. In fact, the New Divinity became so identified with the area that it was sometimes referred to as the "Berkshire divinity."[5] Lyon was raised and began her teaching career in small western Massachusetts towns where Edwardsian and New Divinity ministers and congregations remained a vital part of the religious culture well into the nineteenth century. Lyon's biography is not only an account of personal hardship and of evolving bonds to a supportive female evangelical subculture; it is also a story of her acceptance into a New Divinity clerical network in New England and her assimilation into a newly forged Edwardsian religious tradition.

At first disrupted by family tragedy, Lyon's personal circumstances then became entangled in larger social changes that propelled rural New Englanders westward and that dispatched farm girls to school teaching and factory work. Lyon's father died when she was five years old, leaving her mother with the management of their farm and the care of a large family (Lyon was the sixth of eight children). Jemima Lyon struggled to run the farm and support the family until Mary was thirteen. Jemima then remarried, moved from Buckland with her youngest daughters, and left the family farm in the hands of her twenty-one-year-old son, with the teenage Mary assigned as his housekeeper. Lyon managed to attend district school while performing domestic chores for her brother. In 1814, the seventeen-year-old Lyon began her teaching career in Shelburne Falls, a town a short distance from Buckland. School teaching increasingly became a means of self-support. Her brother's departure with his own family for New York left Mary to fend for herself.[6] School teaching became a livelihood for her rather than temporary employment until a suitable mate came along.

Scraping together enough money from her meager wages as a teacher and housekeeper and from her sale of handmade quilts, Lyon entered Sanderson Academy in Ashfield in 1814. Founded by a bequest from Alvan Sanderson, the local Edwardsian minister, the academy educated both males and females, rejecting the "ornamental" skills that were common in many schools for girls. Lyon later acknowledged that Sanderson's was "the school where I was principally educated, and to which I feel no small degree indebted."[7] Yet, a second Edwardsian minister and his school were to have an even greater influence on Lyon, particularly with respect to shaping her plans and aspirations for Mount Holyoke.

Lyon and students of her life have commented on the critical role that Reverend Joseph Emerson and the Ladies Seminary in Beverly, Massachusetts, played in the development of her pedagogy, a pedagogy that combined academic and spiritual instruction. Yet, scholars have ignored the assertive Edwardsianism that was a hallmark of Emerson's ministry and of his educational efforts. Emerson was one important New Divinity minister who made major contributions to the revitalization of Edwards's cultural authority in the Second Great Awakening and who was a tireless promoter and publisher of the eminent divine's works. Emerson had studied for the ministry under the redoubtable New Divinity theologian and revivalist Nathanael Emmons (1745–1840) of Franklin, Massachusetts, who trained upward of one hundred clergymen in the late eighteenth and early nineteenth centuries. Ordained as the pastor of Beverly's Third Congregational Church in 1803, Emerson then joined other New Divinity men in invoking Edwards's authority, reprinting his works, and issuing unpublished Edwardsian material – all in response to the religious controversies provoked by the Second Great Awakening. As we have already seen, Emerson was responsible for the first publication of Edwards's private "Resolutions" for spiritual and moral development as a separate text.[8]

Emerson made other contributions to the renewal of Edwardsianism.

In 1809, he authored an orthodox catechism, *The Evangelical Primer*, for use in schools and homes. Endorsed by Emmons and other prominent New Divinity ministers, *The Evangelical Primer* was reprinted frequently in the first half of the nineteenth century and became a popular text in the orthodox village schools that Mary Lyon attended and in which she taught. By 1835, more than 200,000 copies had been published.[9]

Lyon came directly under Emerson's influence at his Ladies Seminary, where she enrolled in 1821. Emerson had established the seminary in 1816 after illness led to his dismissal from the Third Church. Emerson's seminary was committed to educating pious female teachers who would make schools an extension of the benevolent empire, whose institutions were so dependent on women's activism. Properly trained teachers, Emerson asserted, would "do more to enlighten and reform the world and introduce the millennium than persons of any other profession except ministers of Christ."[10] His respect for women's intellect, as well as for their self-denying spirituality, led him to urge Edwards's works on his students. "Most of Edwards's works," his students were informed, "may be read, and read, and read again, with great advantage."[11] When Lyon began raising money for Mount Holyoke in the mid-1830s, she did so while simultaneously sponsoring a subscription for a new edition of Edwards's *History of the Work of Redemption*, one of the many Edwardsian works that Emerson enthusiastically recommended to his students.[12]

Lyon's experience at Emerson's seminary was a turning point in her development as an educator. She later reflected that "she owed more to Mr. Emerson than to any other teacher." In his relationship with women, Lyon recalled, "There was no needless gallantry – no apparent consciousness of stooping – or of condescension." Above all, she recollected, Emerson as a teacher instilled in his female students "a modest confidence, not only in their individual powers, but also in the native abilities of their sex." Her experience at Emerson's school undermined for Lyon the conventional "assumption," as she put it, that females "were never designed to be literary or scientific, and that they cannot be without injury to themselves and others."[13] Emerson's tutelage also proved critical to Lyon's religious life. She had been raised a Baptist; she claimed to have experienced conversion in 1816. In 1822, however, Lyon joined the Congregational church in her hometown of Buckland.[14] Her conversion to Congregationalism signified her increasing assimilation into the Edwardsian evangelical religious culture of New England and into its clerical network, which would prove to be a major source of public support for the establishment of Mount Holyoke Seminary.

Between her experience with Emerson and her efforts in the mid-1830s to establish Mount Holyoke, Lyon spent thirteen years teaching in Ashfield, Buckland, and Ipswich, Massachusetts, and in Londonderry, New Hampshire. In Londonderry and Ipswich, she established female academies with Zilpah Grant, whom she had met at Emerson's seminary. Finally, in 1834, Lyon left teaching to devote herself to fund-raising for Mount Holyoke. The seminary's financial arrangements (a substantial endowment and low costs) and the availability of three years of rigorous academic training distinguished Mount Holyoke as a new departure in higher education for women.

Modeled after Amherst College, which was founded in 1821 and whose faculty taught at Mount Holyoke, Lyon's seminary was designed to provide an orthodox, moderately priced academic education to evangelical females from rural and small-town New England. Thus, the founding of Mount Holyoke, like the establishment of Amherst, received strong support from Edwardsian ministers, particularly in western Massachusetts. Though women's societies and female benevolent institutions were the major audience for her financial appeals, prominent orthodox clergymen in western Massachusetts, who drafted fund-raising circulars and served on the board of trustees, helped legitimize Lyon's "unwomanly" activities in the service of evangelical religion. Northampton's John Todd, pastor of the new Edwards Church, served as the first president of the seminary's board of trustees. Todd suggested Mount Holyoke as the name for the seminary, and he delivered the address at the laying of the cornerstone for the school, just as he had done with the Edwards Church. Todd was joined on the board by other orthodox clergy, including Joseph Penney of Northampton's "old" Edwards Church and Rosewell Hawks, who took a leave of absence from his church in Cummington to raise funds for the seminary, an assignment that turned into a twenty-year career as a full-time fund-raiser for Mount Holyoke.[15]

Lyon herself traveled unescorted across New England, wrapped in a buffalo robe to ward off the cold of New England winters, directly soliciting financial support for Mount Holyoke.[16] Her nineteenth-century biographer and energetic patron, President Edward Hitchcock of Amherst (a ministerial disciple of Edwards), observed that some viewed Lyon "as a sort of Amazon, of strong mind and inflexible purpose, but wanting in those tender and delicate feelings which are appropriate to women."[17] Hitchcock, Emerson, Todd, Penney, Hawks, and other orthodox male benefactors seem to have recognized and accepted how Lyon embodied what has been called the "central paradox" of the Second Great Awakening for women: namely, how evangelical religion "idealized feminine attributes of self-denial, humility, submission, purity and meekness" while sanctioning female benevolent activities that "were not very submissive, humble, meek, self-denying or even pure."[18] Mount Holyoke thrived as a result of such a paradoxical appropriation of evangelical religion.

From the seminary's opening in 1837, Lyon was besieged with far more applicants than she could admit. By 1839, there were 400 students seeking admission to the 100 slots that were available. The seminary attracted young women with backgrounds like Lyon's. The student body was comprised overwhelmingly of pious females from modest rural backgrounds. They were drawn to Mount Holyoke primarily from the hills and valleys of interior New England. Emily Dickinson, the seminary's most famous student, was pleased to discover that her countrified Mount Holyoke sisters were not totally deficient in social refinement. "I expected to find rough and uncultivated manners and to be sure I have found some of that stamp," she reported to a correspondent, "but on the whole, there is an ease and grace, a desire to make one another happy, which delights and at the same time, surprises me very much."[19] Many students had acquired considerable education on their own, as the young Mary Lyon had; some were already teachers when they entered Mount Holyoke. Students used earnings from teaching or mill work to help pay for their Mount Holyoke education, sometimes alternating years of work and study. The seminary attracted both the converted and those seeking rebirth. "It is harder to be a Christian anywhere than at Mount Holyoke"[20] became a familiar description of the seminary as its reputation for piety grew. Lyon added the male role of revivalist to that of college founder. Indeed, Lyon's success as a revivalist at Mount Holyoke is perhaps the best example of how she found in evangelical religion and in Edwardsian tradition the inspiration and legitimation for a new level of female self-assertion.

Between the opening of Mount Holyoke in 1837 and Lyon's death twelve years later, revivals were more common and numerous at the seminary than at any other institution of higher education in New England and perhaps in America. Eleven revivals swept through the student body during those twelve years, and as the Reverend Heman Humphrey (the second president of Amherst College and another Edwardsian clerical supporter of Lyon) noted, several of these revivals were "so general and powerful, that nearly all who were without hope, in several classes gave evidence of passing from death to life." Amherst College experienced considerably fewer revivals than Mount Holyoke – ten between 1821 and 1840 – and another orthodox New England college, Williams, was the scene of ten revivals between 1795 and 1840.[21] At all of these institutions, teachers, not students, promoted conversion as part of their educational mission. Lyon assumed the primary responsibility for getting up revivals at Mount Holyoke.

Of course, spiritual instruction in conjunction with academic preparation had been common in the schools Lyon had attended and in which she taught. It was at Emerson's Ladies Seminary, however, that Lyon was fully exposed to the Edwardsian revivalistic tradition and to the evangelical techniques that she would employ at Mount Holyoke. At the start of each year, Emerson asked his students to classify themselves according to whether or not they had experienced conversion. In 1821, Lyon joined those students at the seminary who professed the hope of salvation. She then observed how Emerson used preaching, private counseling, and evangelical readings – including works of Edwards – to bring the unconverted into the fold.[22]

Lyon adopted such techniques, employed Edwardsian revival rhetoric, and urged Edwards's works on her students at Mount Holyoke. "We can even now, after the lapse of years," co-teacher Fidelia Fisk recalled, "see her loving eye resting upon us after the names have been taken of those who had professed Christ publicly, of those who had not done this, but still had some hope; then of those who had no hope."[23] The recollections of Fisk and of Mount Holyoke graduates confirm that Lyon was skilled in invoking Edwardsian rhetoric, sometimes nearly lifting passages from Edwards's most famous revival sermon, "Sinners in the Hands of an Angry God." She compared the classification of students to "the last great day of separation," invoked the inevitability of death and judgment, and posed a series of rhetorical questions that appealed directly to her students' affections. "If death should come to us tonight," she asked at the classification ritual, "would the separation be the same as this now made?" Singling out the unconverted, Lyon then liked to echo Edwards's most graphic revivalistic rhetoric and imagery: "How vain to resist God! Did you ever see the little insect fall into the flame; see it struggle and strive to escape? – how vain! Just so you are in the hands of an angry God. What if you do resist?

What are you[,] a feeble worm of the dust? Oh, how vain! How much better to submit."[24] Clearly, Lyon was a shrewd and historically informed revivalist. Steeped in Edwards's works and evangelical techniques, Lyon was also schooled in the Edwardsian revivalistic tradition that had been one of the major cultural inventions of the Second Great Awakening. Lyon was determined to draw on and impart this tradition to her students.

In addition to her revivalistic efforts, she preached to students several times a week on Scripture and religious doctrine, often, one observer recollected, "with Edwards's History of Redemption in her hand."[25] Lyon's success as a revivalist and her influence on her students derived not only from her knowledge and skills as an Edwardsian teacher and preacher. Mount Holyoke's regimented religious culture of required Bible study, fast days, concerts of prayer, private meditation, "anxious meetings," and active benevolence – all closely supervised by Lyon – established a structure for the flourishing of her evangelical religion within the seminary student body. The seminary's intensive regimen of worship, study, and work was controlled by a system of bells and rules. Bells sounded from sunrise to late evening, dictating the rhythm and orderly efficiency of the seminary. "We use to run at every bell, but we have got used to them," one student reported, "and we know just when we ought to go to any . . . exercise."[26] Seventy rules controlled all phases of student life, requiring whispering in the laundry room, for instance, and prohibiting unofficial group meetings as well as rising before the morning bell. Such a regulated system, one student confided to outsiders in 1844, reflected Lyon's character, which was "noble, generous, and refined, well spiced with genuine *Puritanism*, that very kind which formed the 'Blue Laws' of Connecticut and . . . make the Bluar [*sic*] Laws of Mount Holyoke."[27]

Some students were overwhelmed by the regimentation and religious intensity of the "convent of Saint Lyons," as the seminarians dubbed their school. "O I shall be glad to get home where I can speak above a whisper," one student complained, "and not have to move by a line and plummet."[28] Even teachers could feel overpowered by the irruption of religious emotions at the seminary. On one day in 1846, thirty-one students experienced conversion and another thirty-four were awakened in the "anxious" stage. "I have felt that though it is good to be here, yet I can say how dreadful is this place," confessed teacher Susan Tolman, who would go on to serve as a foreign missionary and to cofound Mills College. "I never passed such a day in my life."[29]

Such tumultuous days, when so many students were laboring under religious convictions, appear to have been exceptional. Yet, outbreaks of
revivalism regularly provided some relief from the intense, highly regimented routine of seminary life. Weeks of fasting, prayer, and preaching
by Lyon usually culminated in a religious outburst precipitated by a
significant event – the departure of teacher Fidelia Fisk for the foreign missions in 1843, for example.[30] At these and other moments, Lyon enlisted
teachers and converted "sisters" in her campaigns to exert communal pres-
sure on those who remained unawakened. Lyon herself, however, was primarily responsible for the revival spirit in the student body. Through her
preaching and private spiritual counseling, she consistently interacted
with Mount Holyoke students. Amherst College's Edward Hitchcock
claimed that "the pastors of our churches" could gain much from studying
Lyon's revival practices. "Why should even ministers be ashamed to learn
wisdom or a subject so important, from a woman," Hitchcock observed,
"especially from one so eminent for wisdom and piety, and whose experience in revivals was so extensive."[31]

Lyon not only impressively assumed the traditional male role of revivalist; she also became the seminary's moral philosopher, the influential
position filled by male presidents of nineteenth-century men's colleges.
Though not a theologian or a doctrinal polemicist, Lyon still used the
classroom and religious meetings as forums to explore and promote her
Edwardsian Calvinist tenets. "She has been taking up for a few mornings
past the great doctrines of the Bible, as Total Depravity, the Nature of Sin
&," one student recorded in 1847.[32] Lyon assigned readings from Edwards,
"always between the morning and afternoon service of the Sabbath,"
teacher Fidelia Fisk recalled. "We are sure that all who learned of Christ
through Edwards and Mary Lyon will thank God throughout eternity for
those blessed seasons."[33] Thus, as both the seminary's moral philosopher
and resident revivalist, Lyon institutionalized Edwardsianism at Mount
Holyoke, contributing to a nineteenth-century religious tradition that was
part cultural invention, part cultural revitalization.

· · ·

The appeal of Edwardsianism to Lyon, the successful way in which she
drew on revivalistic tradition, and the strong support that she received
from Edwardsian clergymen all suggest an important theme in the history
of the feminization of nineteenth-century Protestantism. Major works fo-

cusing on the "bonds of womanhood," on evangelical religion and canons of domesticity, and on the Second Great Awakening as a "women's revival" have all contradicted the provocative thesis of Ann Douglas. In *The Feminization of American Culture*, Douglas argued that a growing proportion of female worshipers in the nineteenth century allied with theologically liberal ministers to dilute Calvinist theology and to sentimentalize American Christianity. Mary Lyon's life not only supports Douglas's critics; it suggests that the surprising staying power of Edwardsian Calvinism and revivalistic rhetoric in nineteenth-century New England may have derived from its appeal to evangelical women.[34] In particular, Lyon and her students appear to have been attracted to Edwardsian notions of disinterested benevolence in an era when an expanding market economy, and the separate spheres of gender activity that accompanied it, made a self-denying social ethic increasingly less relevant to men's lives. Paradoxically, however, Lyon and her students were empowered by a religious culture of disinterested benevolence to transcend the gendered social experience that made Edwardsian self-denial appealing in the first place.

Edwards's frequently reprinted writings on personal piety popularized his views of disinterested benevolence. Some of these works show an increasing attention to female spirituality. Abigail Hutchinson was one of the two key conversions discussed in *A Faithful Narrative of the Surprising Work of God* (four-year-old Phebe Bartlett was the other). The central conversion described in *Some Thoughts Concerning the Revival of Religion in New England* was that of Edwards's wife, Sarah, whose narrative he edited into an exemplary account of experimental religion, benevolence, and spiritual humility. Edwards A. Park, Samuel Hopkins's nineteenth-century biographer, and Sereno Dwight claimed that the famous views on "divine submission" of Edwards's closest disciple were suggested by conversations with Sarah Edwards. Hopkins himself preached to a largely female congregation in Newport, Rhode Island, in the late eighteenth century and published the memoirs of two exemplary Christian women in his church.[35]

Such attention to female spirituality coincided with an increasing Edwardsian concern for the erosion of New England's traditional moral economy in the face of an emergent free market order based on self-interest. Hopkins, for example, mounted a devastating critique of the interconnection of selfishness, commerce, and slavery in late-eighteenth-century Newport; and Hopkins drew his inspiration from Edwards. As Mark Valeri has recently argued, after a close examination of unpublished Northampton

sermons, Edwards called for moral restraint in the marketplace and displayed a premodern mentality that "hedged commerce with so many re-
strictions that his prescriptions stood as a critique of . . . individualism and
an attendant laissez-faire economic system."[36] Edwardsian social ethics
and the doctrine of disinterested benevolence, far from being disembodied
doctrinal positions, were rooted in a traditional moral economy of restraint and self-denial that was under assault from an emergent capitalist
commercial order. Edwardsian social ethics seem to have appealed to individuals who were on the margins of or disturbed by the new commercial
economic order. The "surplus" rural females from orthodox homes who
matriculated at Mount Holyoke were particularly susceptible to Lyon's invocation of disinterested benevolence and her reaffirmation of the moral
economy of the New England village. The seminary developed as a kind of
female communal experiment that stood as a critique of the existing commercial order and that harkened back to an earlier self-sufficient household economy.

In her circulars calling for the establishment of Mount Holyoke, in her
fund-raising activities, and in her sermons to students, Lyon drew on Edwardsian notions of disinterested benevolence, reaffirmed the values of the
traditional moral economy of rural New England towns that was such an
important part of her social experience, and criticized the behavior promoted by a now advanced market economy. Lyon's most public statement
of her own disinterested benevolence and of her aspiration to institutionalize it in a new seminary was offered in a fund-raising circular of 1836:
"Had I a thousand lives, I could sacrifice them all in suffering and hardship
for its [the seminary's] sake. Did I possess great fortune, I could readily re-
linquish it all, and become poor if its prosperity should demand it. Its
grand object is to furnish the greatest possible number of female teachers
of high literary qualifications, and of benevolent, self-denying zeal."[37] For
Lyon, who never married, domesticity did not provide a morally and spiritually adequate outlet for self-denial. Mount Holyoke was not designed to
prepare women for "republican motherhood"; she rejected women who
confined their disinterested benevolence to "their own family circle."[38]
Her primary support came from female benevolent societies comprised
of women who had already extended their self-denial beyond the family
circle. As with the promotion of revivalism, women were urged to persuade their market-oriented husbands, brothers, and sons of the claims of
disinterested benevolence and of a traditional moral economy.

At times Lyon appealed directly to men, chiding them for their worldly preoccupation. She informed husbands in Ipswich, where she had taught and had many female supporters, "that she had come to get them to cut off one little corner of their estate and give it to their wives to invest in the form of a seminary for the daughters of the common people."[39] As this statement suggests, Lyon invoked the language of the marketplace to advocate benevolent, anticommercial goals. In a fund-raising circular of 1835, "To the Friends of Christian Education," she reiterated that the site of Mount Holyoke was chosen in part for "economy"; that "economical" charges would free higher education from the ability to pay; and that the seminary would instill self-denying "habits of domestic economy . . . without which all other parts of education are purchased at too dear a rate."[40] Daily life in the seminary was organized as a traditional subsistence family economy, a communal alternative to the commercial order that Lyon saw emerging around her and that plunged into depression in 1837.

Lyon repeatedly expressed – and displayed in her simple dress and unpolished deportment – a kind of rural Puritan-republican worldview. "Let the people there [in the cities] just give up their extravagance, and live as they do in the country," she observed in 1843, "and there would be no more lack of funds for benevolent objects."[41] A new commercial-industrial order, however, had even penetrated to Mount Holyoke's door-step by this time. South Hadley boasted paper mills, woolen mills, a tannery, and other factories.[42] Confronted with a changing rural world, Lyon idealized family and village life of the past, including her own. In 1843, she recalled the "wild romantic little farm" of her youth where natural beauty and agricultural abundance converged to create a pastoral idyll. She celebrated a mother who could be "found busy, both early and late," in whose "little domain, nothing was left to take its own way. Everything was made to yield to her faithful and diligent hand." Lyon's embroidered recollections portrayed a self-sufficient, though fatherless, farming family "gathered around, that simple table, [where] no one deserved a richer supply than was furnished by the hand of that dear mother."[43]

At Mount Holyoke Lyon created an extended rural household, a throwback to the village moral economy and family cooperation and self-sacrifice that she ascribed to her youth. Unlike male colleges, Mount Holyoke did not allow servants and did not permit students to commute or board out. The seminary was run as a household with family members engaged in cooperative work. One hired male chopped wood, but students performed all the domestic chores, including cooking, cleaning, and laundry.[44] By institutionalizing a cooperative domestic economy, Lyon reduced the cost of a Mount Holyoke education. Moreover, she was able to demonstrate the benefits of a traditional moral economy and to inculcate in her students industry, frugality, cooperation, and self-sacrifice. In her vision, the seminary would produce a cadre of self-denying women like herself, who, Lyon frequently informed students, should set a moral example and "not expect a large compensation for teaching," advice she also offered to prospective ministers' wives in the Mount Holyoke student body.[45] Lyon's benevolent, but intrusive and highly regimented, religious matriarchy required students to see themselves as duty-bound "daughters" who should be selflessly devoted to the well-being of their Mount Holyoke "family." Lyon admitted significant numbers of siblings and cousins, blood ties that reinforced the family social ideal that she cultivated. Even Emily Dickinson, who resisted Lyon's religious indoctrination and left the seminary after a year of study, acknowledged the caring she encountered at Mount Holyoke. "One thing is certain," Dickinson reported to a correspondent, "& that is, that Miss Lyon & all the teachers seem to consult our comfort & happiness in everything they do & you know that is pleasant."[46] Of course maternal solicitude and the personal examples of disinterested benevolence that Lyon and her teachers exhibited were intended to press guilt and the moral claims of self-denial on the seminary's daughters. Such caring, then, could be experienced as oppressive moral watchfulness, though even Dickinson seems not to have responded that way.

Lyon socialized students into the seminary's household economy and culture of self-sacrifice; she nurtured a self-denying ethic, sensibility, and set of habits that graduates then brought to religious causes that fell beyond the traditional sphere of domesticity. In her advocacy of the foreign missionary movement, Lyon most clearly displayed both her encouragement to women to transcend the traditional family circle and her commitment to Edwardsian notions of disinterested benevolence. All Mount Holyoke graduates were instilled with a missionary ethic; prospective teachers or ministers' wives were taught to internalize self-denying disinterested benevolence in ways that encouraged female self-assertion on behalf of evangelical religion. But the spiritual economy of disinterested benevolence designated foreign missions as the most challenging and rewarding field of work. Not surprisingly, in the religious culture that Lyon nurtured, foreign missionary work became one of the chief "vocational phantasies"[47] of the student body. As a result, Mount Holyoke emerged as a sister school to Andover Seminary, the institutional center of the foreign missionary movement in America that had been dominated by the New Divinity at its founding in 1808 and that remained strongly Edwardsian, as we shall see, into the 1860s.

Lyon's only publication, with the exception of fund-raising circulars, was devoted to the foreign missionary movement. *A Missionary Offering* was published in 1843, when the antislavery cause and abolitionist criticism of foreign missions threatened to erode support for and contributions to proselytizing efforts. Lyon laced *A Missionary Offering* with familiar Edwardsian revival rhetoric. Her enthusiasm for foreign missions was provoked by a vision that "beheld the worm that never dies and the fire that never is quenched. I heard the unutterable groans of the forever lost, and I saw the smoke of their torment."[48] On the whole, though, she presented missionary work in the tradition of the *Life of Brainerd*, as the religious battlefield where the loftiest acts of disinterested benevolence were played out.

Lyon also incorporated missionary disinterested benevolence into a millennial perspective that she absorbed from *A History of the Work of Redemption*, one of her favorite Edwardsian texts. Edwards saw the era preceding the arrival of the millennium as a time when "this vast continent of America, that is now so covered with barbarous ignorance and cruelty, [shall] be everywhere covered with glorious gospel light and Christian love."[49] Such a vision informed Lyon's initial interest in training converted Christian teachers for the American west. But Edwards's *History of Redemption* drew a global map of the work of redemption that increasingly stirred Lyon's imagination. Edwards foresaw a time when the entire world would be "united in peace and love in one amiable society; all nations, in all parts, on every side of the globe, shall then be knit together in sweet harmony, all parts of God's church assisting and promoting the knowledge and spiritual good of one another."[50] This universal prospect inspired Lyon to install maps throughout the seminary that illustrated the progress of the Gospel around the world. In a Mount Holyoke adaptation of the concert of prayer, which Edwards had enthusiastically endorsed, Lyon dedicated daily devotions to the work of foreign missions around the world, naming the missionaries, identifying their locations, and compounding Edwardsian benevolence and millennialism to frame an aggressive evangelical moral agenda. Foreign missions, Lyon exulted in *A Missionary Offering*, were "our nation's great feature of the morally sublime" that stood as the ethical equivalent of nature represented by Niagara Falls[51] – a perspective that reveals how the seeming universalism that Lyon derived from Edwardsian millennialism and disinterested benevolence remained rooted in mid-nineteenth-century American nationalism.

For Lyon, sublime acts of disinterested benevolence that furthered the work of redemption were not restricted to missionaries in the field. *A Missionary Offering* enumerated self-denying deeds that were almost invariably inspired by women – daughters, wives, widows – such as the wife who awakened her husband in the middle of the night to "reveal her midnight plan of repairing her old carpet, that the money for the new one might be given to the [missionary] cause." Similarly, Lyon praised the young daughter, "running with the throbbing heart to her widowed father and asking that she might repair her old bonnet for the season, and send the money for the new bonnet to Ceylon." In Lyon's moral drama, women usually spurred men to acts of disinterested benevolence that served the work of redemption. *A Missionary Offering* described a world in which women had to press the claims of disinterested benevolence on males, such as the individual who "passed among his neighbors as a rich man, though his wealth lay more in paper, ink, and lands, treasured up for future generations."[52]

The sublime appeal of the missionary vocation itself far outstripped acts of financial self-denial in support of foreign missions. Lyon promoted the romance of missions in numerous ways at Mount Holyoke, including establishing a missionary library – a common practice at evangelical colleges and theological seminaries in the nineteenth century. In *A Missionary Offering*, Lyon acknowledged that, as a young girl, she had found life stories of missionaries "one of the richest fields of thought, of meditation, and of feeling."[53] By the 1830s, as we have already seen, the missionary memoir had become a well-developed and immensely popular subgenre of religious biography. Used to raise money, to encourage concerts of prayer, and to recruit young men and women, the missionary memoir became a staple of inspirational library collections such as Mount Holyoke's. Works of personal piety and of millennial optimism did so as well. As one would expect, then, Edwards's writings found a useful place in the missionary libraries of Mount Holyoke, Andover, Amherst, Williams, and similar schools. Indeed, an 1845 survey of the "cultivation of the missionary spirit" at colleges and theological seminaries singled out the importance of Edwards's works in missionary libraries. The author of the survey, E. W. Hooker, insisted that Edwards "had his heart set on the missionary cause," a commitment that was reflected in his works. In particular, Hooker noted the importance of Edwards's *Life of Brainerd*, the account of the heroic Edwardsian disciple "whose fervent piety carried him into the missionary field." [54]

In the *Life of Brainerd*, Edwards alluded to his daughter Jerusha, who nursed Brainerd in the final months of his life. Jerusha died four months after Brainerd; she was buried next to him in the Edwards's family plot, her gravestone standing in front of the missionary's. Edwards did not indicate in the *Life of Brainerd* that his daughter and the heroic missionary were engaged to be married, but he did describe her as possessing "much the same spirit as Mr. Brainerd." [55] It was the nineteenth century that added to the romance of Brainerd's life and to his and Jerusha's deaths the view that they were betrothed. Pious pilgrims to the Northampton gravesite – including Mount Holyoke students, who were encouraged to visit the shrine on seminary-sanctioned outings – and nineteenth-century biographers of the missionary associated Jerusha and Brainerd in life and death, describing how the self-denying couple "had anticipated great happiness in married life." [56] The symbolism of their physical and spiritual unions and their sacrificial deaths spoke to the needs and the risks that nineteenth-century missionary-minded men and women faced.

The American Board of Commissioners for Foreign Missions strongly discouraged and even prohibited single missionaries, male or female. Only in exceptional circumstances were single males commissioned, and single women were almost totally banned until the 1840s. The board believed that married couples were better able to cope with the emotional and physical hardships of mission life and to resist the sexual temptations that appeared particularly strong in Polynesia. Couples exemplified for their missionary subjects middle-class Christian domestic values. The missionary wife not only served the physical and emotional needs of her husband; she was designated "Assistant Missionary" and was charged with teaching women and children. [57] Together the couple braved the perils of the missionary vocation, from debilitating voyages to distant posts to the risks of disease. Death at an early age became an accepted fact of missionary life and part of what one might call the hagiography of disinterested benevolence. Nineteenth-century readers and promoters of the *Life of Brainerd* (perhaps with evangelical women such as Mary Lyon in the forefront) grafted on to Edwards's heroic account of the missionary the romantic tale of his female soulmate's spirituality and self-sacrifice.[58]

In nineteenth-century missionary martyrology, women even came to surpass men, succumbing in large numbers to early sacrificial deaths in the tradition of Brainerd and Jerusha Edwards. Women missionaries not only confronted the perils of childbearing; they also faced the multiple and often emotionally and physically debilitating responsibilities of wife, mother, and assistant missionary. Thus, like Brainerd's life of self-sacrifice, the human cost that the missionary movement exacted from women was sometimes deplored as religious enthusiasm in the service of "missionary madness." As Joan Brumberg has persuasively argued, "What critics of foreign missions failed to understand, however, was the evangelical sensibility – which was touched rather than angered, by youthful death in the cause of religion."[59]

Mount Holyoke cultivated such an evangelical sensibility. The seminary's regimen, which was intended to prepare students for a life committed to advancing benevolent causes, took its own toll in student illness and deaths which only seemed to feed the fires of revivalism at Mount Holyoke. Lyon regularly admonished her students, "go where no one else will go, do what no one else will do."[60] She intervened with widowed mothers, reluctant to allow their Mount Holyoke daughters to enlist in the missions and face the likelihood of death. She contributed nearly half of her small annual salary to the missionary movement, and she aggressively promoted a student subscription for the missions that raised impressive sums of money from a group of such modest means.[61]

Lyon did not romanticize missionary work. She presented it in Edwardsian terms: as a spiritual test of true virtue, of disinterested benevolence, of a willingness to die for the good of Being in general. "First to India and then to Heaven," a departing Mount Holyoke graduate informed her family and friends.[62] The seminary graduated nineteenth-century versions of Jerusha Edwards for the missionary movement, producing more pious wives for foreign missionaries than any other female seminary and functioning as a sister institution to Andover. Some young missionaries developed relationships with Mount Holyoke women, often arranged by intermediaries, well in advance of departure to the field. Other young men, after years of study and preparation, graduated and were sponsored by the American Board of Commissioners on the condition that they find a pious bride in the two or three months before departure for the missions.

The Board developed a network of teachers and ministers who provided names of "missionary-minded" women who were "young, pious, educated, fit and reasonably good-looking."[63] Mount Holyoke was a major part of this network. By the time of Mary Lyon's death in 1849, the seminary had sent nearly forty students and teachers to foreign missions. In addition, the seminary enrolled numerous daughters of foreign missionaries, who followed the established custom of sending children back to America to be educated.[64]

As the popularity of the David Brainerd–Jerusha Edwards story within the missionary movement suggests, evangelical leaders sought historical precedents and inspirational models for nineteenth-century religious crusades, a search that sometimes required the rewriting of history. The era of the colonial awakening proved to be a fertile ground for evangelical historical rummaging, especially after Edwards and his writings acquired renewed authority. Jerusha was not the only Edwardsian woman who was culturally rehabilitated in the nineteenth century and who spoke to the concerns of Mary Lyon and Mount Holyoke students. Abigail Hutchinson and Sarah Edwards were two others.

Edwards's *Faithful Narrative*, which contained a detailed description of Hutchinson's conversion in the Northampton revival of the 1730s, was reprinted frequently in the nineteenth century; moreover, the account was important enough to be published separately. Beginning in 1816, both the New England and the American Tract Societies printed eight editions and thousands of copies of the *Account of Abigail Hutchinson, A Young Woman, Hopefully Converted at Northampton, Mass., 1734.*[65] At the same time, the evangelical community displayed increasing interest in Edwards's wife, Sarah. The numerous nineteenth-century biographies of Edwards held up Sarah as a model of disinterested benevolence who served as an assistant and spiritual "companion" to her husband. Sarah visited parishioners, organized women's prayer meetings, and counseled ministerial aspirants studying with her husband. In these religious activities, as well as in her life as a whole, the author of the American Sunday School Union's *Life of Edwards* enthused, Sarah revealed an exemplary Christian character: "her deep and uncommon piety and devotedness to God, her solemn self-dedications to his service and remarkable discoveries of the divine perfections and glory, . . . enabled her, in an unexampled manner, to bow down in humble and silent resignation to the will of God." The nineteenth-century evangelical admiration for Sarah, which reflected the larger Edwardsian cultural revival, even led one marriage manual to urge wives to emulate her "true greatness . . . in rendering others useful, rather than in being directly useful herself."[66] Sarah, Jerusha, and Abigail Hutchinson were all part of a larger nineteenth-century female hagiography that allowed evangelical leaders, like Mary Lyon, to fashion and bestow on the rising generation a religious tradition that linked the colonial and Second Great Awakenings.[67]

.   .   .

Perhaps as much as any foreign missionary Mary Lyon tested the limits of her physical and emotional endurance at Mount Holyoke. Revivalist, moral philosopher, and college founder who continued to supervise Mount Holyoke's expansion, Lyon also screened applicants, counseled students, and worked to place them in positions where they could satisfy the demands of disinterested benevolence. Exhaustion and illness increasingly disrupted Lyon's efforts and finally took her life in 1849. Amherst College's Edward Hitchcock soon began work on a biography of Lyon. *The Power of Christian Benevolence Illustrated in the Life and Labors of Mary Lyon* was first published in 1851 at Northampton. It went through twelve editions by 1860 and was added to the American Tract Society's publication list, where it joined the memoirs of the male and female foreign missionaries whom Lyon so admired. The popularity of Hitchcock's biography, the continuing loyalty of Mount Holyoke to its founder's principles, and the establishment of "Little Holyokes" in the West all served to perpetuate Lyon's legacy.[68]

Lyon's life and the founding and early history of Mount Holyoke, as Kathryn Kish Sklar has argued, compel historians to reexamine the assumption that "the ideological context in which female institutions first achieved collegiate parity with male colleges was the secular or scientific milieu of the last third of the nineteenth century, when Vassar, Smith and Wellesley were founded."[69] But Mary Lyon and the founding of Mount Holyoke also suggest the need to reexamine assumptions about nineteenth-century religious development as well. The nineteenth-century cultural resurgence of Edwardsianism, whose theology, piety, and rhetoric so influenced Lyon and the early history of Mount Holyoke, certainly raises questions about the alleged utter demise of Calvinism in the nineteenth century.

Lyon left no significant body of published writing; she did not compose a diary or autobiography. Perhaps the absence of such sources explains how scholars have ignored or downplayed her attraction to Edwardsian Calvinism. Or perhaps students of Lyon's life and of Mount Holyoke's history, like scholars in general, have viewed the Calvinist tradition in too narrow theological terms – thereby excluding women as contributors to it – rather than in relationship to what nineteenth-century Edwardsianism actually was: a nascent discursive formation rooted in doctrine but embracing as well rhetorical conventions, standards of piety, a view of history, elements of a traditional moral economy, and a latter-day New England Puritan sensibility. Lyon inherited a distinctive view of disinterested benevolence that descended directly from the era of the colonial awakening, but she joined orthodox Congregational ministers in contributing to an Edwardsian tradition that was far more a creation of the nineteenth century than a lineal, continuous evolution from the eighteenth.

Lyon's life and the history of Mount Holyoke under her leadership also reveal some of the limits of the Edwardsian tradition that she absorbed from canonized works and orthodox ministers and that she adapted for her own purposes. Lyon resisted fully extending the moral claims of disinterested benevolence to the antislavery movement. While sympathetic to the cause, she steered Mount Holyoke clear of controversy, cultivated the seminarians' idealism, energy, and self-sacrifice, and harnessed the moral power she aroused to missionary work, thus containing it and protecting public support for her institution. Lyon did not admit black women to Mount Holyoke, and she insisted that the salvation of American slaves had to await the conversion of the "heathen."[70] Still, it might be argued, she contributed to a powerful moral current that, ultimately, was mobilized on behalf of slaves and then in the service of uplift for freedmen.

If Lyon was not an abolitionist, neither was she a feminist. Yet, in evangelical religion and Edwardsian tradition, she found the empowerment to transcend accepted gender roles. Referring to Mount Holyoke, one clerical supporter of Lyon observed, "If she were more of a woman, she could not have done all this."[71] Both in terms of providing inspiration and legitimation for her activities as a college founder, moral philosopher, and revivalist, evangelical religion enabled Lyon to become more of a woman.

5
. . .

THE CREATION AND COLLAPSE OF
THE NEW ENGLAND THEOLOGY

EDWARDS A. PARK AND ANDOVER SEMINARY,

1840 – 1881

Mount Holyoke College and Andover Seminary institutionalized a shared culture of disinterested benevolence and an Edwardsian commitment to the missionary movement and religious reform. Unlike its sister institution, however, Andover's faculty and students engaged in the postgraduate and "manly" study of systematic theology. The rise of seminaries in the first half of the nineteenth century transformed the study of theology and preparation for the ministry. Theological instruction became academized and professionalized; ministerial aspirants abandoned the colonial practice of studying with their local clerics or journeying to the parsonage of a distinguished theologian, pastor, or revivalist.

The professionalization of theological study and discussion extended beyond the seminaries' role in preparing candidates for the ministry; these postgraduate institutions established academic journals that informed clergy of work in biblical interpretation, theological analysis, and church history. A new clerical species, the seminary minister-professor, emerged and recast the old town parson-metaphysician's claim to intellectual pre-eminence.[1] Theological study and discussion retreated to the seminary classroom and journal, to the separate sphere of a professionalized ministry. To be sure, seminaries stamped their graduates with distinctive doctrinal orientations that were not lost on congregations when they faced selecting a new minister. Moreover, antebellum theological discussion and interpretation were obviously bound up with and responsive to the revivalism, practical piety, and religious reform that infused a broad, "Methodized" lay evangelical culture. Yet, seminaries contributed to the professionalization of doctrinal discussion and to the creation of a theological discourse that occurred largely over the heads of the laity.

Certainly debate over Edwards's theological legacy became part of a highly specialized and contested nineteenth-century religious discourse that sometimes even befuddled members of its professional audience. As one prominent nineteenth-century professor of theology observed in the midst of academic polemics over Edwardsian theology, "Thus the words, satisfaction, impute, ability, inability, &c. &c. are kept going up and down like a juggler's balls, until no man can tell what they mean, or whether they have any meaning at all."[2] The efforts of seminary professors to come to terms with Edwards's theological legacy focused not on his works of practical piety that were popular with a lay audience, but on his major Calvinist doctrinal writings of the Stockbridge years, particularly *Freedom of the Will* (1754), *The Nature of True Virtue* (1755), and *Original Sin* (1758). "Edwards on the will," as nineteenth-century polemicists often put it, towered above its competitors to stand as the most formidable intellectual monument in the Edwardsian canon. Regularly reprinted past the middle of the nineteenth century, *Freedom of the Will* went through more editions than any other work of Edwards with the exception of the *Life of David Brainerd.*[3]

Into the 1860s, Edwards on the will endured as far more than a cultural artifact, a theological memorial to intellectual genius dissipated in the service of an outmoded orthodoxy. Even when historians have grudgingly acknowledged that Edwardsian theology persisted as a vital tradition into the nineteenth century, they have interpreted the emergence of Nathaniel William Taylor (1786–1858) and the New Haven theology in the 1820s as the "waning of Edwardsianism." Taylor's "certainty with the power to the contrary" modified Edwards's determinism and allegedly "silenced the ghost" of the American Aquinas and of *Freedom of the Will*.[4]

And yet, Edwards on the will – and Edwards on sin, imputation, the atonement, decrees, and virtue – remained central to theological discourse at Congregational and Presbyterian seminaries through the 1860s. Seminary journals swelled with essays – the new stock in trade of an academic ministry – on Edwardsian theological tradition. Andover's Edwards A. Park emerged by midcentury as the most prolific and knowledgeable historical authority on Edwards and his New Divinity disciples. Park served Andover from 1836 to 1881, first as professor of sacred rhetoric and then for thirty-four years as the prestigious Abbot Professor of Theology; he also edited the seminary's journal, *Bibliotheca Sacra*, for thirty years. By family background and education, Park was a Hopkinsian, a partisan of the "exercise scheme," which held that there was no "taste" or spiritual substance behind the will; sin and virtue consisted of exercises of the will. Park found in an Edwardsian exercise line of thought, which he traced from Samuel Hopkins to Nathanael Emmons, a theology that reconciled divine sovereignty and human accountability and that offered a "Consistent" Calvinism appropriate for the revivalist, activist evangelical culture of the nineteenth century. Park's Consistent Calvinism steered Andover between the Old Westminster Calvinism of Princeton and the liberal Calvinism of New Haven.

Park became the lightning rod at midcentury in a seminary paper war over Edwardsian tradition; his writings staked out the historical ground on which the theological debate was conducted. Trying to determine whether Park or his critics were more loyal Edwardsians, however, is not an especially rewarding line of inquiry; it simply reinscribes the nineteenth-century participants' framing of the controversy. Rather, Park's life and work show how Edwardsian theology remained vital, but contested, into the middle of the nineteenth century. Traditions are created, not passively inherited or discovered, and Edwardsian theological tradition was no exception. Moreover, traditions are mediated by institutions and cultural brokers. A new academic-professional clerical culture furnished the institutional infrastructure that enabled Park to create and transmit his influential construction of Edwardsian theological tradition. In addition, Park's unrivaled knowledge of New England theological history and his position as Abbot Professor at America's oldest and largest postgraduate seminary secured his cultural authority as a guardian of Edwardsian tradition.

Park continually withdrew to historical grounds, compelling his Presbyterian opponents, in particular, to further study of Edwards and the New Divinity. Park's journal essays, lectures, and books comprised the first "genetic" history of Edwardsian theological tradition. Park's apologetic strategy was to "traditionalize" one hundred years of New Divinity improvements, including his own, by rooting them in Edwards or, when necessary, in Edwardsian "germs" developed by his closest disciples. In turn, Park used an organic interpretation of the New Divinity to present Edwardsian tradition as developmental, though consistently Calvinist, and distinct from Taylorism and the New Haven theology. Indeed, Park sought a name that would traditionalize the New Divinity of Edwards's disciples – Hopkins, Bellamy, Edwards the Younger, Emmons – and distinguish it from the "New Divinity" of Taylor. The now familiar historical designation "the New England theology" was essentially created and propagated by Park and Enoch Pond (1799–1882), a Hopkinsian ally who served successively as professor of theology and church history and president at Bangor Seminary and who is now an all but forgotten figure in American religious history.

Park's historical narrative of the New England theology, the hundred year old Edwardsian theological tradition, provoked detailed replies from seminary critics, particularly from Edwardsians at Princeton, Union (New York), and East Windsor who mounted a counter-narrative of the history of New England theology. Seminary agitation over Edwards and the New England theology peaked in the early 1860s after Park published imposing historical works on the atonement (1859) and on the life and thought of the controversial exerciser Nathanael Emmons (1861). By 1870, however, the debate had receded as had, finally, Edwards's theological figure. Still, Park's students would be the first to write comprehensive, nonpolemical histories of the New England theology, histories that nevertheless perpetuated major aspects of Park's narrative of Edwardsian tradition.

Andover and the Ministerial Profession

Park was born in Providence, Rhode Island, in 1808, the second son of an orthodox family. His father, Calvin Park, was professor of moral philosophy and metaphysics at Brown. The elder Park was an admirer of Samuel Hopkins and had studied for the ministry under Nathanael Emmons (1745–1840). The father named his first son Calvin Emmons, reserving Edwards for his second born. Young Edwards was introduced early to the doctrines he would later celebrate as the New England theology. "I was at ten years of age somewhat of a theologian," he recalled as an adult, "and a rigid Calvinist; had a great reverence for Dr. Emmons and Dr. Hopkins."[5] Though Hopkins had already been dead five years when Park was born, Emmons would live until 1840 and persist as a personal and intellectual presence in Park's life. In his youth, Park listened to Emmons preach in

Franklin, Massachusetts, twenty-five miles from Providence, and the well-known minister visited the Park household regularly.[6]

Park enrolled at Brown at the age of thirteen, already schooled by his father in the classics and Reformed theology. After Park graduated from Brown in 1826, he spent six months teaching school in Weymouth, Massachusetts, where he experienced conversion as part of a vocational crisis as he tried to decide whether he should be a teacher or a minister.[7] Settling on the ministry, Park spent a year studying theology with his father and enrolled at Andover in 1828.

Founded in 1808 as America's first postgraduate theological school, Andover resulted from a compromise that was almost stillborn. After negotiations that nearly collapsed over the language of the new seminary's creed, Old Calvinists and Hopkinsians united in a marriage of anxiety over the Unitarian menace emanating from Harvard. The Associate Creed of Andover, to which professors were required to subscribe every five years, lumped together the Westminster Shorter Catechism and New Divinity "improvements" of doctrines, such as original sin. The language of the Associate Creed was tediously negotiated, however; the final product was a document that partially masked New Divinity alterations of the received Westminster faith and fully satisfied no one. Old Calvinists insisted that the Associate Creed was "too favorable to the Hopkinsian sect." Some New Divinity men, such as Emmons, viewed the compromise as producing an "amalgamated" creed that did not adequately acknowledge "the principles that distinguished Hopkinsians from Calvinists."[8] In spite of periodic expressions of discontent, the Associate Creed proved to be a supple, yet substantial, document almost to the end of Park's long affiliation with Andover. It would provide theological cover for his New Divinity improvements while continuing to tether him to orthodox Calvinism.

Leonard Woods (1774–1854) was chosen as the first Abbot Professor of Theology and charged with safeguarding the doctrinal compromise of the Associate Creed. Usually, Woods has been identified as a Hopkinsian, but in his *History of the Andover Theological Seminary*, he distanced himself from controversial positions of Hopkins and Emmons, such as the willingness to be damned for the glory of God and good of the universe.[9] Park saw Woods as insufficiently Hopkinsian; in his teaching and in his arguments with Unitarians, the first Abbot Professor was reluctant to draw on Edwards and the New Divinity to offer a Calvinist apology that "consistently" reconciled divine sovereignty and human accountability.

Park graduated from Andover in 1831, turned down an offer to teach biblical literature at Bangor Seminary, and accepted a temporary call to the Congregational Church in Braintree, Massachusetts. Almost immediately Park led a revival that continued for four months and won him a local reputation as an uncommon preacher.[10] Park's interest in systematic theology did not preclude a commitment to and participation in revivalism. Like the Edwardsian disciples whose works and lives he studied so closely, Park preached an evangelical theology that balanced divine sovereignty and human accountability, that promoted immediate repentance, and that placed the New Divinity in the front ranks of the Second Great Awakening in New England.

Park left Braintree after two years and turned down offers from churches as well as from the New School Presbyterian Seminary in Auburn, New York. He spent the winter of 1834–35 at Yale, where he listened to the lectures of Nathaniel W. Taylor. Unlike the cautious Woods, Taylor offered bold and original arguments on human accountability, the benevolence of the deity, and the atonement in response to the Unitarian offensive against Calvinism. There is no question that Taylor influenced Park, but not by transforming him into a liberal Calvinist. Park never accepted Taylor's efforts to establish the self-determining power of the will, for example, nor the New Haven divine's view that God could not prevent sin in a moral system.[11] Rather, Park adapted elements and arguments of Taylorism to his Edwardsian New Divinity, whose theology, he believed, provided a Calvinist framework that reconciled divine sovereignty and human accountability in ways that refuted the Unitarians.

In 1835, Park accepted a position at Amherst College that required him to teach several subjects, including mental and moral philosophy. After only a year at Amherst, Park returned to Andover as Bartlett Professor of Sacred Rhetoric, succeeding Ebenezer Porter (1772–1834), the New Divinity author of *Letters on the Religious Revivals*.[12] Park represented a second generation of seminary instructors who had themselves been educated in seminaries, who had traveled abroad, and who were aware of and often open to new scholarship on Scripture and church history. The creation of scholarly seminary journals was the achievement of Park's generation. Shortly after he returned from his first European trip in 1844, Park and his colleague Bela Bates Edwards (1802–52) established the *Bibliotheca Sacra*, one of the major seminary publications of the nineteenth century. A quarterly journal of religious scholarship designed, Park and Edwards announced, to address "the needs of theological students and clergymen,"[13] *Bibliotheca Sacra* was not narrowly sectarian in its contents. It published the works of European, particularly German, scholars and accepted contributions from a variety of religious perspectives, even from Unitarians. Yet, *Bibliotheca Sacra* provided a forum for the dissemination of Park's views on preaching, divinity, and theological history. "It is the most elaborate, erudite and authoritative organ of the Puritan or Calvinistic denomination of Protestants we are acquainted with," Catholic Orestes Brownson reported in 1845, "though it wants the lively and interesting character of the *New Englander*."[14] The Andover journal became central to Park's efforts to create the New England theology and to defend his construction of Edwardsian tradition against criticism from rival journals at Princeton, Union, and Yale.

When Park succeeded Woods as Abbot Professor in 1847, Andover remained America's preeminent seminary; however, as the Second Great Awakening subsided and new seminaries emerged, increased competition for students had reduced peak enrollments. From an initial class of 36 in 1809, admissions climbed to more than 80 by the mid-1830s, and then declined to 50 in 1840. Andover's total enrollment was 153 that year, substantially larger[15] than the enrollment at other seminaries, including Bangor (44), East Windsor (29), Harvard (20), Princeton (110), Union of New York (90), and Yale (72). Part of Park's responsibility as Abbot Professor was to attract students, the way the aged Woods had been unable to during his last years. It was common for seminary professors to take to the college lecture circuit in the interest of recruiting students. Even before he secured his reputation as an authoritative interpreter of Edwardsian theological tradition, Park's eloquence in the pulpit and behind the lectern proved to be an asset for Andover in the competition for students. After Park spoke in Amherst in 1853, Emily Dickinson was unrestrained in her praise, which she conveyed to her brother: "We had such a splendid sermon from Professor Park – I never heard anything like it, and don't expect to again, till we stand at the great white throne, and he reads from the Book, the Lamb's book."[16]

Park's influence on a clerical generation cannot be measured simply by the number of seminarians he taught; it must also include the diverse professional roles that Andover graduates assumed. The aspirations and career paths of Andover students reflected a transformed ministry from the days of Edwards, Hopkins, and Bellamy. Park's career itself suggests the dimensions of the nineteenth-century transformation of the ministry. He served as a parish minister, local revivalist, college instructor, seminary professor, and journal editor. Only the clerical role of agency missionary or reformer eluded his experience. Perhaps as many as two-thirds of Andover graduates served in the nonpastoral positions that proliferated in the nineteenth century, many alumni devoting large parts of their careers to college and seminary teaching, publishing, missionary activities, and benevolent society work.[17] As a third generation Hopkinsian, Park imparted to his students a theological tradition derived from Edwards and the New Divinity that offered a defense of Calvinism consistent with human accountability, and thus with the tone and character of nineteenth-century evangelical culture. As a creator of tradition, rather than as an original thinker, Park was not only the last major Consistent Calvinist; he was also the first to imbue the term "New England theology" with historical meaning.

The New England Theology

The phrase "New England theology" originated in the doctrinal compromise that led to the founding of Andover and that was embodied in the seminary's Associate Creed. How to sum up the theological orientation of the seminary with a descriptive name or doctrinal shorthand proved problematic. The available terms – Old Calvinism, New Divinity, Hopkinsianism – threatened to reopen the factional disagreements that had only been resolved by the diligent negotiation of the Associate Creed's language. "New England theology" emerged as a useful compromise, simultaneously historical and imprecise, evoking tradition but not weighed down with the doctrinal freight of the past. But, like the Associate Creed itself, the "New England theology" seemed unsatisfactory to both Old Calvinists and Hopkinsians, and the label was not used extensively within or beyond Andover during the early nineteenth century. In fact, the seminary's creed was usually referred to as "Andover Calvinism."[18]

Park revived the term "New England theology" in the 1830s, after he returned to Andover.[19] By 1852, when Park published a lengthy and learned historical exposition in the *Bibliotheca Sacra*, titled "New England Theology," the metonymic transformation of the label was far advanced; it had become widely recognized as denominating the one-hundred-year-old New Divinity movement. Moreover, the New England theology now had a historical narrative that legitimized its claim as the exclusive school of Edwards. Of course such a claim was challenged by seminary journals, whose contributors sometimes ratified the New England theology even as they tried to pry Edwards loose from it.

At midcentury, Park was not a solitary academic voice fashioning a history of the New England theology and using the *Bibliotheca Sacra* as a kind of personal platform for his views. Former students and ministerial associates contributed to the journal and to the creation of the New England theology.[20] Above all, Park relied on a steadfast theological confederate at Bangor Seminary. Enoch Pond, now an obscure figure, followed a course into the ministry that paralleled Park's. Born in Wrentham, Massachusetts, in 1791, Pond graduated from Brown in 1813, studied theology with Nathanael Emmons, served as a pastor in Ward, Massachusetts, and worked as an editor of Lyman Beecher's *Spirit of the Pilgrims*. Like Park, Pond was a Hopkinsian shaped by Emmons's exercise doctrines. In 1832, Pond joined Bangor Seminary, a small New Divinity institution and outpost of Andover founded in 1814, as professor of theology. He also served as professor of church history and president of the seminary. In nearly forty years on the faculty, Pond instructed hundreds of students and came to be called "the second founder" of the seminary. Pond also contributed dozens of articles, perhaps two hundred in all, to seminary journals and religious periodicals.[21] Many of these pieces reinforced and appear to have been coordinated with Park's publications on the history of New England theology. In the 1850s, for example, Pond published a series of articles in the *Congregationalist* that offered a general evangelical audience a narrative history of the New England theology that was consistent with, but more accessible than, Park's scholarly version in the *Bibliotheca Sacra*. Pond's essays were subsequently published as *Sketches of the Theological History of New England*.[22]

Park and Pond appropriated the term "New England theology," constructed a genetic doctrinal history under its rubric, and removed "the obloquy of the name which it has worn for more than fifty years, the name of 'new divinity.'"[23] Edwards, of course, was the "father of New England theology," but from the perspective of one hundred years of theological history, "he had only laid the foundation of the tradition." In the aftermath of Edwards's premature death, new patriarchs – from Hopkins to Edwards the Younger – continued his work. Edwards and these "fathers," Park observed, conferred on "New England a theological character, not faultless indeed but one that we love to eulogize."[24]

But far more than historical eulogy was at stake in the creation of the New England theology. Grounded as Park and Pond were in the writings and thought of the progenitors of New England divinity, Andover and Bangor held a historical advantage in the seminary paper war over Edwards's theological legacy. As Mark Noll has pointed out, Old School Presbyterians "did not possess the same intimacy with Edwards," let alone his New Divinity disciples, as did New England Congregationalists.[25] Even closer to home, the dogmatic history of Park and Pond disrupted claims to Edwardsian tradition. By appropriating the term "New England theology," Park and Pond not only attempted to neutralize the "obloquy" of the past; they also endeavored to distinguish their school from the "New Divinity" of the present, the Taylorism of Yale, whose journal – the *New Englander* – claimed to continue Edwards's "spirit" and "bold" "new method" of theological inquiry.[26]

Still, the cultural significance of the creation of the New England theology extended beyond seminaries and the new professional academic ethos they embodied. Park and Pond contributed a theological chapter to the invention of the "Great Awakening." The first hundred years of theology in New England were hardly worth recording; they bore witness to a derivative Calvinism that was slowly Arminianized, a doctrinal development that paralleled the moral and spiritual declension of the region. Edwards and the Great Awakening arrested such moral and spiritual decay and marked the birth of American revivalism and of the New England theology. Moreover, just as the New England revival was reified into a great *American* awakening, so too Park and Pond saw the Edwardsian school as "the American theology," as it was known in Reformed circles abroad. The only original school of Calvinism produced in America, it was called New England theology, Park argued, simply "to distinguish it from the systems that have prevailed in other parts of the land."[27] Thus, the creation of the New England theology joined other religiously based nineteenth-century cultural constructions – the Great Awakening, the invention of the Pilgrims, and what Lawrence Buell has called the "reinvention of the Puritans" – that interpreted the American past through the prism of New England thought and experience.[28]

Park drew on his seminary learning and his knowledge of German and Scottish scholarship to fashion the first "New England" dogmatic canon derived from one hundred years of Edwardsian theological development. Park was sympathetic to the study of church history, then emerging as a

distinct seminary discipline. In the "Duties of a Theologian," a lecture delivered at Dartmouth College in 1839, Park stressed that history was crucial
for "the stability and weight of character" that it contributed to a theologian's work. On his first trip to Germany, he listened to the influential
Berlin church historian J. W. A. Neander, who reinforced Park's interest in
a developmental, organic interpretation of theology.[29]

From the Scottish tradition, Park adapted commonsense principles that
informed his historical exegesis of the New England theology. Park accepted the notion that humankind shared common "universal feelings"
which offered "a test for our faith."[30] But such intuitive religious truth
needed to be consistent with or to be translated into theological statements of commonsense reasonableness, which for Park meant balancing
divine sovereignty and human accountability. In his most famous discourse, presented to the Massachusetts Convention of Ministers in 1850
and titled "The Theology of the Intellect and That of the Feelings," Park
argued for two "forms" or "representations" of religious truth. "When an
intellectual statement is transferred to the province of emotion, it often
appears chilling, lifeless," Park insisted, "and when a passionate phrase is
transferred to the dogmatic, it often appears grotesque, unintelligible, ab-
surd."[31] Park's view that doctrinal controversy might be diminished by
more attention to modes of representing religious truth and to differences in language only ignited the mid-nineteenth century's most heated
and famous seminary journal dispute with Princeton's Charles Hodge
(1797–1878).[32] Park undermined his own positions and aroused the fury of
his antagonists when he repeatedly and sometimes disingenuously invoked the distinction between the theology of the intellect and the feelings
to maneuver around any historical doctrine of the New England theology,
such as the willingness to be damned, that did not pass the test of commonsense reasonableness. While remaining a Hopkinsian Calvinist, Park
nevertheless had to "improve" the improvers of Edwards to construct a
dogmatic canon with the appropriate proportions of divine sovereignty
and human accountability.

"The Wens and Protuberances of Calvinism"

Recent scholarship has begun to revise our understanding of Edwards's
New Divinity disciples. For too long scholars uncritically accepted Joseph
Haroutunian's magisterial neo-orthodox interpretation of the movement.

In *Piety versus Moralism: The Passing of the New England Theology* (1932), Haroutunian all but dethroned the New Divinity men as legitimate theological heirs of Edwards. Hopkins, Bellamy, and the arid scholastics who followed in their train and reproduced themselves, drone-like, in their students, corrupted Edwards's theology and moralized his high Calvinism. Park was dispatched as a "liberal Calvinist" in a footnote which seemed to be all that the Andover professor deserved in Haroutunian's "history of degradation."[33] In Haroutunian's hands, the New England theology served as a case study of a larger religious capitulation in American culture: the triumph of ethics over transcendent faith.

Confounded by the way contemporary criticism assailed the New Divinity for both its hyper-Calvinism and its Arminianism, historians have often too easily accepted Haroutunian's explanation: Edwards's followers truly believed they were upholding his theology even as they bled his thought of its Calvinist content. Revisionists have offered a different answer: Drawing on Edwards's distinction between natural and moral necessity in *Freedom of the Will*, New Divinity men espoused a "consistent" Calvinism that securely established God's sovereignty and thus enabled them to preach up human ability.[34] To achieve this theological consistency in a comprehensive way, Emmons noted (in a statement that Park and Pond frequently quoted), the New Divinity men had "to pare off" the "mere wens and protuberances . . . from true Calvinism";[35] they had to preach not only the sinner's natural ability but modify such doctrines as original sin, imputation, and a limited atonement. Still, revisionist historians have stressed, the New Divinity men remained Calvinists, loyal Edwardsians, and spokesmen for a doctrinal synthesis that survived into the early nineteenth century and that promoted immediate conversion and revivalism.

Park, whose historical writings have provided a basis for revisionist work, enables one to extend recent interpretations of the New Divinity. For in spite of his seminary learning, his rationalistic tone, and his excising of the New Divinity's own "wens," Park remained a Consistent Calvinist, committed to a historic Edwardsian theology that balanced divine sovereignty and human accountability. Hence, Park's career and influence suggest that the New Divinity persisted as a vital theology much longer than even recent revisionists have indicated. Moreover, his historical work on three generations of New England theology discloses that the New Divinity's Consistent Calvinism moved considerably farther from Edwards's positions than revisionists, who have stressed his disciples' orthodoxy, have acknowledged. Finally, in defining and systematizing the dogmatic canon of the New England theology, Park had to negotiate historic doctrinal differences between "exercisers" and "tasters," Hopkinsians and Edwardsians, differences that qualify both old and new interpretations of a monolithic New Divinity.

In "New England Theology," published in the *Bibliotheca Sacra* in 1852 and republished as a separate text the same year, Park summarized the consistent Calvinist framework of the New Divinity that has been rediscovered by recent scholars. The New England theology offered a comprehensive "Edwardean scheme" that

> unites a high but not an ultra Calvinism, on the decrees and agency of God, with a philosophical, but not an Arminian theory, on the freedom and worth of the human soul. Its new element is seen in its harmonizing two great classes of truth; one relating to the untrammelled will of man, another relating to the supremacy of God. Because it has secured human liberty, it exalts divine sovereignty; and its advocates have preached more than others on predestination, because they have prepared the way for it by showing that man's freedom has been predestined. They insisted on an eternally decreed liberty, and on a free submission to the eternal decrees.[36]

Clearly, Edwards's *Freedom of the Will*, with its famous distinction between natural and moral necessity, provided theological propulsion for the New England theology and its creators.

For Edwards, natural necessity referred to physical and intellectual capacities, to the "necessity as men are under through the force of natural causes." Individuals suffered under a necessary natural inability if they faced "some impeding defect or obstacle that is extrinsic to their will, either in the faculty of the understanding, constitution of body or external objects."[37] A man cannot lift a thousand pound boulder; an infant cannot solve complex mathematical problems. Such "cannot" of the natural world differed, however, from the "will not" of the moral realm. Moral necessity referred to the certainty between the "inclination," "disposition," or "motive" of the will and "volitions and actions." Moral necessity meant that individuals acted voluntarily, according to the disposition of their hearts or wills. Human beings were free as long as they could do as they willed, that is, as long as they could act according to the inclination of their will. Sinners were naturally able to repent; their moral inability was only "the want of an inclination, or the prevalence of a contrary inclination"; their cannot was merely a will not.[38]

Edwards's distinction between natural and moral necessity was critical to Park and to the preaching and doctrinal improvements of his New Divinity predecessors. From Hopkins's rejection of a gradual approach to conversion dependent on the means of grace to Park's position that "an entirely depraved man has a natural power to do all which is required of him," natural ability was the "far-famed" doctrine of New England theology.[39] *Freedom of the Will* bequeathed to the New Divinity both a Calvinist definition of liberty and an evocative, manipulable vocabulary that supported the evangelical work of the pulpit. By teaching that "sinners *can* do what they certainly *will* not do,"[40] the New Divinity developed a theology that reconciled determinism and accountability, that promoted conversions and revivalistic religion, and that remained vital through the middle of the nineteenth century.

New Divinity men consistently advanced Edwardsian positions on natural ability and the voluntariness of sin in ways that antagonized Old Calvinists and that have led modern scholars to argue for the moralization of Edwardsianism. Emmons claimed that "Every sinner is as *able* to embrace the gospel as a thirsty man is to drink water, or a hungry man to eat the most delicious food." Edwards the Younger maintained that "men have the physical power to remove their moral inability."[41] For Park, Edwards's *Freedom of the Will* laid the foundation for the "'three radical principles'" of the New England theology: "that sin consists in choice, that our natural power equals, and that it also limits, our duty."[42] The New Divinity men were sometimes set upon as Calvinists who "frequently preach like Arminians."[43] But the Consistent Calvinists did not conflate natural and moral ability, succumb to arguments for the self-determination of the will, or abandon Edwards's necessitarianism. God "so constitutes and circumstances men," Park wrote, that their moral inability assures "they will certainly do evil."[44] Park upheld the moral depravity of the human race and divine sovereignty, as his explication of the New Divinity's position on imputation made clear.

Edwards's on the will remained what has been described as the "cantus firmus"[45] of the New Divinity. Yet as Edwards's disciples developed a comprehensive system of Consistent Calvinism derived from his notion that all sin is voluntary, they ventured beyond both orthodox and Edwardsian doctrinal formulations. The history of the doctrine of imputation in New England theology offers the most important case in point. Reformed theologians held that God created Adam as the "natural and covenantal" head of humanity; on the basis of this relationship, his sin was immediately imputed to his progeny. Humans were born with a double guilt – Adam's sin and a moral corruption that is a "penal consequence" of that sin.[46]

The Reformed doctrine of immediate imputation emerged for the New Divinity men as one of the most conspicuous "wens" of orthodox Calvinism. Imputation contradicted the Edwardsian position that all sin was voluntary and undermined the theological relationship between natural ability and moral accountability that was presented in *Freedom of the Will*. As Park argued, Adam's sin "eludes our natural power" and we cannot be held accountable for it. We do not have the natural ability "to go back six thousand years and refuse to eat the apple," nor can we go back "one week before birth, and unmake our natures." For Park and his New Divinity predecessors, Edwards's "enigmatical"[47] book on *The Great Doctrine of Original Sin* (1758) did not adequately reconcile the consequences of Adam's sin with the central arguments of *Freedom of the Will*.

Edwards had turned to the idea of the federal unity of Adam and the human race to modify the doctrine of immediate imputation. "God, in each step of his proceedings with Adam, . . . looked on his posterity as being one with him." Such a personal identity, or "literal oneness," between Adam and his descendants resulted from "the immediate continued creation of God," the fact that God continually constitutes or renews humanity at "every moment." The divinely constituted ontological unity of the human race led Edwards to argue that Adam's apostasy did not belong to sinners "merely because God *imputes* it to them; but it is *truly* and *properly* theirs, and on that ground God imputes it to them."[48] Sinners labored under only one guilt; the guilt derived from their divinely decreed oneness – their constitutional moral identity – with Adam.

"The idea of our literal oneness with Adam is indeed a strange phenomenon in mental history,"[49] Park wrote, echoing a long-standing dissatisfaction with *Original Sin*, from Hopkins to Emmons, in New England theology. Discarding Edwards's idea of personal identity, New Divinity men insisted that sinners could only be held accountable for transgressions in which they *consciously* participated. Adam's sin was not imputed to his

posterity, Hopkins argued, nor were they "guilty of the sin of their first father, antecedent to their own sinfulness."[50] Still, New Divinity men drew
on Edwards's ideas of divine constitution to establish a connection between Adam and his sinful posterity. God used Adam's sin as the "occasion" for constituting his posterity with a corrupt nature – a moral inability – but not as "a punishment or penalty" for the first sin.[51] All sin and
guilt resulted from personal, voluntary, and conscious choices or "exercises" of the will. The divine constitution that originated with Adam established the certainty of sinners' choices, namely, "that they should sin as
Adam had done," Hopkins argued, "and fully consent to his transgression,
and join in the rebellion which he began."[52]

At midcentury, the expositions of Park and other writers in the *Bibliotheca Sacra* systematized, codified, and summarized the historical development away from the doctrine of imputation in New England theology. As a
result, Park provoked a verbal fusillade from orthodox Calvinists, particularly Old School Presbyterians, who had rejected Edwards's notion of personal identity but on behalf of a traditional Reformed interpretation of
original sin. Princeton's Lyman Atwater (1813–83) dismissed the New Englanders' views on original sin as a sterile though "ingenious attempt to
eliminate from the doctrine its unwelcome ingredients – imputation,
hereditary sinfulness, and inability – and yet to keep its substance, viz. that
men inherit from Adam a vitiated nature, which insures that they sin to
their utter and eternal ruin, until through grace they become creatures in
Christ."[53] The New England interpretation was an ingenious reconciliation of natural depravity, divine sovereignty, and human accountability
that Park viewed as much more than an abstract doctrinal seminary lesson. Rather, like the arguments of *Freedom of the Will*, he claimed, the
New England understanding of original sin preserved Calvinism, dis-
armed Arminian critics, and offered a practical divinity that encouraged
moral exhortation and conversion.

The New Divinity men also transformed the standard interpretation of
the atonement to extend their Consistent Calvinist reconciliation of divine sovereignty and human accountability. The accepted doctrine held
that Christ substituted for sinners, paid the penalty of their guilt, and
satisfied the claims of "distributive justice" (the moral debt that was owed
to God). As a consequence, Christ's righteousness was imputed to a limited portion of humankind, the elect, who would be saved. But the New

Divinity men had already rejected the idea of imputation; sin was personal; moral evil and good were not transferable. Furthermore, the limited consequences of the atonement seemed to undermine the argument that all sinners possessed the natural ability to repent and be saved.[54]

The governmental theory of the atonement resolved these inconsistencies. Sin was a transgression of the divine law; a punishment had to be exacted to defend that law and the sanctity of God's moral government. Christ's death was necessary to uphold the divine law (general justice), not to pay the moral debt of sinners. Moral evil and good were not transferable. Christ's righteousness was not imputed to the elect; rather, his death enabled God, "consistently with his honor," to offer salvation to sinners – even to "pardon the whole world." The atonement, Park wrote, eliminated "all the obstacles . . . against the salvation of the non-elect as well as the elect."[55] The New Divinity men protected divine sovereignty, since God was not obliged to save a single person. In addition, the governmental scheme emphasized that salvation was an immediate, direct act of a sovereign God, not something mediated by imputation. The governmental, "Edwardean," or "New England" theory of the atonement, as it finally came to be denominated in the nineteenth century, represented a significant and controversial attenuation of orthodox Calvinist Christology. The theory presented Park with sufficient theological and historical problems of explanation that he devoted a weighty volume of 600 pages to it. *The Atonement: Discourses and Treatises* was published in 1859 and reissued a year later; it has proved indispensable to modern students of the atonement in New England theology.

The governmental theory of the atonement emerged fully in response to the Universalist vogue of the 1780s. Jonathan Edwards, Jr. (1745–1801), and other second generation New Divinity men, whose writings were collected in Park's *Discourses*, fully developed the theory and removed another doctrinal wen on inherited Calvinism. But Park needed to establish the origins of the governmental theory in Edwards the father and his closest disciples, for he wanted to show that the "New England" theory was not "new divinity" but part of an organic, developmental Edwardsian tradition. Park composed a lengthy introductory essay to the *Discourses*, entitled "The Rise of the Edwardean Theory of the Atonement," that offered the first systematic history of the governmental theory in Edwardsian thought and therefore became a canonical text for supporters of the New

England theology. Park combed through the writings of Edwards, Hopkins, and Joseph Bellamy and isolated the "germs" of the governmental theory that were "strewed" through the work of the "fathers" of the New England theology.[56]

Park acknowledged that Edwards "adopted, in general, both the views and the phrases of the older Calvinists, with regard to the atonement." Yet, Park insisted, "he made various remarks which have suggested the more modern theory."[57] Park tried to build his case by the frequency and weight of his references to Edwards, rather than by their *direct* connection to the governmental theory. For in his writings, Edwards, in fact, never significantly modified the orthodox understanding of the atonement or embraced governmental ideas. While it is true that Edwards's alteration of the doctrine of Adam's imputed sin *suggested* the governmental theory's modification of Christ's imputed righteousness, and the Edwardsian notion of natural ability *implied* that the traditional interpretation of a limited atonement needed to be improved, Park did not cite such implicit connections between Edwards and the governmental theorists.

Instead, Park turned to the first generation of New Divinity men to buttress the Edwardsian lineage of the New England theory; here Park clambered on to firmer ground. Bellamy, for example, broached both the idea of God as a moral governor and a general atonement in *True Religion Delineated* (1750). Edwards read the work in manuscript, Park noted, and wrote the Preface to the treatise. Edwards's "exalted" recommendation of the volume confirmed that he endorsed emerging aspects of what would become the full-blown New England theory. (Edwards's thought, though not his published writings, may have been moving in a governmental direction under the influence of his closest disciples, as some scholars have suggested.)[58] Even more than Bellamy, Park saw Samuel Hopkins as "an invaluable witness to the *essential* coincidence between the school of the elder Edwards and the school of the younger Edwards, in regard to the atonement." Hopkins's "peculiar relations . . . to the elder and younger divines of New England," Park observed, "make him in some respects the most important of all our theologians." Hopkins's massive *System of Doctrines*, published in 1793, incorporated "numerous" aspects of the New England theory, Park pointed out, and offered no criticism of the governmental interpretation of the atonement that the Younger Edwards had fully developed during the Universalist controversy of the 1780s. The "great triumvirate of the New England theologians" – Edwards, Hopkins, and Bellamy – were "fathers" of Edwards the Younger and thus of the New England theory of the atonement.[59]

Presbyterian and Congregational critics assailed both Park's historical method and his seemingly wire-drawn conclusion in the *Discourses*. Such criticism expanded to Park's entire dogmatic, narrative history of New England theology and launched a modest counter-narrative that attempted to reclaim Edwards from, as one seminary journal writer described it, the "perversions" of his "successors."[60] Park's enterprising historical work supplied a large, inviting target to such critics, for he moved well beyond the history of natural ability, original sin, and the atonement in New England theology. He linked major Consistent Calvinist improvements on these doctrines to an exercise scheme that he molded into an Edwardsian tradition suited to mid-nineteenth-century evangelical America.

Exercisers and Tasters

In the interests of commonsense reasonableness and the need to maintain the proper "proportions" of divine sovereignty and human accountability, Park's historical apologetic for the New England theology sometimes explained away "eccentric" positions of particular New Divinity divines. With some justification, his opponents accused him of "cutting off the claws"[61] of his Consistent Calvinist subjects. Consider the famous Hopkinsian idea that salvation "implies a willingness to be damned . . . for the glory of God," one of the many doctrinal positions that prompted criticism of the New Divinity, not for its Arminianism, but for its hyper-Calvinism. Park invoked his distinction between the theology of the intellect and of the feelings to explain Hopkins's position. Hopkins's views of divine submission represented less a rational, doctrinal formulation than a mystical expression of the feelings "with regard to the endurance of *pain* for the divine glory."[62] So, too, when New Divinity theologians suggested that divine sovereignty extended to God's authorship of sin, Park attributed it to the theology of the feelings. "Such a phrase as 'God is the author of iniquity,' has recommended itself to them by its *strength*, and not by its philosophical exactness," he insisted. "It is unfaithful to their precise meaning, and belongs to the style of excitement and impression, rather than to that of calm discussion."[63] Though a partisan of Hopkins and Emmons, Park attempted to create a canon of historic dogma that represented a middle ground of New England theology. His Consistent Calvinism led him to develop a doctrinal and historical reconciliation between Edwardsians and Hopkinsians, tasters and exercisers in New England theology.

New Divinity men shared a common set of theological positions derived from Edwards, but genealogy ran along different lines. Joseph Bellamy trained many Connecticut ministers who identified themselves as New Divinity but Edwardsian to distinguish themselves from particular Hopkinsian doctrinal formulations. Bellamy's historical and doctrinal authority became institutionalized at Connecticut's East Windsor Seminary. The Hopkinsian clerical line, to which Park belonged, was more influential in Massachusetts, was extended by Nathanael Emmons, and found a home at Andover. The taste-exercise divergence tended to coincide with these divisions. Tasters held that a spiritual substance, "taste," "relish," or "disposition," lay behind the will and governed choice; such a depraved taste, which was sinful itself, also led sinners certainly to choose sin. Exercisers denied knowledge of a spiritual substance in back of the will; choice was the immediate exercise of the heart or will without an antecedent passive principle or taste. "All sin consists in sinning," Emmons, the most controversial exerciser, asserted.[64] From the *Religious Affections*, to *Freedom of the Will*, and *True Virtue*, Edwards used language – "taste," "relish," "exercises of the heart," "sensible exercises of the will" – that was invoked to endorse both positions.

Still, Edwards's immediate disciples did not become embroiled in the exercise-taste controversy. Hopkins confided to New Divinity minister Stephen West in 1770 his fear that the "new notion of no spiritual substance" would split Edwardsians "into divisions among themselves."[65] The debate between exercisers and tasters has not fared well in the hands of most historians of the New England theology. The belated emergence of the dispute – after Hopkins and Bellamy had passed from the scene – can easily be interpreted as a kind of New England doctrinal glossolalia or as a metaphysical sideshow of a cultish movement devolving into obfuscation. While it is true that the exercise-taste controversy involved metaphysical issues, there were major dogmatic implications to the dispute. How else can one explain Park's historical and apologetic engagement in its particulars? The *Bibliotheca Sacra* continued to discuss the history of the exercise-taste debate into the 1860s; and Park devoted two lengthy memoirs to Hopkins and Emmons, who represented the exercise genealogy.

Emmons came to be seen as the father of the exercise scheme because he was so bold in advancing its positions. Drawing on Hopkins, Emmons sometimes stopped short of denying the existence of a taste behind the will, claiming that we could only know with certainty the exercises of the heart, the choices of the will. At other times, Emmons incorporated taste into exercise; he suggested that taste or disposition were not distinct from the will but simply, as Edwards often indicated, the activities or operations of the will. This line of reasoning, however, led Emmons to make God the "efficient" cause of moral exercises; that is, God acted directly on the will. "God," Emmons argued, "exerts his agency in producing all the moral and voluntary exercises of every moral agent." Even Adam's volitions resulted from a "divine energy [which] took hold of his heart and led him to sin." [66] While Emmons never described the soul as a "chain of exercises" sustained by divine efficiency, as his critics often claimed, such an interpretation was a legitimate conclusion from his most radical statements that no spiritual substance, principle, or taste lay behind the will.

Emmons's exercise scheme incorporated Edwardsian notions of human accountability and divine sovereignty. Rejecting the position of the tasters, Emmons adopted the Edwardsian view that free will, and therefore moral accountability, resided in choice, not in the cause or inclination behind choice. Emmons's exercise notions also drew on Edwards's idea of "continual creation," the view that God sustains the universe and every person and thing in it through continual new exertions of the divine will. [67] But Emmons's exaltation of divine sovereignty often ignored Edwards's views of the laws of nature and the constitutional arrangements through which God exercised sovereignty over His creatures and creation.

Nineteenth-century Hopkinsians like Park could not endorse hyper-Calvinist exercise arguments about divine efficiency that made God the author of sin. But neither could they fully accept the views of tasters such as Asa Burton, author of *Essays on Some First Principles of Metaphysicks, Ethicks, and Theology* (1824), who located moral agency not in the will, but in a taste behind the will that governed its choices. Park resisted Burton's substitution of a threefold division of the mind into the understanding, will, and sensibilities (taste) for Edwards's twofold division of the understanding and will. [68] For Park, acceptance of the notion of a corrupt involuntary taste or sensibility undermined the Edwardsian idea that all sin resulted from a voluntary choice, or exercise, of the will. As Park put it, "If all sin be caused by that which is sin, then sin exists as a cause, before it exists at all." [69] That is, one could not use sin to explain sin. At issue for Park in the exercise-taste controversy was the very marrow of the New England theology: the balance or "harmony" between divine sovereignty and human accountability and the interpretation of sin, virtue, and regeneration that flowed from this dual emphasis and promoted practical Edwardsian divinity.

Park's historical and doctrinal reconciliation of the exercise and taste schemes drew on constitutional and occasionalist explanations of causality in New England theology that derived from Edwards. Park appealed to Hopkins, who had argued that taste, "disposition, or frame of mind, which is antecedent to all right exercises of the heart, and is the foundation and reason of it, is wholly to be resolved into divine constitution or law of nature."[70] Taste was used in New England theology, Park insisted, primarily to describe the law of nature or the "foundation" or "occasion" of choice, not a passive sinful principle or faculty behind choice. Taste, disposition, relish referred to a divine constitution, a "neutral occasion," that furnished the foundation for sinful exercises of the will. Moral agency remained in the will, not in a new faculty behind the will, as Burton and other tasters claimed. When pressed, the most Park would concede was that "there is lying back of our sinful choices and occasioning them" a divinely constituted taste that "our emotions often prompt us to stigmatize . . . as itself sin." But our intellects tell us differently; "antecedent to choice," we cannot be "guilty for the very make of our souls" or for the "natural existence" of constitutional principles like taste.[71]

Human beings were constituted sinners, but they were not guilty until they actually sinned. Park's arguments, as psychologically suspect as they may have been, salvaged the crucial exercise position that "all sin consists in sinning" (in voluntary choice, not passive involuntary taste) but avoided Emmons's hyper-Calvinist statements about divine efficiency. Drawing on Edwardsian notions of causality, Park could argue that God was certainly the "ultimate" author of sin – as He was of everything – but He was not the immediate "efficient" author of sin because He worked through secondary causes, laws of nature, and constitutional foundations such as "taste."

Moreover, not only sin, but virtue, resided in voluntary exercises of the will rather than in a passive taste or disposition distinct from or behind the will. "Where there is no exercise of heart, nothing of the moral inclination, will or choice," Park asserted, "there can be neither sin nor holiness."[72] Edwards and Hopkins had defined true virtue as disinterested benevolence toward Being in general. This Edwardsian or New England theory did not locate virtue "in something prior to benevolent choice, viz. in a taste or relish for holiness, or . . . holy things on account of their moral beauty or excellence . . . ," though Edwards's works, Park and other writers in the *Bibliotheca Sacra* acknowledged, sometimes suggested such an interpretation. But taste in itself was neither virtuous nor sinful; it furnished the foundation or occasion for holy, or sinful, exercises. Edwards repeatedly described virtuous affections, Park correctly pointed out, as "modes of exercise of the will" and as "*vigorous* and *sensible* exercises of the inclination and will." True holiness consisted in benevolent, voluntary exercises of the will – in a "free choice of the general above the private good." [73]

Regeneration, then, involved a change of the will from sinful and selfish exercises to benevolent ones. Here again, Edwards could be read in support of the taste scheme. For Edwards did say, a writer noted in the *Bibliotheca Sacra*, that "regeneration consists in imparting to the soul a new spiritual taste, relish, or principle which is prior to, and which lays a foundation for, holy exercises." But this involuntary change of taste was not in itself moral or virtuous; for taste only described the law of nature through which God worked. Thus, the change in taste that took place in regeneration simply supplied the occasion or foundation for virtuous voluntary exercises of the will. As Park described the new taste imparted by regeneration, "Unless it be *exercised*, the man who has it as a passive quality, will not be saved." [74] Park and other Andoverian exercisers appealed to no less of an authority on Edwards than Samuel Hopkins to clarify the "New England" theory of regeneration. Hopkins had distinguished between "regeneration," in which an individual passively receives God's grace, and "active conversion," in which an individual achieves salvation by holy exercises and actions. Following Edwards and Hopkins, nineteenth-century exercisers preached that the sinner not only possessed the natural ability to repent, but could "actually . . . renew his own heart under the operations of the Spirit" in active conversion. [75]

Several points seem to be clear concerning Park's interpretive efforts to establish the Edwardsian origins of the exercise scheme in New England theology. Park interpreted Edwards through Samuel Hopkins, not through Nathaniel Taylor as some students of nineteenth-century theology have suggested. [76] At critical points in his exposition of the exercise doctrines of Edwardsianism – imputation, sin, virtue, regeneration – Park invoked Hopkins. No wonder the Abbot Professor wrote to the historian

George Bancroft in 1859, "I am more convinced that Hopkins was a great man, that he had great influence over Edwards, and that in many respects he is of more *historical* importance than any other American divine, unless Pres. Edwards himself be excepted." That same year, Harriet Beecher Stowe, whose husband was Park's Andover colleague, accused the Abbot Professor of overintellectualizing Edwardsian tradition by constructing a "dry, shingle palace of Hopkinsian theology." Park, Pond, and their supporters in and outside of Andover and Bangor were identified by their critics as "Hopkinsians." [77]

The exercise scheme was central to the "new" Hopkinsianism and to efforts to define the distinctiveness of the New England theology. Park "improved" Edwards, Hopkins, and Emmons, explaining away controversial positions that he often attributed to the theology of the feelings. But he preserved and developed the exercise emphasis on natural ability, active conversion, and the personal, voluntary nature of all sin and virtue, Edwardsian doctrines suitable for the Methodized evangelical culture of the nineteenth century. Even the term "exercise," though it referred primarily to interior movements of the heart or will rather than to external action, nevertheless resonated with the discourse of activism, voluntarism, and moral energy that pervaded nineteenth-century evangelical culture. However, to recognize that the New Divinity men could not jump out of their cultural skin is far different from arguing, as Haroutunian did, that they willy-nilly engaged in a wholesale capitulation of Edwards's thought to humanism and moralism. Some of the interpretive problems that confronted Park demonstrate that Edwardsianism was not a monolithic, fixed, or static theological tradition as Haroutunian simply posited. Edwards's thought *became* a tradition, and a contested one at that, in the hands of his interpreters. Park invoked Edwards to traditionalize exercise tenets, but he also made the scheme pass the test of commonsense reasonableness. As a result, exercise doctrines gave vitality to the New England theology through the middle of the nineteenth century, yet in a framework that "harmonized" an emphasis on human accountability with an Edwardsian recognition of divine sovereignty.

From Theological Tract to Biography

Park's biographical works added to his reputation as the preeminent authority on the New England theology. He employed biography as a dogmatic weapon to promote among ordained and prospective Edwardsian ministers a self-consciousness that the New England theology was a school with a historic, but still vital, doctrinal tradition. Park labored on memoirs of Edwards, Hopkins, and Emmons, the three individuals who represented the main line of doctrinal development that he explicated in his general works on the New England theology. He completed biographies of Hopkins and of Emmons and worked unsuccessfully on his study of Edwards almost to the end of his life. In addition, Park contributed numerous short biographies of New Divinity ministers to the religious reference works, such as William B. Sprague's *Annals of the American Pulpit* and Philip Schaff's *Religious Encyclopaedia*, that were common in the second half of the nineteenth century.[78]

At midcentury, biographical interest in Edwards spilled over to his disciples, offering suggestive evidence of the continuing relevance of the New Divinity. Between 1842 and 1861, memoirs and collected works of all the major New Divinity disciples of Edwards were published: Jonathan Edwards, Jr. (1842), Nathanael Emmons (1842 and 1861), Joseph Bellamy (1850), and Samuel Hopkins (1852). Emmons was the subject of two biographies – Park's and minister Jacob Ide's. Hopkins was examined in three memoirs, Park's and two that preceded his work. Hopkins's antislavery essays were also collected and published in 1854 as *Timely Articles on Slavery*. At the same time, major works in the history of the New England theology – Bellamy's *True Religion Delineated*, for example – were reprinted as individual volumes. In fact, on the eve of the Civil War, all of the volumes listed above and many other New Divinity works were on the list of the Congregational Board of Publication in Boston.[79] Clearly, Park did not "manufacture" the historical and doctrinal interest in the New Divinity at midcentury; but, under the heading of the New England theology, he defined dogmatic traditions that extended its influence.

Park's *Memoir of the Life and Character of Samuel Hopkins, D.D.* focused on the Edwardsian protege's ministry and activities as a reformer rather than on his theology. Perhaps because Park drew so heavily on Hopkins in explaining the New England theology, he saw no need to examine in detail Hopkinsian doctrines. Park did, however, reaffirm that the "germ of Emmonism" was found in Hopkins's view that "it is difficult, and perhaps impossible, to form any distinct and clear idea . . . [that a] principle, taste, temper, disposition or habit"[80] exists passively behind the will. When Park came to some of the more controversial aspects of Hopkinsianism, he trotted out his apologetic workhorse – the distinction between the theology of the intellect and that of the feelings.

Hopkins's life provided Park with an opportunity to refute Princeton's belittling of the so-called New England theology as a "School of Metaphysics" comprised of Edwards's "dwindled progeny" under whom "a winter reigned in the theology of the land, second only to the scholastic age."[81] For Park, Hopkins exemplified how the New England theology, far from being a scholastic scourge, engaged the world – its exercise religion of the heart lengthening into external action on behalf of reform. Park extolled Hopkins's stands against slavery and the slave trade, embellishing his actions and circumstances to create a heroic account of a benevolent Edwardsian minister "rising up before his slave-holding congregation, and demanding, in the name of the Highest, the 'deliverance of the captive, and the opening of prison doors to them that were bound!'"[82] Even a reviewer critical of the New England theology praised Hopkins's courage and "commended" his example "to those pastors and doctors, who, within the last three years in their zeal for compromise and political expediency, have shown themselves recreant in the cause of liberty."[83] Hopkins emerged from Park's memoir as "Old Benevolence," a soulmate of David Brainerd who illustrated the historical conscience of the New England theology.

Park's memoir also offered a detailed account of Hopkins's thirty-year effort to send freed slaves as missionaries to Africa. Such labors were largely unsuccessful, but they helped establish Park's main point: Hopkins was not a closeted metaphysician who simply spun theories of benevolence and interiorized true virtue in exercises of the heart. As a sympathetic reviewer concluded, Park's *Memoir of Hopkins* demonstrated that the "great movement of New England theology" was not to found a school of metaphysics but "to secure results as true regeneration, eminent sanctification, benevolent activity and enterprise, and the conversion of the world."[84] But, unlike his mentor Edwards and New Divinity leaders such as Bellamy and Emmons, Hopkins was a failure as a revivalist, a shortcoming mistakenly attributed to the metaphysical bent and preaching of the New England theology. Hopkins's vain efforts as a revivalist, Park reported, derived from personal deficiencies, a lack of pulpit eloquence, and a nasal tone that, as one auditor described it, "approached a cracked bell."[85] Park ended his *Memoir of Hopkins* with the start of the Second Great Awakening; he correctly pointed out that the prominence of

New Divinity men in its local revivals, while deepening Hopkins's sense of failure, bore out the loyalty of the New England theology to Edwards's evangelical piety.

Reprinted in 1854, Park's *Memoir of Hopkins* was sympathetically, though not widely, reviewed, perhaps because the antislavery issues were too controversial in some quarters of evangelical America.[86] In contrast, Park's *Memoir of Nathanael Emmons*, published in 1861, attracted the critical notice of seminary controversialists. Park's work on Emmons was twice as long as his study of Hopkins and included an elaborate theological defense of the leading exerciser in New England theology. Union Seminary's Henry Boynton Smith (1815–77), a New Side Presbyterian critic of Park and the exercise scheme, conceded that the nearly 500-page memoir constituted "the most entertaining, ingenious and finished piece of ecclesiastical biography which New England has as yet sent forth in honor of her religious patriarchs."[87] Indeed, in the canon of pious memoirs of the "ancient Divines" of the New England theology, only Sereno Dwight's *Life of Edwards* surpassed Park's *Memoir of Emmons* in its maze of detail and in the comingled hagiographic-apologetic elements of its plot.

As an undergraduate at Yale in the 1760s, Emmons had read Edwards on the will, "with close attention" and "more than common satisfaction," he recalled, and upon graduation was drawn into the New Divinity movement and attracted to Hopkins's writings. During his long, stable ministry of more than six decades in Franklin, Massachusetts, Park stressed, Emmons's Hopkinsianism inspired his energetic leadership of or involvement in an array of benevolent activities. A "representative of the old Massachusetts and Connecticut divines" who, like Edwards and Hopkins, devoted long hours to theological study and writing, Emmons nevertheless helped found the Massachusetts Missionary Society, served as editor of its journal, and was actively engaged in such benevolent institutions as the America Board of Commissioners for Foreign Missions and the American Education Society. In addition, Emmons's Hopkinsian preaching sparked conversions; he led four revivals in Franklin during his ministry. For Park, Emmons's life was a paean to the heroic Farmer Metaphysicians of New England theology, "a sermon on the blessedness of country ministers" who promoted doctrinal study, practical piety, and benevolent activity.[88]

Moreover, Emmons stood for the preseminary-era theological teachers who instructed students in their parsonages. In this regard, Emmons, who continued to educate ministers even after seminaries were established, loomed as a New England "giant, with a hundred athletes in his train." No other theological teacher "in the land," Park observed "has come so near as Emmons to spreading out his pupils through an entire century."[89] Park dedicated forty pages of the memoir to biographical sketches of many of Emmons's nearly one hundred students and documented the diverse and influential positions they filled. Emmons lived until 1840. From the founding of Andover and Bangor to the early stages of Park's and Pond's seminary careers, his personal and intellectual influence infused New England theology. Yet historians have uniformly relegated his exercise scheme to the margins of the nineteenth-century theological world and dismissed Emmons as the New Divinity's Bartleby – an eccentric, uncompromising curiosity who could not even command significant sympathy from those in his immediate circle. How, then, did he attract one hundred students? Why did Park toil on a voluminous memoir of such a seemingly singular thinker? Why did Enoch Pond dedicate his *Lectures on Christian Theology*, published six years after Park's memoir, to Emmons?[90]

Emmons's exercise notions and vocabulary actually came to permeate New England theology in the nineteenth century; all sin consists in sinning became something of a doctrinal motto at Andover. In a fifty-page critical essay on Park's *Memoir of Emmons* in the *American Theological Review*, Henry Boynton Smith, who had studied at Andover and Bangor, perceptively observed that "Isolated and peculiar as he [Emmons] seems to be, his scheme is vitally interwoven with antecedent theories and it has affected subsequent speculations."[91] Park was a case in point. In his teaching and writing the Abbot Professor incorporated Emmons's ideas and terminology but shunned the controversial "exercise" designation in favor of "the New England theology"; moreover, as we have already seen, Park employed Edwardsian occasionalist causality and Hopkinsian constitutional arguments to chisel out a place for "taste" in the exercise scheme and to sidestep Emmons's view of divine efficiency. Emmons himself sometimes reverted to Edwardsian and Hopkinsian positions; he did not always describe moral exercises as the consequence of God's *direct efficient* power.

Park's interpretive challenge in composing the *Memoir of Emmons*, then, was to show that Emmons's exercise theology achieved an appropriate balance between divine sovereignty and human accountability. Thus, Park drew on all of his seminary-acquired exegetical abilities to moderate Emmons's statements on divine efficiency and to amplify his seeming acknowledgments of Edwardsian occasionalism and constitutionalism. Park

conceded that Emmons "adopts a severe method of describing certain divine arrangements." But, as with the Bible, certain passages needed to be
studied in a historical context, with an awareness of "peculiarities of dic-
tion." Because he lived until 1840 and "conversed with friends who are yet
in the noon of their life," Park explained, "men have interpreted his words
by the standard of the present age, instead of interpreting them by the age
to which he belonged." Furthermore, like "idiomatic phrases of the He-
brew Bible," Emmons's language was often figurative, not literal. His
"metaphorical," "feminine" expressions of doctrine exemplified the wisdom of distinguishing between the theology of the intellect and that of the
feelings.[92]

For when Emmons used language that suggested divine efficiency, or
when he adopted Hopkinsian phrases on divine submission, he was – like
the French mystic Fénelon – merely "expressing his religious emotions,"
his disinterested love of a sovereign God. Translated into the theology of
the intellect, divine "efficiency" simply meant divine "independence."
Good Edwardsian that he was, Emmons denied the self-determining
power of the will: "Man does not begin his moral action by choosing to
choose." For Park, Emmons's divine efficiency boiled down to the fact
"that all other choices are put forth by the intervention of powers which
absolutely depend on the first external choice of the First Cause."[93]

Having tempered Emmons's doctrine of divine efficiency, Park went on
to reaffirm his Edwardsian recognition of the secondary causes and laws of
nature through which God operated. Park admitted that Emmons, in his
desire to assert divine sovereignty, had not given adequate notice "to the
mode in which God executes" his decrees. But Park was still able to assemble passages from Emmons's works that invoked the laws of nature and
secondary causes. One crucial passage confirmed for Park why Emmons
tended to ignore the "modes" of divine operation: "God employs so many
secondary causes in bestowing blessings upon mankind, that they are ex-
tremely apt to overlook the *primary* and *supreme Cause* from which they
flow."[94] Similarly, Emmons spoke and wrote as if there was nothing behind exercises of the will, because he did not want sinners to plead that an
involuntary, corrupt nature or taste presented, as he put it, "an *insur-
mountable* obstacle or natural inability, in the way of their loving God, re-
penting of sin, or doing anything in a holy manner." Emmons followed
Hopkins in arguing that "it is impossible to conceive of a corrupt and sinful nature, *prior to*, and *distinct from*, corrupt and sinful *exercises*."[95] But

such a perspective, Park suggested, did not preclude the existence of a spiritual substance or taste as a morally neutral constitutional foundation of choice.

Through an interpretive process that involved tugging and tucking Emmons's thought and snipping and pasting from his works, Park restored a balance between divine sovereignty and human accountability in the theology of the most famous exerciser. He also reasserted Emmons's essential Edwardsianism, underscored the Franklin divine's Hopkinsian line of descent, and assimilated him into the mediating exercise theology of Andover and Bangor. In the *American Theological Review*, Enoch Pond lauded the memoir of his teacher and endorsed Park's explanation of Emmons's exercise theology. "Prof. Park," Pond enthused, "has erected a monument . . . to the memory of his friend, and his father's friend – a monument that will stand, and be studied and admired, in years and generations yet to come."[96] Other reviewers, however, heaped criticism on Park. Indeed, his *Memoir of Emmons* renewed seminary efforts to redeem Edwardsian tradition from the creators of the New England theology.

Counter-Narrative

The period from 1850, when he delivered his convocation address on "The Theology of the Intellect and That of the Feelings," to 1861, when he published his *Memoir of Emmons*, comprised Park's most productive years and the high-water mark of the New England theology. Park created an Edwardsian theological tradition by codifying a dogmatic canon and constructing an organic doctrinal history; his publications displayed, perhaps, unsurpassed knowledge of the lives and works of the theologians, from Edwards to Emmons, who contributed to that tradition. Park's efforts brought notoriety to him and Andover. In 1853, he was chosen president of the faculty; at the same time he turned down the presidency of Amherst College. Park's reputation also stimulated new student interest in Andover beginning in the early 1850s.[97]

Critical outbursts from rival seminaries heightened the intellectual excitement of these years. Seminary journals provided the forum for a paper war over the New England theology and Park's "provincial" and well-nigh clannish appropriation of Edwards. Critics mounted a nascent counter-narrative of New England theological history that did not achieve the breadth or depth of Park's work. This counter-narrative remained confined to seminary journals; it did not produce books that challenged Park's publications. Furthermore, whereas Park and Pond developed a coherent historical narrative that became institutionalized at Andover and Bangor, critics of the New England theology were more diffuse. They were affiliated with different seminaries, whose varying doctrinal emphases shaped their view of Edwardsian theological tradition. Princeton's Charles Hodge and Lyman Atwater, Union's Henry Boynton Smith, and East Windsor's Edward A. Lawrence emerged in the 1850s and early 1860s as among the most combative critics of Park. Despite their doctrinal differences and disparate knowledge of New England theological history, they offered commentary on Park's publications that often overlapped and that aimed to retrieve an essentially orthodox Edwards from the historical "distortions" of his successors.

Park's use of the term "New England theology" became a focal point of contention. His critics continued to use the labels "New Divinity," "Hopkinsianism," and "Emmonism" to distinguish Edwards from his boldest disciples. Lyman Atwater railed that "New England theology" only suggested the "local, temporary, provincial, idiosyncratic" and therefore "false" doctrines of the New Divinity – an amalgam of "new things that are not true, and true things that are not new." Park's popularizing of "the assumed title of New England theology," Atwater insisted, furnished the protective "shield" of Edwards's "mighty name" for "propounders and abetters of all the schemes of ephemeral divinity."[98]

Other critics castigated Park for dismissing more than one hundred years of New England religious history. The New England theology, Edward Lawrence complained, consisted of "the system of doctrines, which from the founding of the colonies, has been held by the Congregational churches in New England." But Park discarded the first one hundred and thirty years of history and restricted "New England theology to the one hundred [years] of the later history." John Calvin, English Puritans, and the colonial founders who adopted the Westminster Confession, both Lawrence and Charles Hodge stressed, had all shaped New England theology before Edwards and New Divinity adherents were even born. From this perspective, Edwards was neither the "*father*" nor the "founder" of New England theology. "It is older than Edwards and the father of him, not he of it."[99]

Such an orthodox historical interpretation of New England theology and of Edwards did not devalue the colonial awakening but merely delimited its theological significance. The awakening remained a "great" event that arrested the religious declension of New England brought about by the Halfway Covenant, Stoddardeanism, and the moralistic erosion of Calvinism. The colonial awakening, Lawrence asserted in 1861, constituted *"the reaction of the pure old New England Theology against an enfeebling amalgam of Pelagian, Socinian, and Arminian elements."* [100] Lawrence, Henry Boynton Smith, and the Princetonians consistently embraced moderate New Divinity men like Bellamy and Leonard Woods as exemplary New England defenders of orthodoxy, but Hopkins proved to be more problematic. Park's critics were determined to establish "the derivative character" of Edwards's theology itself, which was not "an improvement, except in its mode of statement and defence." Park's history of improvements in New England theology from Hopkins to Emmons demonstrated how Edwards's "progeny . . . devoured its parent." [101]

Commentators on Park turned to his historical exegesis of the New England theology to establish their case. Park's method of interpretation, a writer protested in the *American Theological Review*, "binds like an India-rubber clasp more or less according to convenience." *The Atonement: Discourses and Treatises* became the prime example for Park's critics of his elastic use of Edwards's name and thought. For while acknowledging that Edwards did not directly endorse the governmental theory, Park "seized upon" nothing more than "some casual expressions, some *obiter dicta*" of Edwards which "have been pressed into the service of the new theory." Park's use of "Edwardean" to describe the New England or governmental theory amounted to "an abuse of Edwards's good name as well as a perversion of the truth of history." Edwards never embraced a theory, Henry Boynton Smith pointed out, that "robbed the believer of half his Savior." [102]

Smith insisted that Emmons's exercise scheme and the emphasis in New England theology on sinners' natural ability laid the foundation for Taylorism and theories concerning the self-determination of the will. This doctrinal indictment of the so-called New England theology found a receptive audience at Princeton, whose Old School Presbyterians Smith was trying to reunite with his New School brethren. Alarmed by invocations of natural ability that seemed to smack of Arminianism and determined to secure Edwards's orthodoxy, the Princetonians and some Old Calvinists in New England even stripped *Freedom of the Will* of any novelty. Edwards's distinction between natural and moral ability, Atwater maintained, was mistakenly held up as "the invention and glory of American theology." But

Edwards was not "the inventor of this distinction"; it was "familiar to theologians, not only before the time of Edwards, but from the time when the heresies of Pelagius first occasioned thorough discussion of the subject of sin and grace." *Freedom of the Will* discussed natural and moral ability as "terms already established" and well known "among divines of the Augustinian school." [103]

Princeton's efforts to deradicalize Edwards by casting him as an essentially orthodox Old Calvinist, while predating the 1850s, acquired an urgent, reactive character at midcentury as Park aggressively advanced his historical interpretations of the New England theology. In their campaign to de–New Englandize Edwards, the Princetonians acknowledged only two novelties, or "peculiar philosophical" positions, in the theologian's corpus. Edwards had put forth "eccentric philosophical" views of humanity's personal identity with Adam and of true virtue "as consisting wholly in love to being in general." But these two minor "eccentricities of his theology and philosophy" did not subvert Edwards's fundamental Old Calvinism; and they certainly did not legitimize "successive forms of the New Divinity," whose alterations of original sin, imputation, and a limited atonement and whose exercise doctrines were "utterly abhorrent" to Edwards's theology. [104]

When Park applied "Edwardean" to such innovations of the New England theology, his critics from Princeton to Connecticut devised a sarcastic but effective historical reply: Park surely meant Edwards the son, not the father. The younger Edwards, after all, even in Park's history, marked the emergence in full garb of the New England theory of the atonement. In addition, the son authored a seemingly authoritative document, "Improvements in Theology, Made by President Edwards, and Those Who Have Followed His Course of Thought." First published by Sereno Dwight in 1829, "Improvements in Theology" was reprinted in the younger Edwards's collected works in 1842; it outlined ten doctrinal improvements, from natural ability to imputation, the atonement, and disinterested benevolence, and became a canonical source for Park and the New Englanders. [105] But for opponents the document only proved that the son and other New Divinity men, and not Edwards, were the principal "improvers" of New England theology. Edwards, Park's critics grumbled, was not the father of the New England theology; he "was only the father of Edwards the son," who was "the true father of the Edwardean theology." [106]

The Edwardsian theological tradition remained an intensely contested historical subject through the middle of the nineteenth century, as the polemical and reactive counter-narrative of Park's opponents reveals. Park and his critics both saw their theology as a product of *the* past at the same time that they constructed *a* past to serve the apologetic needs of the present. One hundred years of doctrinal improvements did not lead to a result that was self-evidently Edwardsian; Park had to return continually to Edwards to traditionalize the New England theology. For their part, his critics sought to traditionalize Edwards by rooting him in an antecedent Puritan past, thereby contesting the "New Divinity" claim to his legacy.

Such competing historical perspectives on theological tradition raise questions about recent interpretations of Edwards and the New Divinity. One revisionist historian has argued that "the New Divinity was hardly more than a set of variations on certain Edwardsian themes." Another asserts, "By 1758 most of the important New Divinity principles had already emerged to public view in the writings of Edwards." [107] In their rush to reestablish the Calvinist and Edwardsian orthodoxy of the New Divinity, revisionists ironically reinscribe old notions about the Consistent Calvinists' lack of originality and their utter intellectual inferiority to Edwards. With the exception of Hopkins, the New Divinity men down to Emmons did not create original systems of theology. Park himself only published sermons and discourses, not works of systematic theology. But, as Park's history of the atonement, original sin, imputation, and the exercise theology suggests – and as critics of the New Divinity protested – first and second generation disciples "improved" Edwards's thought in significant and original ways while endeavoring to maintain his reconciliation of divine sovereignty and human accountability.

The Passing of the New England Theology

Park resigned as president of Andover's faculty in 1868, the same year that Old and New School Presbyterians reunited. Soon Park stopped attending faculty meetings, in part because of poor health, in part as a protest against changes at Andover that signalled the beginnings of the "Progressive Orthodoxy" that would transform the seminary and dislodge the New England theology from its influential institutional base. New faculty appointed in the 1860s initiated curriculum changes to modernize instruction at Andover. Egbert C. Smyth (1829–1904) was installed as Brown Professor of Ecclesiastical History in 1863. Smyth would emerge as one of

Andover's leading liberals who would hasten the passing of the New England theology at the seminary.[108] Smyth and his fellow liberals sought a theology more receptive to science and the higher criticism than Park's and less attached to doctrinal creeds of the past. Park was hardly reassured by Smyth's fondness for saying of Edwards, "We shall not go back to him, nor yet go forward without him."[109]

In 1870, Park, whose wife was a great-granddaughter of Edwards, acquired the major collection of the theologian's manuscripts, which had passed down from Hopkins, through the Dwight family, to Sereno Dwight, and then to Tryon Edwards. Egbert Smyth, who had also married into the Edwards family, possessed other manuscripts. Andover became the major repository of Edwards's papers precisely at the time it was moving away from his theological tradition.[110] Through the 1880s, absorbed in the controversies surrounding Andover's abandonment of the New England theology and afflicted with poor health, Park was unable to pursue work on his memoir of Edwards or edit the theologian's manuscripts for publication.[111]

Park resigned from the Abbot Professorship in 1881. As Leonard Woods had done thirty-five years earlier, Park nominated his successor – Frank H. Foster, a recent student who had been groomed for the position. Foster was rejected. Three years later the *Bibliotheca Sacra*, which had been such an essential organ for the "creation" of the New England theology, was transferred to Oberlin.[112]

In retirement, Park continued to resist the Andover liberals and the Progressive Orthodoxy propagated through the seminary's new journal, the *Andover Review*. Park organized alumni groups against the new faculty, spoke out publicly in opposition to the seminary's heterodoxy, and republished the Associate Creed of Andover's founders. Since all faculty had been required to subscribe to the creed every five years, Park pressured the seminary's board to make subscription binding as the founders had mandated. Such legalistic arguments and the overall desperation of his efforts to resist change brought Park full circle from the irenic and commonsense reasonableness of "The Theology of the Intellect and That of the Feelings."[113]

Park's exasperation only underscored his attachment to tradition; the dissolution of the New England theology and the palpable doctrinal irrelevance of Edwards, both in and outside of Andover, after 1870 undoubtedly contributed to Park's failure to complete his final historical projects.

Park saw defenses, explanations, and refutations of Edwards, which had reached a high point at midcentury, decline sharply in the decades after the Civil War. Editors and readers of seminary journals fixed their attention on new controversies and theological issues that accompanied the emergence of liberal Protestantism. The audience for redactions of Edwards's writings dwindled, and in 1892, the American Tract Society, that paper mill of Edwardsianism, removed the theologian's works from its publication list.[114]

Major elements of Park's historical perspective on the New England theology, however, persisted into the post-Edwardsian era through the work of his students. In 1899, George Boardman, retired professor of systematic theology at Chicago Theological Seminary (founded by Congregationalists in 1858), published *A History of New England Theology*, the first post-Calvinist overview of the subject. Boardman drew on Park's publications and praised him as a teacher and theological interpreter: "I still turn to the notes taken in my student days for suggestions and arguments concerning the faith once delivered to the saints."[115] Boardman ignored New England theology before the colonial awakening, described the practical piety promoted by a dominant Hopkinsian strain, and emphasized the New Divinity's Edwardsianism and Calvinism.

Boardman's study was followed by a much more ambitious work – that of Frank H. Foster, Park's failed nominee for the Abbot Professorship, who had served as professor of theology at Pacific Seminary, founded by California Congregationalists in 1869. Foster had begun working on *A Genetic History of the New England Theology* (1907) before Park's death in 1900. Foster acknowledged Park "for much help of a historical character, both personal and through his historical writings, as well as for the dogmatic view of the whole period." Foster praised Park as "the profoundest student of the history of the New England theology that has yet appeared."[116]

Foster's volume remained the standard work on the New England theology for a generation – until the publication of Joseph Haroutunian's *Piety versus Moralism*. Haroutunian's study replied directly to Foster; it offered a neo-orthodox gloss on the nineteenth-century counter-narrative of Park's critics and reasserted the New Divinity's betrayal of Edwards and Calvin. Indeed, one can almost detect the echo of Charles Hodge and Lyman Atwater in Haroutunian's pronouncements: "The chief aim of the Edwardean theology was not to formulate a theory of the will; it was inspired by a piety which sought to glorify God and His sovereignty over man."[117] Recognizing how and why the twentieth-century scholarly debate over the New England theology replicates nineteenth-century controversy should encourage scholars to press on to new perspectives. These new perspectives will need to acknowledge both the vitality and complexity of Edwardsianism and examine how doctrinal traditions rooted in Edwards's thought were constructed and contested through the middle of the nineteenth century.

6

• • •

COLONIAL REVIVAL

EDWARDS AND PURITAN TRADITION IN
AMERICAN CULTURE, 1870–1903

Neither the postbellum dissolution of the New England theology and of Calvinism in general, nor the attendant emergence of social Christianity, which increasingly supplanted revivalistic evangelical religion in mainline Protestant churches, proclaimed the end of American culture's engagement with Jonathan Edwards. Quite the contrary, the passing of the New England theology established new interpretive opportunities for the creation of a post-Calvinist Puritan tradition that met the cultural needs of the present. The formulation of a usable post-Calvinist Puritan past was part cultural consolidation, part cultural reaction. New England–based or –bred elites sought narratives of the origins of American culture that consolidated the political and military victory over the South. Moreover, in the face of the urban, industrial, and ethnic transformation of America these same secular and religious elites spearheaded an interest in and nostalgia for a heroic colonial past – a heavily reactionary perspective that, while acknowledging Puritanism's imperfections, still celebrated its spirit and achievements as the most important moral and cultural presence in the founding and development of America.[1] As the "last" or "greatest" Puritan, Edwards remained central to new narratives of the relationship between religious tradition and the shaping of American culture.

Shortly before and after the Civil War, Harriet Beecher Stowe and Henry Ward Beecher completed novels in which they attempted to come to terms with their Edwardsian and Puritan heritage. In their flight from Calvinism, both Stowe and her brother clung to Puritanism as a moral and

cultural force; they displayed an ambivalence toward their religious tradition – an ambivalence that would not be completely erased in later post-
Calvinist assessments of Puritanism by individuals who were more culturally distant from that heritage than the children of Lyman Beecher. Between 1852 and 1864, Stowe lived in Andover, Massachusetts, where her
husband, Calvin, served on the seminary faculty. The Stowes were friends
and neighbors of Edwards A. Park; Stowe read the Abbot Professor's biographies of Hopkins and Emmons, discussed the works with him, and
used them in two historical novels in which she began to retrieve Puritanism as a moral and cultural force from its thralldom to Calvinism.

The Minister's Wooing (1859) is set in Newport, Rhode Island, in the
1790s with Samuel Hopkins, "the patron saint of the Negro race" in the
town, as "the hero." Stowe does not temper Hopkins's hyper-Calvinist
views of divine sovereignty, as Park did; she rejects them, as she does "the
refined poetry of torture" in Edwards's sermons. Yet, Stowe embraces disinterested benevolence, especially as it informed the ethos of the Edwardsian ministry: "Their whole lives and deportment bore thrilling witness to
their sincerity. Edwards set apart special days of fasting, in view of the
dreadful doom of the lost. . . . Hopkins fasted every Saturday. David Brainerd gave up every refinement of civilized life to weep and pray at the feet of
hardened savages, if by any means he might save one."[2] Hopkins's disinterested benevolence inspires two heroic acts of self-sacrifice in The Minister's Wooing. He challenges slaveowners and slave traders in his own congregation, and he gives up his fiancée, Mary Scudder, when her young
beau, who had been presumed drowned, returns to Newport. Even as
Stowe uses fiction to negotiate her retreat from the faith once delivered to
the saints, she extols the "nobility" and the "grand side" of the "strivings of
the soul" encouraged by New England theology, and she eulogizes the
"lives of eminent purity and earnestness" of its "noblest" representatives.[3]

In the mid-1860s, Stowe moved to Hartford, Connecticut, and joined
the Episcopal Church. The second of her four New England novels, Oldtown Folks (1869), drew on her husband's childhood recollections to evoke
life in a small Massachusetts community at the turn of the nineteenth century. Oldtown Folks is offered as a memoir by an adult male narrator. Ho-
race Holyoke was orphaned as a boy and taken in by his Grandmother
Badger, a severe but loving Puritan matriarch whose favorite reading, her
precious "blue book," was Joseph Bellamy's True Religion Delineated.
Oldtown's Calvinist minister, Dr. Moses Stern, was none other than Na-

thanael Emmons, Calvin Stowe's teacher. Stern's theological system was comparable to a "skillful engine of torture" powered by "the mental anguish of the most perfect sense of helplessness, with the most torturing sense of responsibility." Still, like Grandmother Badger, Oldtown's throwback to the Puritan patriarchs of ancient times possessed redeeming virtues that gave him a certain nobility. If Stern's "devotion to the King Eternal" exhibited "something terrible and painful," it also displayed qualities which were "grand and in which we can take pride, as fruit of our own nature."[4]

Seemingly inspired by his sister, Henry Ward Beecher turned to local color fiction to separate the theological dross from the precious elements in his New England religious heritage. In 1867, Beecher published *Norwood; or, Village Life in New England*, a novel set in a town that closely resembles Northampton. Norwood is located twenty miles north of Springfield and situated on a hill overlooking the Connecticut River Valley. Moreover, like Northampton, Norwood was established "not far from thirty years after the Pilgrims' landing." Norwood's minister, Jedidiah Buell, is portrayed as an Edwardsian thinker, "a high and noble man, trained to New England theology, but brought to excessive distress by speculations and new views."[5] Buell is presented as an embodiment of a tradition of logical theology that has left New England Calvinist thinkers, "Edwards, perhaps, excepted," deficient in poetic sensibilities and poorly prepared to address the moral and emotional needs of Christians. Yet Beecher shares his sister's pride in New England's religious heritage and social ideals. He sees hope for Buell and his Norwood parishioners in the liberation of Puritan tradition from the constrictions of Calvinism. Beecher's spokesman, medical Dr. Reuben Wentworth, even praises New England theologians for dealing "with the great moral truths in such a manner that the imagination of their people has been powerfully developed."[6]

Stowe and Beecher, of course, differed in several ways from late-nineteenth-century colonial revival interpreters of Puritan and Edwardsian tradition. Lyman Beecher's offspring wrestled with an intensely personal religious past. They also belonged to a generation that had become embroiled in controversies over Calvinist theology and revivalism. In addition, when Stowe and Beecher published their novels, Edwardsianism remained a vital, if receding, presence in American religion. The cultural and religious disengagement from Calvinism during the last three decades of the nineteenth century enabled writers and thinkers to reassess the

Puritan heritage with even more sympathy than Stowe and Beecher displayed. There were dissenters, to be sure; and most respectful interpreters of the Puritans were ambivalent enough about the past to accept the wisdom of Hawthorne's historical perspective: "Let us thank God for having given us such ancestors; and let each successive generation thank him not less fervently, for going one step further from them in the march of ages."[7]

But the Puritan past became usable precisely because it was now distant. In a post-Calvinist, postrevival era, Unitarians and Anglicans joined Congregationalists and Presbyterians in a new "politics of Puritan historiography"[8] that addressed the cultural needs of the moment and that led to the first outpouring of Puritan studies. Scholars developed Puritan origins narratives for American history and literature. Pilgrim and Puritan monuments proliferated on the landscape, visual narratives of the tradition and spirit that had triumphed in the Revolution and the Civil War and to which immigrants required acculturation. Commemorations of historic colonial events and of town and church foundings provided occasions for lay and religious elites to perorate on America's glorious Anglo-Puritan past and to invoke religious tradition against such Victorian era symptoms of moral degeneration as political machines, labor strife, saloons, and consumerism. "A foreigner might think," Oliver Wendell Holmes observed in a biographical sketch of Edwards in 1880, "that the patron saint of America was Saint Anniversary."[9]

In the aftermath of the demise of the New England theology, Edwards endured as a dominant cultural figure in newly constructed narratives examining the Puritan origins of American history and American literature. Furthermore, Edwards became the subject of a major and highly successful late-nineteenth-century biography, part of the larger Victorian interest in and appreciation for the virile character, rock-ribbed sense of duty, and spiritual aspirations embodied in the lives of Puritan leaders. Stockbridge and Northampton issued new calls for Edwards's services. Rapidly changing communities, the sites of Edwards's pastorates, commemorated him, erected monuments in his honor, and preserved or invented Edwardsian "antiquities." Saint Anniversary in Stockbridge and Northampton demonstrates not only the vigor of the colonial revival impulse at the local level; it reveals the cultural backlash that Puritan ancestor worship became.

·   ·   ·

Even before the convening of their Pilgrim Memorial Convention in 1870, American Congregationalists, who held special claim on Puritan tradition and Edwards, sought to stress a common history and ecclesiastical practice, not Calvinist theology, as a denominational bond. Meeting in Boston in 1865, the National Council discussed a statement of faith and debated whether it should include a proposed acknowledgment of "the system of truths which is commonly known among us as Calvinism." [10] Opposition from a minority of the more than five hundred delegates assembled threatened to divide the Council and to jeopardize continuing denominational work in the West and new religious opportunities in the recently defeated South. An excursion to Plymouth, where the representatives reconvened on Burial Hill, appears to have established the historic atmosphere that helped fashion a compromise. The "Burial Hill Declaration" omitted any reference to Calvinism; it also offered a statement so general that, as one denominational historian observed, the document seemed "better suited to an address on an historic occasion than to a creed for local and permanent use." [11]

Five years later, the commemoration of the two hundred and fiftieth anniversary of the founding of Plymouth Colony ushered in what can only be called the golden age of Congregational historiography. From the ruins of the New England theology, denominational energy was diverted to collecting, preserving, and interpreting historical evidence, an early stage of the colonial revival creation of a usable Puritan past. Led by Henry Martyn Dexter (1821–90) and Williston Walker (1860–1922), denominational historians hailed Edwards as "so saintly a man" and as the "father of modern Congregationalism" [12] who overturned Solomon Stoddard's Presbyterian church practices; they also moved far beyond doctrinal history to recover the Puritan as a moral and cultural figure. Dexter graduated from Yale and Andover, served churches in New Hampshire and Boston, and edited the *Congregationalist*, a denominational journal of history and biography. Dexter published his monumental *The Congregationalism of the Last Three Hundred Years as Seen in Its Literature* in 1880. Over 1,000 pages long, Dexter's volume included a 300-page bibliography of published material and manuscript items that stimulated historical research on Congregationalism. Dexter boasted that in his veins "were blended the blood" of a "restless and sometimes testy Puritan" founder of Massachusetts Bay with the blood of Plymouth's Pilgrim leaders. "I began almost to esteem it a filial duty," he confessed, "to study closely our primitive annals." In *As to Roger Williams, and His "Banishment" from Massachusetts Plantations* (1876), Dexter's esteem for his Puritan ancestors even led him to defend them as wisely acting out of self-preservation in expelling the famous religious dissenter.[13]

Dexter also inspired the historical work of Williston Walker, a graduate of Yale (where he served as professor of church history) and Hartford Seminary, who claimed that Congregationalism "contributed far beyond any other polity to the fashioning of the political ideals of the United States."[14] Through such works as *Creeds and Platforms of Congregationalism* (1893), *A History of the Congregational Churches in the United States* (1894), and *Ten New England Leaders* (1901), which included a long, sympathetic essay on Edwards as a latter-day Puritan, Walker succeeded Dexter as the leading authority on the history of Congregationalism.

The development of Congregational House – a denominational headquarters and library – paralleled the historical work of Dexter and Walker. Originating at midcentury under the advocacy of Edwards A. Park, the Congregational Library Association grew into the Congregational House in Boston, which by the 1890s possessed thousands of books and pamphlets and became the major repository of material on denominational history. In 1898, a new, stately eight-story Congregational House was completed on Beacon Hill to accommodate expanding historical interests and denominational needs. Four bas-relief tablets depicting major historical events in the founding of New England were commissioned for the front of the building: the Mayflower Compact, the Pilgrims worshiping on Clark's Pond in Plymouth Harbor, the founding of Harvard College, and John Eliot preaching to the Indians.[15]

Such visual representations of the Pilgrim-Puritan origins of America multiplied – like the saloons that sprouted in ethnic working-class neighborhoods – across New England and outside the region as well. While the Pilgrims and Plymouth became "national" historical icons in the late nineteenth century, Puritan history occasioned far more commemorations, casting of bronze, and molding of granite. Augustus Saint-Gaudens sculpted the most impressive Puritan statue, which was unveiled in Springfield, Massachusetts, in 1887 (Figure 1). Saint-Gaudens's nine-foot bronze statue, "The Puritan," both humanized and aggrandized his subject, creating a visual analogue for colonial revival interpretations of the

FIGURE 1. Augustus Saint-Gaudens, "The Puritan" (1887),
Springfield, Massachusetts. Photograph by T. Conforti.

Puritan character. Pennsylvania's New England Society even commissioned Saint-Gaudens to sculpt a replica of the Springfield statue for Philadelphia.[16] Moreover, Saint-Gaudens's work clearly influenced subsequent Puritan statuary, such as Salem's bronze of Roger Conant.

The erection of statues and monuments to such Puritan stalwarts as John Harvard, John Winthrop (Figure 2), and John Eliot (Figure 3) accompanied the progress of Saint Anniversary in New England. Edwardsian tradition became part of a seemingly indulgent celebration of a glorious past that was in part a response to Victorian excesses of a different sort. In the late nineteenth century, residents of Enfield, Connecticut, dedicated a rock-monument on the town green consecrating the site where Edwards delivered "Sinners in the Hands of an Angry God" (Figure 4). A short while later, Haddam citizens erected a plaque on the homesite of John and David Brainerd (Figure 5). In addition, as we shall see, the historically minded leaders of Stockbridge and Northampton scattered Edwards and colonial memorials throughout their communities. Puritan artifacts, which were placed in public places and not just on church grounds and private property, were far from simply objects of nostalgia that reassured Anglo-Puritan descendants buffeted by change. Rather, they were civic-religious monuments that appropriated public space, linked place to past, and through such historicizing sought to stabilize the present by, among other things, promoting a respect for tradition and interest in Americanization among growing numbers of non-Anglo citizens.

Furthermore, bas-reliefs, bronze statues, granite monuments, memorial boulders, and commemorative plaques composed a visual narrative that buttressed the emergent Puritan origins lines of interpretation in public addresses, magazine articles, and American history and American literature texts. In the post-Calvinist era, Congregationalists had to share their interest in and appreciation for America's Puritan heritage with former religious opponents, even Unitarians. The Puritans "believed that a free people should govern itself by a higher law than their own desire," George Hoar, Massachusetts's Unitarian senator, declared. "Duty and not self-indulgence, and future good in this world and the other, and not a present and immediate good, were the motives upon which they acted."[17] Descendants of the Puritans, like Hoar, contributed to a colonial revival historical perspective that appealed across denominational lines – fusing as it did nostalgia, ancestor worship, Anglo-Saxon racialism and jeremiad-like criticism of the perceived degradation of Victorian America.

FIGURE 2. Richard S. Greenough, "John Winthrop" (1880), Boston.
Photograph by T. Conforti.

FIGURE 3. John Rogers, "John Eliot Preaching to the Indians" (1889), Natick, Massachusetts, Historical Society. Photograph by T. Conforti, with permission of the Natick, Massachusetts, Historical Society.

FIGURE 4. Boulder marking the site of "Sinners in the Hands of an Angry God" (ca. 1890), Enfield, Connecticut. Photograph by T. Conforti.

Such an ideologically charged view of the past informed a spate of books – scholarly and popular – that constituted the first flowering of Puritan studies. Even leaden tomes like George Ellis's *The Puritan Age in Massachusetts, 1629–1685* (1888) prospered through several editions. More popular was a run of Puritan biographies which seemed to begin with Alexander V. G. Allen's highly successful 1889 study of Edwards (discussed below) and which continued through the 1890s.[18] Barrett Wendell's *Cotton Mather, The Puritan Priest* (1891) ranks among the most interesting and controversial of these biographical works; it shows how descendants carefully picked the bones of ancestors and thereby fashioned a usable Puritan past. Mather had been the Unitarian whipping boy whose behavior in the Salem witch trials predicted the revivalistic "fanaticism" of the Calvinist-inspired awakenings of the eighteenth and nineteenth centuries. During the bicentennial year of the witchcraft trials, however, Harvard English professor Barrett Wendell published an admiring biography of Mather that did not flinch from his involvement in the episode but at the same time suggested some exculpatory evidence: witchcraft was a popular belief, as was confidence in spectral evidence, which Mather rejected. Mather was never "deliberately dishonest," for throughout his life "he never ceased striving, amid endless stumblings and errors to do his duty." Wendell, who believed New England life was "the source of what is best in our America," showered praise on Mather for "strenuously" and "devoutly" pursuing what he thought was right. Wendell, as one scholar has observed,

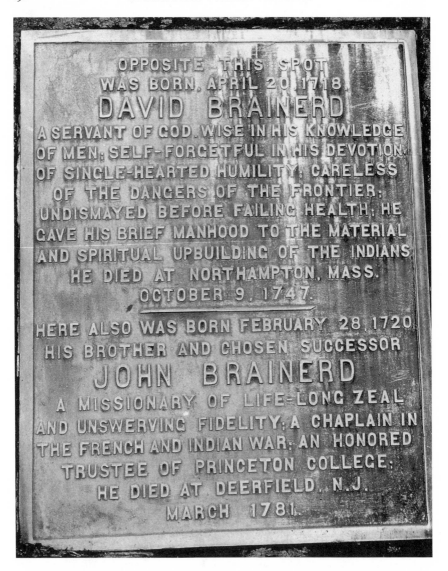

FIGURE 5. Brainerd birthplace plaque (1905), Haddam, Connecticut.
Photograph by T. Conforti.

"identified the Puritan spirit with little more specific than the strenuous life." [19] In the hands of interpreters like Wendell, colonial history – as Puritan iconography suggested – became the fount of restorative moral and cultural values for the maladies of Victorian society.

Boston minister Ezra Hoyt Byington was one successful historian of the

Puritans who extended Wendell's line of interpretation. In *The Puritan in England and New England*, which went through four editions between 1896 and 1900, Byington partially excused the Puritans' persecution of witches while conceding that the religious founders of America were not "perfect models" for his contemporaries because they were "not as tolerant as we have learned to be." But despite such limitations, the Puritans were still "in the best sense progressive, and our age owes very much to their fidelity to truth and to freedom." If the Puritans had embodied the "gentleness" and tolerance of the Pilgrims, the New England character, whose traits were now under cultural assault and social abandonment, "would not have given its impress to a great nation like this republic." [20]

The popularity of *The Puritan in England and New England* led Byington to complete a second volume, *The Puritan as a Colonist and Reformer* (1899), which contained a long chapter on "Jonathan Edwards and the Great Awakening." Byington's work was a response to what he saw as the "increasing interest" in and "higher appreciation" of the "Puritan spirit." Byington infused this spirit with Anglo-Saxon racialism, and he lauded the "freedom," "enterprise," and "faith" that cultivated an English "instinct" for successful colonization. Edwards and the Great Awakening, he asserted, represented an extension of the reforming Puritan tradition that had colonized America. The distinguished divine's preaching and writing revitalized spirituality and theology in New England and reversed the "remarkable declension of religious life in the Puritan churches." [21]

Byington did not call for a new Edwards or a new Mather, but at least one participant in a major church symposium, entitled *The New Puritanism*, held in 1897, was unable to summon such restraint. A colonial revival Puritan tradition emerged not only from the books of clerical and academic historians; it was forged in the addresses, publications, and commemorative artifacts of church, town, and historical anniversaries. The semicentennial of the prestigious Plymouth Church in Brooklyn was one such occasion. Lyman Abbott, who succeeded Henry Ward Beecher as the pastor of Plymouth Church, carefully sifted through New England history to distinguish the "Old" from the "New" Puritanism. Abbott applauded Edwardsian tradition for its encouraging among Christians "a profound sense, if a somewhat morbid sense, of their guilt and sinfulness," as well as a "very profound, if not altogether healthful, reverence for God." But the "fatalism" of Edwards's *Freedom of the Will* separated the Old and the New Puritanism; the latter began to evolve in the nineteenth century as the moral energy and "social conscience" of Puritanism and Edwardsianism were rescued from Calvinist theology.[22]

In an address on "Puritan Principles in the Modern World," New Jersey minister Amory Bradford went beyond Abbott and called for a "revival of Puritanism." Bradford seemed uninterested in distinguishing between old and new phases of religious tradition. He praised powerful Puritan figures from Cromwell to Edwards, while berating Victorian America for its "vice," "luxury and effeminacy" and for producing literature that was "in great part becoming mere dirt." Bradford issued a call for the reaffirmation of "traditional" Puritan values: "for character; for clean living as a condition of public service; for recognition of responsibility to God; for the supremacy of the spirit."[23]

Alice Morse Earle was probably among the auditors in the Plymouth Church listening to Abbott, Bradford, and others descanting on the New Puritanism. One of many transplanted New Englanders living in Brooklyn Heights, Earle devised her own historical response to the changes that so disquieted Bradford; she reveals yet another dimension to the colonial revival creation of a usable Puritan past. A prolific author of enormously popular historical works, Earle adapted the techniques of local color fiction to produce richly textured, evocative studies that lauded the virtue and stability of the colonial world. In her skilled hands, a nostalgic glow and descriptive detail often carried – and sometimes masked – the same ideological freight with which Bradford overburdened his audience. *The Sabbath in Puritan New England* was one of Earle's most successful works; first published in 1891, it went through twelve editions in little more than a decade. The book's conclusion resonated with the positive rhetoric and nostalgic historical appraisal that characterized the late-nineteenth-century colonial revival view of the Puritans: "Patient, frugal, God fearing and industrious, cruel and intolerant sometimes, but never cowardly, sternly obeying the word of God in the spirit and the letter, but erring sometimes in the interpretation thereof, – surely they had no traits to shame us, to keep us from thrilling with pride at the drop of their blood which runs in our backsliding veins."[24] It was only a short step from such a seemingly balanced, yet laudatory, assessment to President Theodore Roosevelt's expression of admiration for Edwards because he "always acted in accordance with the strongest sense of duty, and there wasn't a touch of the mollycoddle about him."[25]

Earle's popular works, like commemorations, monuments, and text-

books written for schools, helped disseminate an elite, almost nativist construction of Puritan tradition to a wide audience. This historical perspective encountered resistance not only from southerners, immigrants, and
citizens of communities with strong New England Societies who could not
trace their origins to the region; the colonial revival view of the past even
provoked dissent among New England's Puritan descendants. Brooks
Adams's *The Emancipation of Massachusetts* (1886), for example, advanced
older notions of an oppressive Puritan theocracy from which his ancestors
were gradually, but thankfully, liberated.[26] Three years later, Harvard historian John Fiske admonished his former student for failing "to define the
elements of wholesome strength" in the Massachusetts theocracy and for
restricting his vision to "its elements of crudity and weakness." The fervent
Puritan, Fiske argued in *The Beginnings of New England* (1889), was also
"in every fibre a practical Englishman with a full share of plain common
sense." Avoiding the pitfalls of medieval "otherworldliness," the New England Puritans sowed the "seeds" of self-government and of American
Constitutionalism. Far from emancipating themselves from colonial religious tradition, Fiske suggested, contemporary Americans needed to reaffirm the "Puritan's ethical conception of society."[27]

. . .

Edwards's life and cultural figure were woven into new colonial revival assessments of Puritan tradition. It is perhaps fortunate that Edwards A.
Park did not complete his long-planned biography of Edwards, which
undoubtedly would have remained fixed in the doctrinal polemics surrounding the New England theology rather than meeting the post-
Calvinist cultural needs of Puritan descendants. So, too, late-nineteenth-
century Puritan ancestors were spared an extended treatment of Oliver
Wendell Holmes's interpretation of Edwards, offered in an 1880 essay that
revealed how the famous poet continued to ride his own one-hoss shay –
an outmoded antebellum Unitarian distaste for the Calvinism and revivalism of New England's Puritan heritage. Edwards's sermonizing, Holmes
observed, showed his skill in the "apparatus of torture"; his life amounted
to a "short and melancholy" existence; his Calvinism was all "Scotch theological thistle." Edwards's God was "not a Trinity but a Quarternity,"
Holmes insisted. "The fourth Person is an embodied abstraction, to which
he gave the name of *Justice*." Edwards's Calvinist system remained "to the
last degree barbaric, mechanical, materialistic, pessimistic." Even mem-

bers of Holmes's Unitarian literary circle objected to such a limited view of Edwards, the "Protestant saint." [28]

Nine years later, the first full-scale Edwards biography of the post-Calvinist era was presented to the public. Alexander V. G. Allen's *Jonathan Edwards*, like Wendell's biography of Mather and the broader historical assessment of Puritan tradition of which it was a part, offered a highly sympathetic, though not uncritical, interpretation of its subject. Allen's study was part of Houghton Mifflin's prestigious "American Religious Leaders" series, described as "Biographies of Men who have had great influence on Religious Thought and Life in the United States." [29] Allen produced a biography that assimilated Edwards's life and thought into the new post-Calvinist recovery of a usable Puritan past; reprinted in 1890, 1891, 1896, and 1899, Allen's study remained the only major modern biography of Edwards until the 1930s.

A native of Vermont, Allen had spent a year at Andover Seminary, with Park as his teacher, while preparing for the Episcopal priesthood. He went on to serve as professor of church history at the Episcopal Seminary in Cambridge, Massachusetts. Allen combined a knowledge of and a distance from Edwardsian theological and revivalistic traditions that enabled him to transcend the historical perspectives of Park and Holmes and to produce a biography that met the colonial revival cultural needs of Puritan descendants. "I have not found myself devoid of sympathy with one who has filled so large a place in the minds of New England people," Allen announced in his preface. "Edwards is always and everywhere interesting, whatever we may think of his theology." While Allen examined Edwards's theology, he defended studying the great Puritan "on literary and historical grounds alone." [30] Not surprisingly, the Edwards who emerged from Allen's biography was, like the colonial revival Puritans in general, more an artifact in the cultural strife of the late nineteenth century than the embodiment of a continuing doctrinal or religious presence in American life.

Allen piled on Edwards's figure "the concentrated vitality and aggressiveness of the occidental people, – of the Anglo-Saxon race in particular, of which he was a consummate flower blossoming in a new world." The product of a "typical Puritan household," Edwards embodied what, from a genteel Victorian religious slant, appeared as an admirable "ascetic tendency" that "entered so largely into the composition of the New England character." Moreover, the "strength and nobility" of that temperament derived from the kind of "conscious self-direction of the will" which Edwards displayed and which "became the characteristic of New England Puritanism."[31] Edwards sprang from the pages of Allen's biography as a flesh and Anglo-Saxon blood typification of Saint-Gaudens's cultural icon.

Allen devoted a lengthy section of his study to the era of the Great Awakening, drawing on Joseph Tracy for details and uncritically accepting his line of interpretation. Writing from a postrevival vantage point, Allen could look back on the awakening as a colonial relic, rather than as an episode directly related to controversies in the present. The awakening represented a response to declension from the "unique and beautiful experiment of the Puritan fathers." Through revivalistic religion Edwards endeavored to reaffirm "the principle of Puritanism." To be sure, sermons like "Sinners in the Hands of an Angry God" overflowed with sulfurous rhetoric. Modern readers, however, needed to view such Edwardsian productions in relationship to a colonial "standard of speech, in accordance with which they should be judged, rather than by the gentler, more sentimental standard of later times."[32]

Beyond such "allowances," Allen conceded, there remained a "vehemence" in sermons like "Sinners in the Hands of an Angry God" that derived from "the fundamental principles of the preacher's theology." Still, Edwards's preaching included expressions of "marvelous tenderness," not just Dantesque descriptions of a divine inferno.[33] Allen's assessment of Edwards the preacher, like so much else in his interpretation of the divine's life, found favor with Williston Walker. In his lengthy sketch of Edwards in *Ten New England Leaders,* Walker followed Allen and argued that, "though the terrors of the law fill a large place in his pulpit utterances, no man of his age pictured more glowingly than Edwards the joys of the redeemed, the blessedness of the Union with Christ or the felicities of the Knowledge of God."[34] Both Allen and Walker seemed to suggest that neither literary interest in the rhetoric of the Enfield sermon, nor the legacy of antebellum disputes over religious enthusiasm, should distort their era's view of Edwards the preacher.

Indeed, a growing disengagement of mainline Protestantism from revivalism enabled Allen to look back at the colonial awakening with a kind of religious detachment. The "morbid tendencies" and "similar phenomena" associated with the awakening "have always attended those epochs when humanity is seen striving in some unusual way to realize the spiritual as distinct from and above the natural." Allen's sympathetic post-

Calvinist, postrevival assessment of the "Great Awakening" did not extend
to David Brainerd, who seemed beyond cultural redemption. Brainerd's
notoriety, Allen observed, had not "entirely faded"; but he seemed the embodiment of a "morbid psychology," not "genuine religious experience." [35]
Walker agreed with the Episcopalian historian; Brainerd's "morbid, intro-
spective self-examinations" and his seesaw emotions amounted to a "sorry
illustration . . . of the noble ideal of the full-rounded, healthful Christian
life." Samuel Hopkins, not Brainerd, stood as the Edwardsian disciple who
seemed to preserve the values – moral courage, self-sacrifice, an iron sense
of duty – that colonial revival students of the Puritan spirit like Allen admired and celebrated. [36]

Allen's discussion of Edwards's theology attempted to disentangle "the
local and the transitory" elements in his thought – namely, Calvinism –
from that which remained "imperishable" and universal – namely, the
quest for transcendental spiritual truth and experience that spoke to the
nondogmatic religious needs of Victorian America. Since the "spell" of
Freedom of the Will finally "has been broken," Allen argued, one could see
that Edwards's enduring works were his study of the *Religious Affections*
and sermons like "A Divine and Supernatural Light," not "Sinners in the
Hands of an Angry God" (a revival-era Calvinist remnant). Indeed, images
of "*light*" and "*sweetness*" so permeated Edwards's writings, Allen claimed,
that the colonial divine was the "forerunner of the later New England
transcendentalism quite as truly as the author of a modified Calvinism." [37]

Two generations before Perry Miller, Allen wed Edwards to Emerson,
establishing the same religious bonds that the distinguished Harvard
scholar delineated. The mystical element in Edwards produced a kind of
transcendental hunger for the "beauty" and "sublimity" of God and the
creation. Edwards's pursuit of divine illumination made light "a word that
controls his thoughts." His "direct vision into divine things" produced
written analyses similar to "transcendental modes of speech." For Allen,
"A Divine and Supernatural Light" in particular seemed to resemble "so
closely the later transcendental thought of New England as almost to
bridge the distance between Edwards and Emerson." [38]

Thus, Allen's biography added a post-Calvinist Edwardsian spiritual
legacy to his positive assessment of Puritanism as a moral-cultural force, a
tradition that he saw distilled and powerfully expressed in Edwards's life.
Andover's Egbert Smyth praised Allen's study for demonstrating that "Edwards is today a living power; Hopkinsianism, Emmonsism, Edwards-

eanism even are outlived." While some unreconstructed Calvinists assailed Allen for transforming Edwards into a pantheist, other reviewers commended him for not allowing his rejection of Calvinism to obstruct a fair historical appraisal of the theologian.[39] Reviewers failed to note that Allen's interpretation of Edwards as a link between Puritanism and transcendentalism drew on work in the emerging field of American literature. Colonial revival–era literary scholars developed their own Puritan origins narrative that reserved a prominent place for Edwards.

· · ·

The development of American literature as a field of study coincided with, and responded to the same cultural needs as, the colonial revival. Not surprisingly, then, the newly established formal study of American literature shaped, and was shaped by, the colonial revival creation of a usable Puritan tradition. As Nina Baym has argued, the post–Civil War New England elites who pioneered the study of American literature "realized that the nation was an artifice and that no single national character undergirded it." Like their fellow historians, from whom they were often indistinguishable, early scholars of American literature offered "the carefully edited New England Puritan as the national type." Historians of American literature hoped to fashion a common heritage – a kind of cultural Puritanism or republicanism – that would inculcate in natives and immigrants alike values deemed "necessary for the future: self-reliance, self-control, and acceptance of hierarchy."[40] Thus, the same needs and opportunities for cultural consolidation and cultural assimilation that informed the historical "recovery" of the Puritan tradition pervaded the study of American literature. An origins narrative emerged that made Puritanism the necessary "prologue" to the great American literature of the nineteenth-century "New England Renaissance," a term coined by Barrett Wendell.[41] Academic descendants of the Puritans dominated the beginnings and early history of American literary study. Some even had clerical backgrounds, a distinct advantage in an era when literature was promoted as a companion and even as a substitute – in the public schools, at least – for religion. Moses Coit Tyler, the "father" of American literary history, was one reborn Congregational minister.

A native of Connecticut, who traced his ancestry back to Plymouth Colony, Tyler graduated from Yale in 1857, studied at Andover Seminary for two years, and served short terms as a Congregational minister in New

York State. Tyler resigned his second church in 1862, and five years later joined the University of Michigan, where he taught English and rhetoric. In 1881, he moved on to Cornell and became professor of American history and literature. Tyler joined the Episcopal Church and was ordained to the priesthood in 1883, the same year he confessed that his soul "constantly says, 'Thou ought to be preaching the Gospel, rather than teaching American history, or writing books about it.'"[42] In fact, Tyler did continue to preach through his textbooks on the history of American literature, joining other descendants of the Puritans in responding to the changing face of the late nineteenth century by celebrating America's colonial foundations.

In 1875, Tyler proposed that his publisher, George Putnam, underwrite the cost of a colonial literature survey that would take advantage of the new interest in the past stimulated by the approach of the centennial of American independence. Such a text would also fill a need created by the emergence of college and high school courses on American literature. Tyler did not meet the centennial deadline; *A History of American Literature* was not published until 1878. The two-volume work – the first extended survey of its kind – provided an account of American literature from its beginnings to 1765.[43] Tyler's work was cited by Alexander V. G. Allen and influenced the biographer's view of Edwards's place in American literature. On a broader level, Tyler's volumes decidedly shaped the major interpretations of American literature down to Wendell's own survey, *A Literary History of America* (1900), and beyond.

After an opening chapter on the English background, Tyler devoted seventeen chapters to American literature, twelve of which focused on New England. "Since the year 1640," Tyler boasted, "the New England race has not received any notable addition to its original stock, and today their Anglican blood is as genuine and as unmixed as that of any county in England." Moreover, unlike other less racially pure parts of America, New England was established as a "thinking community." Though this "thrifty and teeming" intellectual society did not produce belles lettres – that is, "real" literature – its voluminous body of writing, which derived from or was molded by religion, became important from the perspective of the history of ideas.[44] First, Puritan writing revealed venerable New England character traits, which Tyler seemed intent on transmitting to his readers. Tyler, like other colonial revival students of the Puritans, acknowledged the "dark side" of his ancestors. But in preacherly pronouncements, he extolled the mental discipline, moral stamina, and earnestness of the Puritans: "They were not acquainted with indolence: they forgot fatigue; they were stopped by no difficulties; they knew they could do all things that could be done."[45]

An appreciation for such enduring "American" character traits constituted one reason for the study of Puritan writing; understanding the source of subsequent American literary expression comprised another. The "narrowness of Puritanism," Tyler observed, "stunted and stiffened" the development of literature in America. The Puritans' creed and the lack of "symmetry" to their culture "crushed down" the elements essential to belles lettres. Yet, the Puritans retained an aesthetic sense, "and in pure and wholesome natures such as theirs its emergence was only a matter of natural growth."[46] Once delivered from the repression of Calvinism, Puritan mental training, moral energy, and spiritual aesthetics found expression through literature. Not Tyler, whose study ended in 1765, but New England scholars who quickly followed in his train picked up the scent and proceeded to "Puritanize" the writers of the nineteenth-century literary renaissance. "Edwards to Emerson" was enfolded in a narrative of Puritan origins and consummation that explained the development of American literature.

Tyler's own treatment of Edwards is revealing. The fifteen pages he devoted to Edwards were only exceeded by the seventeen he gave to Cotton Mather. Tyler held up Edwards as the product of the "gentlest and most intellectual New England stock." His early life and youthful intellectual accomplishments illustrated how the "thinking community" was sustained by "educational efforts wrought on the people of New England by their rugged theological drill." Edwards's "Resolutions," though marred by "puerile severity," bore witness to "traits of a personal character full of all nobility."[47]

In a succession of vivid images Tyler brought Edwards to life as the "logical drill-master of innumerable minds." Edwards's power as a preacher derived from his attention to the "minuteness of imaginative detail." His words, descending from the pulpit like "drop after drop of the molten metal, of the scalding oil, fell steadily upon the same spot, till the victim cried out in shrieks of agony." Of course, Edwards's imaginative impulse was constrained by "that ganglion of heroic, acute, and appalling dogmas named after John Calvin." Nevertheless, Edwards displayed "the fundamental virtues of a writer" even if he did not produce beautiful literature.

The "precision, clearness, and simplicity" of much of his writing and his "bold, original, and poetic imagery" suggested how Puritanism was a sort of cultural quarry whose moral sense, intellectual rigor, and religious imagination supplied the building blocks for American literature.[48]

Tyler's *A History of American Literature*, like the bronze and granite totems being hoisted into place by his contemporaries, was in its own way a monument to the Puritans. Tyler's volume, though far from uncritical of his New England ancestors, resounded with the colonial revival appreciation of the Puritans that was emerging in more strictly historical works. Tyler's study proved to be monumental in another sense; it shaped the study of American literature for more than a generation. Tyler's publisher, for example, issued the first comprehensive survey of American literature from the beginnings to the late nineteenth century in 1887. Authored by the New England born and educated Dartmouth College professor, Charles F. Richardson, *American Literature, 1607–1885* consisted of two volumes: one devoted to American thought and the other to poetry and fiction. American "literature," Richardson claimed, was "only about eighty years old," but colonial religious treatises, sermons, and "records of sight and experience" represented "index figures pointing to future triumphs." In fact, Richardson claimed, the Puritans stood as "the direct precursors and the actual founders of most that is good in American letters."[49]

Other influential professorial descendants of the Puritans put the issue more bluntly. New England's "intellectual activity," Barrett Wendell submitted, "so far exceeded that of any other part of the country that literary history of other regions may be neglected." Wendell's "New England Renaissance" was really an "American Renaissance," as it would be renamed by a later Harvard professor. Wendell also proposed the now canonical pairing of Edwards and Franklin "as representing two distinct aspects of American character." Edwards embodied ideals of religion and morality "inherent in the lasting tradition of the English Bible." Franklin illustrated political and social ideals, "equally inherent in the equally lasting tradition of the English law."[50]

In the two decades after the publication of Tyler's seminal text, American literary histories multiplied. Authors responded to both an expanding educational market for such volumes and to the cultural needs of their era – promoting national pride, a respect for tradition, even a moral code. As Wendell's *A Literary History of America* suggests, Edwards's cultural figure undergirded the Puritan origins narrative that circulated from text to text. Consider Frances Underwood's *The Builders of American Literature* (1893). A Unitarian literary critic, Underwood authored *Quabbin: The Story of a Small Town with Outlooks on Puritan Life* (1893), a richly textured, almost local color, history of his home community that stands as arguably the finest colonial revival–era New England town history. In *The Builders of American Literature*, Underwood did not allow his Unitarianism to interfere with his assessment of the Puritans and of Edwards. It was certainly true, Underwood conceded, that the "unloveliness" of the Puritans' temperament, "the severity of their discipline, and their disdain for sentiment" impeded literary expression in New England. But the Puritans did not journey to America "to indite poems and romances" or "to dance around Maypoles." The Puritans undertook "the great work of founding the colonies on an enduring basis," and for this task their religious spirit and values served them – and posterity – well. For Underwood, Edwards hovered over the colonial era as "the last great Puritan divine." As the "flower of the Puritan race and culture in New England," Edwards demonstrated colonial religion's abiding virtues as well as its antiquated defects. Ensnared in Puritanism's "gloominess, asceticism, narrowness, and provincial spirit," Edwards also exemplified its "logic, its inflexible purpose; its reverence, personal holiness, and steadfast faith."[51]

In the literary histories of the 1880s and 1890s, Edwards became not only an exemplar of the two sides of Puritanism; he emerged as a sort of cultural sepulcher in which Puritan tradition was deposited and held for safe transmission to the nineteenth century. "The dignities of a whole corp of Puritan ancestry are centered in him," one literary historian declared in 1897; "they bridged him over boyhood: he must have strode across the years of fun and pranks on the stilts of his forefathers." Since he was an "intellectual saint rapt into high communion with the Invisible," as another turn-of-the-century literary scholar observed, Edwards's writing was approached as a cultural switchback slowly moving American literature toward its highest expression in the nineteenth-century renaissance. Edwards, the author of *An Introduction to American Literature* (1898) asserted, "is both the spiritual descendant of Cotton Mather and of Michael Wigglesworth, and the spiritual ancestor of Dr. Channing, the great leader of New England Unitarianism, and Emerson, the thinker of later times."[52] Edwards appeared as a towering canonical figure in these early literary texts that valued the history of ideas, that privileged New England writing, that approached colonial works as the prolegomenon to the nineteenth-

century renaissance, and that used literature to promote cultural nationalism and Anglo-Puritan moral values.

· · ·

Monuments, commemorative addresses, historical studies and biographies, and literary histories – these were all cultural productions influenced by the late-nineteenth- and early-twentieth-century interest in and
appropriation of the colonial past. Monuments, historical sites, and the
homes of famous figures also stimulated the cultural appetite of a growing
traveling public – consumers of what is now called heritage tourism. Pilgrimages to colonial shrines and to restored or preserved homes and villages brought temporary relief from the dizzying changes of the late nineteenth century, while arousing nostalgia and respect for a seemingly more
simple and virtuous past.

In guidebook accounts that paralleled the narratives in American history and literary texts, the New England past came disproportionately to
define the cultural heritage for which tourists went in search. Boston's Edwin Bacon, for instance, published two large and successful guidebooks at
the turn of the century: *Historic Pilgrimages in New England* and *Literary
Pilgrimages in New England*. Both works employ the visit of a young Western friend of the author who makes summer journeys to the East to acquire cultural knowledge and reaffirm ancestral roots. Advertisements described *Historic Pilgrimages* as follows:

> This is the vivid story of early New England, told while standing upon
> the very spots where the stirring Colonial drama was enacted. The fa-
> mous places where the Puritans and Pilgrims planted their first homes,
> the ancient buildings, and the monuments to the wise and dauntless
> founders of the great commonwealth are visited, and, while in the at-
> mosphere of the association, the thrilling narrative of the past is re-
> corded.[53]

Literary Pilgrimages takes the author and his culturally starved young companion to the homes and "haunts" of New England writers as well as to the
"scenes of their writing."[54]

Stockbridge and Northampton were two of these literary shrines; here
the travelers tarried and reflected on "the great eighteenth century metaphysician, who has been called the last and finest product of the Puritans
of America." The sojourners recorded their encounter with Edwardsian

monuments, markers, and artifacts, even reproducing some of them in the guidebook.[55] In fact, when Bacon published *Literary Pilgrimages* in 1902, the residents of Stockbridge and Northampton were still in the process of consecrating their townscapes with new Edwards mementos, a process that had begun after the Civil War and that had tracked the progress of the colonial revival. Stockbridge and Northampton afford a view of the colonial revival interest in the Puritan past from the local level. Very different communities in the late nineteenth century, they exemplify varied aspects of the colonial revival, of the renewed interest in Puritan heritage, and of the process of commemoration at the local level that erected less grand monuments to religious tradition than Saint-Gaudens's "Puritan."

Though encircled by mill villages in the river valleys of the Berkshire Hills and by Irish millhands and railroad workers, Stockbridge developed in the post–Civil War era as a fashionable and quaint resort town. The sense of antiquity encouraged by new, cultivated historical associations enhanced the appeal of such "ancient" New England towns. As early as 1868, the First Congregational Church in Stockbridge dedicated four tablets to its first ministers, including Edwards and Stephen West, his New Divinity successor. At the commemoration address, Reverend Nathaniel Eggleston, First Church's pastor, noted that the "Edwards Place abides yet," reference to the theologian's home in Stockbridge which became a late-nineteenth-century landmark. At the time, Eggleston voiced concern over such privately owned "landmarks of our ancestors," fearing that they might cease "to function as aids to memory." Churches, however, offered a location to "erect memorials that will remain when dwellings, subject to the laws of private property, shall be gone."[56] Public space as well, the citizens of Stockbridge would soon discover, presented a more visible and dominant civic location for memorializing a glorious past.

Colonial revival sentiment in Stockbridge received a boost not only from the arrival of major New England historical anniversaries; it drew impetus from the first gathering of the Edwards family, which was held in the town in 1870. Nearly two hundred descendants of Edwards responded to the invitation to attend the meeting. Two days of celebration ensued; between lectures about their distinguished progenitor and ancestral self-congratulations, the descendants visited Edwards shrines, such as the theologian's home on Main Street. Edwards's alma mater furnished a large tent under which his ancestors came together for food and refreshments. Yale also sent President Theodore Dwight Woolsey, himself a descendant of

Edwards, who served up appropriate commemorative fare. "He [Edwards] and others among the best Puritans of New England," Woolsey proclaimed, "succeeded in the crowning struggle of the human soul to rise above earthly things, and to lead a spiritual life on the principles of Christ's gospel."[57]

Some speakers, though not direct descendants of Edwards, took pride in a personal connection to the theologian and contributed to the meeting's ancestor worship, as well as to distress about the preservation of the past. Boston minister I. N. Tarbox was, like Edwards, a native of East Windsor, Connecticut, and he reported on disquieting changes in the town – the kind of alterations that provoked colonial revival guardians of the past. The Edwards homesite in Connecticut was "now occupied by one of our adopted fellow-citizens from Ireland, by the name of Christopher McNary." While the Irishman resides on a "spot that is famous," Tarbox complained, "he seems not aware of the privileges in this regard." Such a benighted fellow was "not well read up in Edwardean history," among his other educational deficiencies. "The association of the past disturbs him not," content as McNary was "raising tobacco."[58]

Colonial artifacts, which became part of the antique mania of the late nineteenth century, functioned like historical monuments to secure associations with the past. Edwardsian artifacts were abundantly displayed, and even manufactured, for the participants in the Stockbridge family meeting. Edwards A. Park, for instance, offered manuscripts showing how Edwards compensated for a shortage of paper by writing in newspaper margins, on advertisements, and even on "paper patterns which his daughters had used for making fans and collars, which they sold in order to defray the family expenses." Edwards's "genius" triumphed though he labored "without the fit apparatus."[59] Beneath portraits of Edwards and Sarah and the insignia of the family coat of arms, sacred relics that ranged from the theologian's Yale valedictory address to his wife's wedding dress were exhibited. Edwards's silver porringer was passed around the dinner table like a communion cup from which his descendants sipped coffee as they imbibed his Puritan spirit – a spirit, one speaker averred, that needed to be preserved and combined "with the advancing science and culture of the age."[60] Wood that had been salvaged from the old Indian meeting house where Edwards had preached was carved into "little useful and ornamental articles" for family members. These sacred Edwardsian keepsakes and a group photograph near the site of the Indian church (Figure 6) would help sustain the ancestral afterglow of the family meeting.[61]

Commenting on the late-nineteenth-century vogue of family reunions and ancestor worship, Michael Kammen has observed that such filio-pietism served "primarily to enhance the living more than to honor the dead."[62] In Stockbridge, Edwards's descendants basked in rhetoric to their ancestor that included gratefulness to Divine Providence for the blood coursing through their veins. Speakers and auditors celebrated everything from the contributions of family members to the Civil War to the clan's D.D.'s and LL.D.'s that, one versifying descendant remarked, were "like leaves in the autumn breeze," if not "thick as peas." In the flush of family celebration, the descendants determined that it was their "duty to raise . . . some enduring monument" to their ancestor that would "remind the traveler, in a distant age, alike of the virtues of the man and the piety of his race."[63] Two years later a large granite memorial monument to Edwards (Figure 7) was unveiled at an intersection on Main Street.

The Edwards commemoration stimulated the placement of other historical markers on the Stockbridge townscape, a sacred place that descendants had voted to designate as the "traditional home of the Edwards family."[64] These visible associations with the past burnished an aura of antiquity and stability into the townscape that added to the quaint village's appeal as a tourist resort; "Olde Stockbridge," an up-to-date past, began to take shape. But neither the cultural needs of colonial revival tourists, nor the ancestor worship of the Edwards family, prevented the demolition of the "Edwards Place" at the turn of the century. On the sacred site, however, a memorial sundial (Figure 8) was erected and from the landmark's boards numerous mementos were fashioned and, apparently, sold to visitors.[65]

When the Edwards family chose Stockbridge as its official "hometown," Northampton had also come under consideration. The rejection of Northampton resulted from more than the fact that the community had turned its back on its illustrious Puritan minister. Post–Civil War Northampton, in its size, economic activity, and ethnic diversity, contrasted sharply with the Berkshire village of Stockbridge. It was precisely this contrast that made colonial revival fascination with the Anglo-Puritan past in general, and with Edwards in particular, so much stronger in Northampton than Stockbridge. Northampton, which shed its town status in 1883, resembled

FIGURE 6. Edwards family meeting (1870), Stockbridge, Massachusetts. Photograph courtesy of the Stockbridge Library.

FIGURE 7. Edwards monument (1872), Stockbridge, Massachusetts.
Photograph by T. Conforti.

FIGURE 8. Sundial, Edwards homesite (1901), Stockbridge, Massachusetts.
Photograph by T. Conforti.

midsized communities like Salem, Massachusetts, whose rich and controversial colonial heritage and rapidly changing socioeconomic order made them focal points of the colonial revival.[66] Certainly, if the native citizens of Salem could retrieve a usable Puritan past from the remains of their colonial history, Northamptonites faced a far less daunting task.

Even before Northampton's interest in the colonial past accelerated in the 1890s, its Yankee citizens confronted many reminders of Edwards and the heritage he represented. Both the First Church, which was held up as the "birthplace" of the colonial awakening, and the Edwards Church, founded in 1833, remained thriving parishes in the center of town. Recently erected obelisks to the Edwards and Dwight families (Figure 9) stood in the old cemetery not far from the bustling civic and commercial district. The Edwards elms, trees that the theologian had planted in front of his home on King Street, were a famous local landmark; they would be photographed or illustrated in books discussing Puritan heritage and be reproduced as postcards (Figures 10, 11). On the homesite stood the Whitney Mansion, which became a boardinghouse for business travelers and tourists and which was often mistaken as the Edwards homestead.[67]

By the 1890s, these and other historical artifacts seemed inadequate to anchor the community to its colonial past. Northampton, with a population of nearly 17,000 by 1895, had a long history of manufacturing on the banks of the Mill River. But the production of cloth, machinery, tools, and items from buttons to toothbrushes grew significantly in the late nineteenth century – until the recession of 1893, from which the city only slowly recovered. Part of this recovery entailed the growth of unions, which increased from seven in 1898 to thirty-five by 1903.[68] Most unsettling of all, perhaps, these changes were accompanied by significant alterations in the ethnic and religious composition of Northampton. Irish Catholics had maintained a strong presence in the city since midcentury, but growing numbers of French Canadians were drawn to Northampton from the 1880s, and they would be followed, from the 1890s onward, by Polish and Italian contract laborers and Russian Jews. By the beginning of the new century, when Polish immigration began to swell, upward of half of the city's residents claimed foreign-born parents. Immigration had already disrupted Northampton's civic institutions, venerable legacies of the community's Puritan past. As early as 1891, for example, Irish and French Catholic schools opened and dramatically affected public school

FIGURE 9. Edwards obelisk (ca. 1895), Bridge Cemetery, Northampton, Massachusetts. Photograph by T. Conforti.

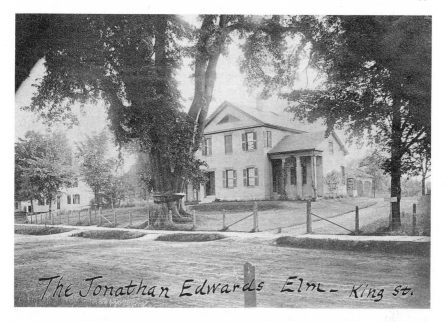

FIGURE 10. Edwards elm and homesite with "Ye Olde Whitney House" (ca. 1890), Northampton, Massachusetts. Photograph courtesy of Historic Northampton, Northampton, Massachusetts.

FIGURE 11. Edwards elm and homesite, Northampton, Massachusetts (ca. 1900), postcard. Photograph courtesy of Historic Northampton, Northampton, Massachusetts.

enrollment: one school was closed down and three others lost half of their students.[69]

In the midst of such changes, Yankee natives responded with more than nostalgia for "Olde Northampton." They also launched commemorative activities that, along with other actions, comprised a significant cultural backlash. Edwards's historical figure took on iconic power in the cultural politics of late-nineteenth- and early-twentieth-century Northampton.

In the mid-1890s, Northamptonites began planning and organizing for the two hundred and fiftieth anniversary of the city, which had been established in 1654. One committee was charged with collecting material and artifacts relating to Northampton's early history. As in other communities, the approach of the city's anniversary and a changing social landscape gave birth to the local historical society. The committee members soon realized that the documents and artifacts gathered for the commemoration would need a permanent home. Moreover, a Northampton Historical Society would arrest the erosion of interest in and knowledge of the city's past that resulted from the influx of immigrants, many of whom could barely speak English. And what better place to establish the historical society than on the homesite of Northampton's most distinguished historical father, shaded by the remaining and well-publicized Edwards elm (the other had blown down in 1885).[70]

The committee began to work to acquire and remodel the Whitney Mansion, or "Ye Olde Whitney House," as it was apparently renamed when it started taking in boarders. Plans called for a combination historical society, museum, and headquarters of the Daughters of the American Revolution, a sort of Northampton heritage center on the location consecrated by Edwards. The commemorative committee and its supporters were unable to complete the legal and financial arrangements to purchase and renovate the Whitney Mansion; the historical society was then established at another location in Northampton. But a historical tablet was placed on the property identifying it as the Edwards homesite (Figure 12).[71]

Other efforts to preserve Northampton's colonial past and commemorate Edwards coincided with the founding of the Northampton Historical Society. In 1898, James Russell Trumbull published the first volume of his celebratory *History of Northampton, Massachusetts from its Settlement in 1654* (the second volume was published in 1902). A full portrait of Edwards graced the frontispiece of the book. Trumbull's history bulged to 1,200 pages, but he did not venture beyond 1800.[72]

FIGURE 12. Edwards homesite tablet (1905), Northampton, Massachusetts. Photograph by T. Conforti, with permission of Historic Northampton, Northampton, Massachusetts.

In 1898, also, what was purported to be Edwards's granite doorstep was hauled from the Whitney Mansion and placed on the lawn in front of the town's impressive and recently completed library (Figure 13), the first of several stone memorials to Northampton's religious heritage.[73] That same year, a local real estate developer – offering his own contribution to the preservation of colonial tradition – laid out Edwards Square. A small development of modest middle-class homes, Edwards Square encircled the Edwards elm and homesite. Almost immediately, Edwards Square became the site of a fortress-like armory (Figure 14), a monument to change that was different from, but not unrelated to, the newly placed colonial markers on Northampton's landscape. Built between 1899 and 1900, the armory served as police headquarters and National Guard barracks. Northampton followed the lead of many much larger communities that built armories in the last two decades of the nineteenth century. Usually located in stable middle-class neighborhoods, armories enabled the National Guard to store arms, drill, and respond effectively to social disorder, including violent strikes.[74] In Northampton, at least, the armory did not become a

FIGURE 13. Edwards's doorstep placed at front of Forbes Library (1898; now covered by shrubs), Northampton, Massachusetts. Photograph by T. Conforti.

FIGURE 14. Armory adjacent to Edwards homesite (1898–1900), Northampton, Massachusetts. Photograph courtesy of Historic Northampton, Northampton, Massachusetts.

nerve center of state repression; rather, it seemed to function not unlike historical monuments, as a reassuring symbol of the community's ability to cope with and contain change.

While sounds of civic and domestic construction reverberated on both sides of the Edwards homesite, members of the First Congregational Church moved ahead with their plans to pay tribute to the theologian. The church established a committee in 1897 to plan an appropriate memorial to Edwards. Money was raised from church members, other residents of Northampton, descendants of Edwards, and admirers in New England and abroad. The committee could not wait until 1903, the bicentennial of Edward's birth, to honor the distinguished divine. They unabashedly decided to memorialize Edwards on the one hundred and fiftieth anniversary of his dismissal from the First Church! In June 1900, an Edwards descendant unveiled a five-by-eight-foot bronze bas-relief of the colonial pastor completed by the sculptor Herbert Adams. Offering an image of Edwards in the act of preaching what some said was his farewell sermon, the bronze tablet commemorated his now heroic figure with flattering biblical verse (Figure 15).[75]

A daylong series of academic and clerical addresses, which were published by Houghton Mifflin as *Jonathan Edwards: A Retrospect*, accompanied the unveiling ceremonies. In his introduction to the volume, editor H. Norman Gardiner, chairman of the Edwards Memorial Committee and professor of philosophy at Smith College, declared that the bronze tablet "represents neither the contrition nor the pride of the local church." Instead, he offered the memorial as recognition of "a widely spread, and to a certain extent, newly awakened regard for the genius and character of its subject" as well as of a "sympathetic interest in what appeared to many as a simple act of historic justice."[76]

Alexander V. G. Allen's address rehearsed the major points of his popular biography. Edwards was an American Dante, with poetic "imagination," "tenderness," and spiritual "insight"; his enduring writings included "the Sermon on Spiritual Light" and his "greatest work," *Religious Affections*. Egbert Smyth offered the Andover view that had not reassured Edwards A. Park years earlier. The memorial tablet stood for "something more than a *return* to Edwards." It meant instead "*a going on* with him," an acknowledgment "that we still have him with us and will continue to have, – *him*, the noblest Roman of us all." Yale's George Park Fisher, dean of the Divinity School, brought Edwards's valedictory address to the com-

FIGURE 15. Edwards bronze (1900), First Church, Northampton, Massachusetts.
Reproduced from H. Norman Gardiner, ed., *Jonathan Edwards: A Retrospect*
(Boston: Houghton Mifflin, 1901).

memoration, just as President Woolsey had to the Edwards family meeting thirty years earlier. Fisher praised Edwards as "the Saint of New England," and stressed that three of the theologian's descendants had served in the presidency of Yale for almost half of the nineteenth century. Yale's acquisition of the major Edwards manuscript collections in 1900 strengthened the special institutional claim on the Edwardsian legacy that Fisher made. Speaking for Northampton, Reverend Henry Rose, pastor of the First Church, reminded the audience that Edwards had described the town as "a city set on a hill." Rose was determined to preserve Northampton's distinctive religious heritage as the famed "centre of the mighty religious phenomena known in history under the name of the Great Awakening."[77]

Other speakers from Northampton, Boston, and Princeton recited hymns that contributed to a kind of colonial revival Protestant version of a beatification ceremony. Yankee Northamptonites and other Anglo-Puritan descendants found new opportunities after the turn of the century to continue commemorating Edwards. Indeed, 1903 proved to be the high-water mark of colonial revival celebrations of Edwards as an embodiment of Puritan tradition.

·   ·   ·

The Northampton commemoration not only gained the notice of the local and denominational press; it was reported in *Harper's* and the *New York Times*. In fact, two weeks before the commemoration the *Times* had editorialized on the need, almost "as a matter of patriotism," for a new edition of Edwards's works and for a biography even "less critical and more human" than Alexander V. G. Allen's.[78] Edwards's induction into the American Hall of Fame in 1900 lent support to the *Times*'s call, reinforced the filiopietistic activities of Northamptonites, and provides additional evidence of Edwards's eminence in American culture.

The Hall of Fame was yet another late colonial revival attempt to define and institutionalize America's heritage in the face of a shifting social order that seemed to lack centripetal cultural force. Built with a gift from an anonymous donor to New York University, the Hall of Fame was intended as a kind of American pantheon "to stimulate patriotism and high endeavor by commemorating those virtues in persons who have passed away and by collecting busts, portraits, and mementos of these our great." Induction was open to distinguished Americans who had been dead for at

least ten years. The benefactor of the Hall of Fame established a careful se-
lection process that was intended to avoid "mistakes of enthusiasm or of
prejudice." Nominations were submitted to a panel composed of one
hundred distinguished men and women. Nominations and elections were
to be held every five years with fifty inductees who had received at least
fifty-one of the judges' votes gaining admission to the historical sanctuary
after they had also been endorsed by the faculty senate of the university.[79]

With the Hall of Fame building completed, the first election was held in
1900. But only 29 of the 234 nominees received more than fifty-one votes.
(They were all men, with Mary Lyon receiving the highest number of votes
among nominated women.) Edwards was among the select group. Indeed,
he outpolled Nathaniel Hawthorne eighty-one to seventy-three.[80]

Little wonder, then, that the bicentennial of Edwards's birth three years
later occasioned extensive commemoration. Widely reported in the religious and secular press, the memorialization of Edwards stretched from
Andover, Northampton, Springfield, and Stockbridge in Massachusetts,
and Hartford, New Haven, and South Windsor in Connecticut, to New
York City, Princeton, and churches from the Midwest to California. Andover hosted the most elaborate commemoration – two days of hymns
and addresses accompanied by a full exhibit of Edwards manuscripts and
artifacts. At Yale, Williston Walker offered the keynote address on Edwards, while in South Windsor the commemorators visited the theologian's birthplace and his father's grave.[81]

Everywhere Edwards was hailed as a sacred Anglo-Puritan, and thus
American, cultural icon. Speaking to audiences both in Stockbridge and
Princeton, Professor John DeWitt, for instance, extolled Edwards as the
notable representative of a northern European "spiritual race." Remind-
ing his auditors that 1903 was also the centennial of Emerson's birth, De-
Witt observed, "The day belongs, not to the great Puritan who gave up the
Puritan conception of the universe for its interpretation by poetry and letters, but to the great Puritan who denied himself the high satisfactions of
literature, that through his distinctively Christian doctrine of God and
men he might be the friend and aider of those who would live in the
spirit."[82] In the shadow of Saint-Gaudens's statue, a speaker in Springfield
allowed that Edwards's theology was antiquated, but the tradition he represented, "the spirit of Puritanism, is bone of our bone, flesh of our
flesh."[83]

In the decades leading up to the Edwards bicentennial, cultural exigencies had sparked colonial revival nostalgia, ancestor worship, and commemoration, which in turn shaped academic studies of America's historical and literary heritage – a "national" heritage of New England origin. The Puritan was refashioned by influential descendants into a kind of post-Calvinist ecumenical figure in whom the moral and cultural spirit of Protestantism, and thus of Americanism, reposed. For many, the Puritan spirit offered the religious leaven for Victorian America. Edwards as "a Puritan of Puritans" was commemorated and enshrined as an American cultural icon.

To a considerable extent, colonial revivalists' uses of Puritan tradition emerged as an effort to construct and impose on a dynamic and seemingly unwieldy nation what can only be described as a civil religion. In celebrating the religious origins of American history and literature, in upholding Anglo-Puritan character traits and moral values, in raising religious or quasi-religious historical monuments, and in using textbooks, public schools, and civic space to accomplish these ends, descendants of the Puritans invoked their heritage to define the American way. Such efforts, however, did encounter significant resistance – and not just from southerners. Northampton Catholics, for example, not only established their own schools; they celebrated their own cultural heritage. In the town's two hundred and fiftieth commemoration, historical floats sponsored by the Knights of Columbus and the St. Jean Baptiste Society joined floats depicting Minutemen and other aspects of Northampton's colonial and Revolutionary past. And when a Polish National Catholic Church was later built on the Edwards homesite, the members rebuffed attempts to preserve the historical tablet that designated the location as hallowed ground.[84] The tablet ended up in the Northampton Historical Society, where it is stored today.

EPILOGUE

• • •

FROM THE PROGRESSIVE TO THE
NEO-ORTHODOX EDWARDS

The publications that poured from presses during the Edwards bicentennial spilled over into 1904. William Harder Squires, professor and dean at Hamilton College in New York, even established a short-lived journal under Edwards's name. Inaugurated in October of 1903 in conjunction with bicentennial celebrations, *The Edwardean: A Quarterly Devoted to the History of Thought in America* anticipated the ongoing publication of Edwards's manuscripts and sought to develop a "native American philosophy" around the esteemed divine's writings. "Edwards does not belong in the list of shelved prophets who have proclaimed a warning message to their times and then passed into oblivion," the first issue of *The Edwardean* enunciated. Rather, Edwards numbered among "those universal thinkers who have discovered and formulated truths that concern all times and challenge the boldest spirits to their contemplation."[1]

The fourth and last issue of *The Edwardean* appeared in July 1904, symptomatic of the bicentennial ebullience that had run its course. Beginning in 1905, publications on Edwards fell below even prebicentennial levels.[2] The New England Puritan lodestar was in the process of being eclipsed by new narratives about America's past. Still, Northamptonites clung to their colonial and Edwardsian heritage. In 1911, for example, Northampton staged four days of historical pageants commemorating the community's heritage. One pageant depicted a colonial wedding; a descendant of Edwards assumed the role of his illustrious ancestor performing the marriage ceremony for Betty Allen, whose name graced the local Daughters of the American Revolution chapter and who was played by one of her progeny (Figure 16).[3]

The early-twentieth-century vogue of historical pageants like North-ampton's suggests how vestiges of the colonial revival view of the past persisted at the local level even while new historical interpretations emerged that challenged entrenched New England origins narratives. Progressive Era scholars of American history and literature turned to the frontier, to Jeffersonian tradition, to an abiding politico-economic conflict between aristocrats and democrats and created their own usable past. Such perspectives radically diminished the influence of religion in general, and of Puritanism in particular, in American history. In the decades surrounding World War I, Edwards's Brobdingnagian cultural figure was reduced to human and sometimes sub-American proportions.

Consider, for instance, the first volume of the *Cambridge History of American Literature* (1917). Taking issue with Barrett Wendell's interpretation of American literature and with the "descent upon . . . [him] of the spirit of Cotton Mather," the editors assigned the chapter on the Puritans to Vernon L. Parrington.[4] His discussion of "The Puritan Divines, 1620–1720," outlined the interpretation that would consume the better part of the first volume of *Main Currents in American Thought*, published ten years later. Parrington approached Puritanism as a movement that "phrased its aspirations in so strange a dialect, and interpreted its program in such esoteric terms, that it appears almost like an alien episode in the records of a practical race." The Puritans' ecclesiastical practice, not their formal religious thought, made a contribution to America's democratic currents. Parrington framed Puritan history almost exclusively in political and class terms: a dogmatic, theocratic, hierarchical Presbyterianism advocated by "gentlemen" warring against a liberal, democratic Congregationalism supported by the "commoners." John Cotton, John Eliot, and the Mathers were locked in battle with Roger Williams, Thomas Hooker, and John Wise.[5]

Parrington's survey stopped in 1720; thus he did not discuss Edwards. But Paul Elmer More's chapter on Edwards followed immediately. While More's analysis was less tendentious than Parrington's, there was little doubt to which Puritan camp the distinguished theologian belonged. Edwards "made terror the chief instrument of his appeal to men"; he "terrified the people of Enfield"; and he "threw away the opportunity of making himself . . . one of the very great names in literature" by adhering to a dogmatic religion. More's literary judgment found sympathy in such Progressives as Charles Beard, who dismissed Edwards's works as "occult writings."[6]

FIGURE 16. Edwards, played by a descendant, performing the "colonial" wedding
of "Betty Allen" (1911), Northampton, Massachusetts. Photograph courtesy of
Historic Northampton, Northampton, Massachusetts.

Beard offered his historical judgment in 1927, the same year Parrington published the first two volumes of *Main Currents in American Thought* and addressed "The Anachronism of Jonathan Edwards." The late colonial New England world in which Edwards was consigned to live offered a society "stewed in its petty provincialism" whose theology was distinguished by "tedious decay"; an archaic creed spoke in "the voice of dogma . . . , not the voice of reason and experience." With his formidable intellectual power and mystical instincts "Edwards was called to be a transcendental emancipator." Tragically, like Cotton Mather and the reactionary theocrats who preceded him, Edwards lent "his noble gifts to the thankless task of re-imprisoning the mind of New England with a system from which his nature and his powers summoned him to unshackle it."[7]

The onrushing currents of American democratic culture rendered Edwards passé as soon as he chose the "path that led back to an absolutist past, rather than forward to a more liberal future." The Great Awakening amounted to a paroxysm of religious reaction – a theocratic crusade of "lurid terrorism" that only hastened the collapse of an oppressive Puritan order. Edwards's preaching aroused "pathological states of mind not far removed from insanity." Equipped with a kind of vernacular Freudianism of the 1920s that arraigned Puritanism for the principle repressions of American life, Parrington turned psychologist. He indicted Edwards and the great revival for exciting a "mob psychology," employing "hypnotic suggestion," encouraging "hysterical possession," and captivating "neurotic" victims. This priest-inspired parade of pathology did awaken the "popular mind" to the reactionary menace of theocrats and New England's residual Calvinism.[8] Thus the revival proved to be a cultural watershed, though not of the kind that Joseph Tracy had offered nearly one hundred years earlier. Instead, the awakening marked the colonial transition toward a liberal, democratic religious order.

With respect to Edwards, the revulsion against Puritanism so characteristic of the 1920s did not reach its fullest expression in Parrington's work. That distinction belonged to Henry Bamford Parkes's *Jonathan Edwards: The Fiery Puritan*, which actually was published in 1930. The first major biography of Edwards since the work of Alexander V. G. Allen, Parkes's study was shaped by Parrington's perspective and the Menckenesque Puritan baiters of the 1920s. A chapter of the biography on the Great Awakening was even titled "Religious Lunacy." Unlike Parrington, however,

Parkes railed against a Puritan spirit that Edwards perpetuated and that persisted as a "blight" on life in America. In his efforts to "make everyone like himself," Parkes lashed out, Edwards "fastened on the necks of his countrymen a Puritanism such as we know to-day." While a patriot, Edwards was "not truly an American"; he spawned disciples who were "intolerant fanatics." Though Edwards's influence was "but a tributary to the flood of American culture," Parkes dropped any pretense of scholarly restraint or balance in summarizing the fiery Puritan's pernicious legacy: "It is hardly a hyperbole to say that, if Edwards had never lived, there would be to-day no blue laws, no societies for the suppression of vice, no Volstead act."[9]

The views of scholars like Parkes, Parrington, and More, the character and small number of publications on Edwards, and the absence of new editions of his works all suggest that, for the first time since the start of the Second Great Awakening, the theologian's figure and relevance receded to the margins of American cultural discourse during the two decades that bracketed World War I. Progressive Era scholars and critics of the 1920s repudiated colonial revival interpretations of America's Puritan past. In turn, new Progressive perspectives furnished the foil for the neo-orthodox "recovery" of the Puritans, of Edwards, and of American religious history that began in the 1930s.[10] In overreacting to their immediate liberal predecessors, neo-orthodox interpreters constructed an Edwards who met their polemical and cultural needs; in the process, however, they diverted modern scholars from the kind of understanding of Edwards's place in American culture that this study has examined. For while they rescued Edwards from the seeming caricature of their Progressive predecessors, neo-orthodox interpreters often substituted a prophetic, almost transhistorical figure devoid of legitimate disciples or of an enduring, vital presence in American cultural development.

With the publication in 1932 of Arthur C. McGiffert's *Jonathan Edwards*, which a reviewer characterized as a "neo-Calvinistic" study,[11] and Joseph Haroutunian's *Piety versus Moralism*, a far more powerful and influential work, the neo-orthodox reassessment of Edwards was launched. Renouncing the "gullibility and sentimentalism" of a liberal religious humanitarianism that failed to appreciate Edwards and the Puritans, Haroutunian called for "a revival of the 'tragic sense of life,' together with the wisdom and sobriety which grow out of it." He believed that his contemporaries needed to "rediscover" the universal religious "truths" that were "signified by the doctrines of divine sovereignty and divine grace, of pre-destination and election, of depravity and regeneration."[12]

But Edwards and the tragic sense of life had fallen victim to America's liberal, democratic, and humanitarian culture; even his closest followers had succumbed to "new political and humanitarian principles."[13] Edwards's theological legacy, far from being grounded in subsequent American history, transcended the corrupting moralism of American culture. Edwards became a great prophet with no legitimate heirs. His New Divinity disciples' professed loyalty to his thought did not inoculate them against the virulent humanitarianism of American culture. Mouthing Edwardsian phrases even as they embraced Enlightenment values, New Divinity men betrayed their teacher, bewildered their congregations, and retreated to the cultural backwaters of New England. With Edwards's death, "authentic" Calvinism was prepared for its own interment. Such a dogmatic neo-orthodox historical dirge amounted to another powerful contribution to a fertile line of created Edwardsian traditions. *Piety versus Moralism* furnished a sweeping historical perspective for neo-orthodox theological critics of American culture; it elevated Edwards to an isolated, prophetic genius; and it created interpretive problems for scholars like H. Richard Niebuhr who saw Edwards as a transcendent figure but who also wanted to write him and religion into (that is, back into) American cultural history.

To Niebuhr, the Great Awakening and the idea of the Kingdom of God in America provided the footing for both a prophetic and a historical Edwards. In *The Kingdom of God in America* (1937), Niebuhr rescued the colonial awakening from what he saw as the historical travesty perpetrated by Parrington. With the idea of the Kingdom of God, he also contributed to a new, twentieth-century phase of the reification of the "great" awakening. Niebuhr presented Edwards as a prophet of what would later be recognized as religious existentialism. Edwards's revival sermons, far from displaying the terrorizing tactics of a fiery Puritan, represented his "intense awareness of the precariousness of life's poise, of the utter insecurity of men and of mankind which are at every moment as ready to plunge into the abyss of disintegration, barbarism, crime and the war of all against all, as to advance toward harmony and integration." Edwards, Niebuhr went on, "recognized what Kierkegaard meant when he described life as treading water with ten thousand fathoms beneath us." The idea of the Kingdom of God "had remained secondary" in American Protestantism prior to the colonial awakening. But as a result of the profound preaching of Edwards and others, the awakening made the "coming Kingdom" the "dominant idea" in American Protestantism.[14]

For all the scholarly acknowledgments of *The Kingdom of God in America* as a seminal work, major analyses of Edwards's millennial thought and legacy – his so-called new departure in eschatology which allegedly anointed America as a "redeemer nation" to the world – did not appear until the high noon of academic scholarship on Edwards a generation later.[15] Part of the problem for some scholars was that Niebuhr, as he recognized, appeared to offer "theology in the guise of history." Against Progressive materialists, Niebuhr was determined to show in a general way how religion functioned "independent" of culture; more specifically he wanted to demonstrate how the "Kingdom which was prior to America" established the moral and spiritual principles to "which this nation, in its politics and economics, was required to conform."[16] Still, with all of its limitations as a historical work and as a study of Edwards's legacy for American culture, *The Kingdom of God in America* did appropriately point toward nineteenth-century evangelical America as a fruitful field for exploring Edwardsian tradition.

Three years later, Thomas H. Johnson completed a major bibliography of the publishing history of Edwards's works that offered powerful, suggestive evidence of the ongoing engagement of the theologian with nineteenth-century American culture.[17] Johnson documented, for example, that the *Life of Brainerd* was Edwards's most popular work, and yet that volume has only recently become the subject of serious scholarly analysis. Why has this been so? Why have Edwards scholars interpretively overinvested in the Great Awakening and its relationship to the American Revolution? Why have literary scholars continued to find Edwards's echo in the nineteenth-century renaissance? Why have scholars ignored or dismissed evidence of Edwardsian traditions in American culture that stretched from the Second Great Awakening to the post–Civil War colonial revival?

A partial answer to these questions is that our view of Edwards and the colonial awakening is still under the shadow of a voluminous body of post–World War II scholarship that was influenced by the neo-orthodox movement and by Perry Miller, an atheist who nevertheless sympathized with a Niebuhrian view of the American past. In the same year that Thomas Johnson furnished his significant bibliographical evidence of the direction that Edwardsian tradition took, Miller published his famous essay "From Edwards to Emerson." With a literary and intellectual authority that few scholars could summon, Miller recycled a line of interpretation that originated in the late nineteenth century. Though he expressed caution, even defensiveness, about the essay when it was reprinted in *Errand into the Wilderness*, "From Edwards to Emerson" became a kind of ur-text for the rapidly emerging American studies movement.[18]

Miller's intellectual biography, *Jonathan Edwards* (1949), provoked a more mixed response. Yet, despite the combined admiration, confusion, and criticism that greeted the work, it carried the authority of America's most distinguished student of the Puritans and its most skilled practitioner of intellectual history. Miller's biography became the starting point for most of the work on Edwards for nearly three decades. As is well known, Miller presented Edwards as a forward-looking psychologist who drew on John Locke to develop a modern understanding of the mind. The folly of this interpretation aside, Miller's views left Edwards a prophet without a tradition. Miller had already retreated from the Edwards to Emerson line of analysis with which he had opened the decade; the transcendentalist received only two brief citations in *Jonathan Edwards*. Miller's conclusion about Edwards was telling – and also regrettable for its impact on subsequent scholarship. It is worth quoting at length.

> Edwards it is true did have followers in the dynasty of New England theologians, who continued his war with liberal theology, but petrified his philosophy into dogma, reduced his revivalism to a technique of mass manipulation, and then destroyed the architecture of his thought by splintering it into factions and schools. By this process Edwards was lost to the American tradition; the belief that he was an anachronism, a retrograde leader of a rear-guard action against science, became a premise of America's opinion about its past. Even in the twentieth century, when the smiling aspects largely ceased to smile, and Hawthorne, Melville, and Mark Twain were re-evaluated, Edwards remained identified with what Dr. Holmes called the "nebulous realm of Asiatic legend," and therefore could not be supposed of value for critical realism. Edwards was thus relegated, through failure of comprehension, even further into an unusable past.[19]

Miller was unable to see beyond Holmes and Parrington or, one might say, beyond the history of Harvard. He reacted to the Unitarian and Progressive derision of Edwards, the only enduring Edwardsian tradition in

American culture that he seemed to recognize. With all the irony that his neo-orthodox perspective on human fallibility would have appreciated, he created a historical strawman of his own. On some level, Miller knew better. The figure who is conspicuous by his absence from Miller's text is not Emerson; it is David Brainerd. Miller was aware of the popularity and long publishing history of the *Life of Brainerd*. But he was unable to see this work as part of a vigorous Edwardsian religious tradition that persisted through the middle of the nineteenth century.

Miller's prolific scholarship on the Puritans in the 1950s and his appointment as general editor of Yale University's project on the *Works of Edwards* augmented his intellectual authority as a new creator of tradition. Established in the early 1950s, the *Works of Jonathan Edwards* published its first volume, *Freedom of the Will*, in 1957. Miller's "General Editor's Note" launched the project with a neo-orthodox panegyric to Edwards that sounded remarkably similar to nineteenth-century evangelical chants of praise. Referring to the crucible of World War II and its aftereffects, Miller explained how recent history had "stimulated drastic reexamination of such complacent assumptions" as the notion that Edwards's religious thought was somehow "retrograde." For Miller, the *Works of Jonathan Edwards* was "itself testimony to the deepening appreciation in the mid-twentieth century of the importance of Edwards to the intellectual as well as the religious history of America." Miller acknowledged his sense of "veneration" for Edwards's "majestic" figure and the "towering" structure of his thought.[20]

The *Works of Edwards* signaled a new moment in what one might call the continuing cultural production of Edwards. The project represented the convergence of a neo-orthodox paradigm and the post–World War II institutional expansion of academic scholarship. Yale's definitive editions of the theologian's works – with their lengthy, informed introductions – joined Miller's biography to spur new scholarly interest in Edwards. Not surprisingly, doctoral dissertations on Edwards doubled each decade from the 1950s onward. Yale itself became, as Andover had been a century earlier, a kind of "guardian" of Edwardsian tradition. The principal repository of Edwards's papers as well as of Edwardsian cultural artifacts, the site of Edwards College, the home of the project on Edwards's *Works*, Yale also trained a group of scholars who produced some of the most influential studies of Edwards.[21]

A post–World War II academic monument to Edwards's genius emerged from the disciplines of history, literature, American studies, philosophy, and religion. Yet the modes of analysis that shaped this scholarly edifice derived from or responded to the magisterial work of the early neo-orthodox interpreters of Edwards – Joseph Haroutunian, H. Richard Niebuhr, and Perry Miller. Consider, for example, the interpretive ties that bind Haroutunian's *Piety versus Moralism* and such an important subsequent work as Conrad Cherry's *The Theology of Jonathan Edwards: A Reappraisal* (1966). Cherry, like Haroutunian, began his study by invoking the views of neo-orthodox thinkers who "reclaimed Augustinian and Calvinist categories in order to prick the contemporary conscience, wean man away from religious sentimentality, and throw him up against the hard reality of a God who judges as well as forgives." Quoting Haroutunian, Cherry went on to show how Edwards "was first and last a 'theologian of the Great Commandment,'" love for a sovereign God. Thus, America's Augustine could have no genuine heirs in America's democratic culture.[22]

Similarly, note again the persuasive influence – for good and for ill – of Perry Miller on Edwards studies. More than any other scholar, Miller rescued Edwards from his Progressive disparagers. Yet, he also saddled a generation of scholars not only with highly problematic interpretations of the modernity of Edwards and of the theologian's links to transcendentalism; but he also plotted a line between the colonial awakening and the Revolution. Focusing on New England, his synecdoche for America, Miller suggested that the Revolution represented a moral and spiritual crisis dominated by religious rhetoric and rituals that drew on a cultural reservoir whose fountainhead resided in the colonial awakening and Puritan tradition.[23] In *Religion and the American Mind from the Great Awakening to the Revolution* (1966), Miller's former student and Harvard colleague, Alan Heimert, dramatically extended his mentor's arguments and perpetuated his role as an academic provocateur in Edwards scholarship. Dedicating his book to Miller, Heimert amassed scores of references to Edwards and attempted to show how the colonial awakening was the opening round of the Revolution. He asserted that Edwards's *Some Thoughts Concerning the Revival* was "in a vital respect an American declaration of independence from Europe"; *Freedom of the Will* became "the Calvinist handbook of the Revolution"; and *History of Redemption* offered "a scenario for American social and political history in the last half of the eighteenth century."[24]

Heimert's strained efforts to situate Edwards within an American tradition matched his mentor's most extravagant claims for the modernity of Edwards and for the Calvinist theologian's links to Emerson. Not surprisingly, a handful of provocative lines of analysis, from Haroutunian to Heimert, have preoccupied Edwards scholars, especially those engaged in assessing the theologian's legacy for American cultural history. Even the most recent collection of essays on contemporary Edwards scholarship reveals a continuing dialogue – often in the form of revision or refutation – with the neo-orthodox Edwards.[25]

Interpreters of Edwards have been too absorbed in exploring his relationship to the colonial awakening, the Revolution, and the nineteenth-century literary renaissance. We need to recognize how this interpretive agenda derived from a constructed tradition that served the cultural and scholarly needs of the mid-twentieth century. Other constructed Edwardsian traditions have not survived, but their recovery revises the conventional understanding of the theologian's place in American culture. From the Second Great Awakening to the mid-twentieth century, interrupted only by the Progressive Era and its immediate aftermath, Edwards remained a central figure in American religious and cultural discourse.

NOTES

INTRODUCTION

1. See Robert W. Jenson, *America's Theologian: A Recommendation of Jonathan Edwards* (New York, 1988).

2. M. X. Lesser, *Jonathan Edwards: A Reference Guide* (Boston, 1981), and Nancy Manspeaker, *Jonathan Edwards: Bibliographical Synopses* (New York, 1981). Lesser has updated his bibliography. His *Jonathan Edwards, 1981–1993* (Westport, Conn., 1994) runs to approximately 200 pages.

3. Gerald R. McDermott, *One Holy and Happy Society: The Public Theology of Jonathan Edwards* (University Park, Pa., 1992). Other very recent studies include John E. Smith, *Jonathan Edwards: Puritan, Preacher, Philosopher* (Notre Dame, Ind., 1993); Stephen R. Yarborough and John C. Adams, *Delightful Convictions: Jonathan Edwards and the Rhetoric of Conversion* (Westport, Conn., 1993); and Barbara B. Oberg and Harry S. Stout, eds., *Benjamin Franklin, Jonathan Edwards, and the Representation of American Culture* (New York, 1993).

4. Nathan O. Hatch and Harry S. Stout, eds., *Jonathan Edwards and the American Experience* (New York, 1988); see also Joseph A. Conforti, "Jonathan Edwards and American Studies," review essay in *American Quarterly* 41 (March 1989): 165–71. For the most recent revisionist contribution to our understanding of the New Divinity, see Mark Valeri, *Law and Providence in Joseph Bellamy's New England: The Origins of the New Divinity in Revolutionary America* (New York, 1994).

5. See, for example, Donald Louis Weber, *Rhetoric and History in Revolutionary New England* (New York, 1988).

6. Franklin B. Dexter, ed., *The Literary Diary of Ezra Stiles, D.D. LL.D.*, 3 vols. (New York, 1901), 3:275.

7. See Lynn Hunt, ed., *The New Cultural History* (Berkeley, Calif., 1989).

8. For a recent study of American religion that draws on Geertz, see David G. Hackett, *The Rude Hand of Innovation: Religion and Social Order in Albany, New York, 1652–1836* (New York, 1991), pp. 159–64; see also William G. McLoughlin's use of Geertz in *Revivals, Awakenings, and Reform: An Essay on Religion and Social Change in America, 1607–1977* (Chicago, 1978), pp. 15–16, 102–3.

9. Clifford Geertz, *The Interpretation of Cultures: Selected Essays* (New York, 1973), p. 5 and chaps. 1, 4, 8; see also Geertz, *Local Knowledge: Further Essays in Interpretive Anthropology* (New York, 1983).

10. Biersack, "Local Knowledge, Local History: Geertz and Beyond," in *New Cultural History*, ed. Hunt, p. 80. Biersack points out that "the webs, not the spinning; the culture, not the history; the text, not the process of textualizing – these attract Geertz's attention" (p. 80).

11. Hunt, "Introduction: History, Culture, and Text," in *New Cultural History*, p. 10. See also Ronald G. Walters, "Signs of the Times: Clifford Geertz and Historians," *Social Research* 47 (1980): 537–56.

12. James Clifford, *The Predicament of Culture* (Cambridge, Mass., 1988), p. 338.

13. H. Aram Vesser, ed., *The New Historicism* (New York, 1989), p. xi. Lynn Hunt argues persuasively that "Just as historians need not choose between sociology and anthropology or between anthropology and literary theory in conducting their investigations, neither must they choose once and for all between interpretive strategies based on uncovering meaning on the one hand and deconstructive strategies based on uncovering the text's modes of production on the other." See Hunt, "Introduction: History, Culture, and Text," p. 16.

14. James Clifford, "Introduction: Partial Truths," in *Writing Culture: The Poetics and Politics of Ethnography*, ed. James Clifford and George Marcus (Berkeley, Calif., 1986), pp. 1–26.

15. Clifford, *Predicament of Culture*, p. 15; see also Werner Sollors, "Introduction: The Invention of Ethnicity," in *The Invention of Ethnicity*, ed. Werner Sollors (New York, 1989), pp. ix–xx, and Eric Hobsbawm, "Introduction: Inventing Traditions," in *The Invention of Tradition*, ed. Eric Hobsbawm and Terrence Ranger (New York, 1983), pp. 1–14.

16. The essays in Vesser, ed., *New Historicism*, offer a good introduction to these issues.

17. Richard Brodhead, *The School of Hawthorne* (New York, 1986), p. 5; Timothy Breen, *Imagining the Past: East Hampton Histories* (Reading, Mass., 1989), chap. 1. Breen offers a "hermeneutical history" that is "fundamentally an interpretive exercise" focusing on the creation of historical meaning (p. 14). See also Darren Marcus Staloff's interesting essay "Intellectual History Naturalized: Materialism and the 'Thinking Class,'" *William and Mary Quarterly* 50 (April 1993): 406–17.

18. Brodhead, *School of Hawthorne*, p. 6.

19. On the process of historicizing texts and textualizing history, see H. Aram Vesser, ed., *The New Historicism Reader* (New York, 1994), esp. p. 26.

CHAPTER ONE

1. Nathan O. Hatch, *The Democratization of American Christianity* (New Haven, Conn., 1989), p. 7. Hatch offers the best recent review of the historiography of the Second Great Awakening (pp. 220–26). Two recent works that examine social change and the democratizing impact of the Awakening are Randolph A. Roth, *The Democratic Dilemma: Religion, Reform, and the Social Order in the Connecticut River Valley of Vermont, 1791–1850* (New York, 1987), and David G. Hackett, *The Rude Hand of Inno-*

vation: Religion and Social Order in Albany, New York, 1652–1836 (New York, 1991).

2. Donald Louis Weber does raise this issue, though he does not deal with it comprehensively or analytically. See "The Image of Jonathan Edwards in American Culture" (Ph.D. diss., Columbia University, 1978), chap. 3.

3. See Hatch, *Democratization of American Christianity*, p. 221. The preceding paragraph draws heavily on the views of Jon Butler.

4. Jon Butler, "Enthusiasm Described and Decried: The Great Awakening as Interpretative Fiction," *Journal of American History* 69 (1982): 308–11 and esp. p. 308n, which discusses how Edwards's correspondence and publications described revivals; see also Butler, *Awash in a Sea of Faith: Christianizing the American People* (Cambridge, Mass., 1990), pp. 164–65. For a different view, see W. R. Ward, *The Protestant Evangelical Awakening* (New York, 1992).

5. Butler, "Enthusiasm Described and Decried," p. 308n. As Harry S. Stout and Frank Lambert have recently argued, George Whitefield became a transatlantic celebrity through publicity and marketing efforts. Certainly the American preaching tour that he launched in 1739 contributed to a perception that something unusual was happening in the religious sphere. Though he was probably better known than Edwards, Whitefield did not stir up a general revival throughout the colonies during the so-called "great" awakening. Moreover, even in New England, Whitefield's subsequent tours did not generate widespread interest. On Whitefield's activities as a revivalist, see Harry S. Stout, *The Divine Dramatist: George Whitefield and the Rise of Modern Evangelicalism* (Grand Rapids, Mich., 1991), and Frank Lambert, *"Pedlar in Divinity": George Whitefield and the Transatlantic Revivals, 1737–1770* (Princeton, N.J., 1994).

6. Quoted in Richard D. Birdsall, "The Second Great Awakening and the New England Social Order," *Church History* 39 (1970): 353. On the start of the Second Great Awakening in Connecticut, see David W. Kling, *A Field of Divine Wonders: The New Divinity and Village Revivals in Northwestern Connecticut, 1792–1822* (University Park, Pa., 1993), chap. 2; Richard D. Shiels, "The Second Great Awakening in Connecticut: Critique of the Traditional Interpretation," *Church History* 49 (1980): 401–15, and "The Connecticut Clergy in the Second Great Awakening" (Ph.D. diss., Boston University, 1976); and Charles R. Keller, *The Second Great Awakening in Connecticut* (New Haven, Conn., 1942), chap. 3.

7. Prominent New Divinity ministers involved in these efforts included Azel Backus (Bethlehem), Alexander Gillett (Torrington), Griffin (New Hartford), Levi Hart (Preston), Asahel Hooker (Goshen), Samuel Mills (Torringford), Ebenezer Porter (Washington), Ammi Robbins (Norfolk), John Smalley (New Britain), Nathan Strong (Hartford), and Benjamin Trumbull (North Haven).

8. C. C. Goen, ed., *The Great Awakening: Some Thoughts Concerning the Present Revival of Religion in America*, vol. 4 of *Works of Jonathan Edwards*, 13 vols. (New Haven, Conn., 1972), p. 507.

9. Donald Mitchell, *Dr. Johns* (1864), quoted in Andrew L. Drummond, *The Story of Protestantism* (London, 1949), p. 207.

10. Joseph A. Conforti, "Joseph Bellamy and the New Divinity Movement," *New England Historical and Genealogical Register* 137 (1983): 126–38; Glenn P. Anderson,

"Joseph Bellamy (1719–1790): The Man and His Work" (Ph.D. diss., Boston University, 1971). Mark Valeri's *Law and Providence in Joseph Bellamy's New England: The Origins of the New Divinity in Revolutionary America* (New York, 1994) is a fine study of the New Divinity in a late-eighteenth-century context that should stimulate new interest in Bellamy's influence.

11. Conforti, "Joseph Bellamy and the New Divinity Movement," pp. 135–38; Percy C. Eggleston, *A Man of Bethlehem, Joseph Bellamy, D.D., and His Divinity School* (New London, Conn., 1908).

12. William B. Sprague, *Annals of the American Pulpit*, 9 vols. (New York, 1857–69), 1:410. On Bellamy and the colonial awakening, see Valeri, *Law and Providence in Joseph Bellamy's New England*, chap. 1.

13. William B. Sprague, *Lectures on Revivals of Religion* (Albany, N.Y., 1832), p. 19.

14. See Joseph A. Conforti, "Edwardsians, Unitarians and the Memory of the Great Awakening, 1800–1840," in *American Unitarianism, 1805–1865*, ed. Conrad E. Wright (Boston, 1989), pp. 31–50.

15. *Circular Letter Containing an Invitation to the Ministers of Every Christian Denomination in the United States to Unite in Their Endeavours to Carry into Execution the Humble Attempt of President Edwards* (Concord, N.H., 1798), pp. 5–6. Edwards's *History of Redemption*, edited by Jonathan Edwards, Jr., was reissued in 1792, and New Divinity minister David Austin reissued Joseph Bellamy's treatise on *The Millennium* (1758) along with Edwards's *Humble Attempt* in 1794. In addition to Edwards's *An Account of the Life of the Late Reverend Mr. David Brainerd* (Boston, 1749), which was republished in 1793, another important biographical study, published a little later, was New Divinity minister Stephen West's *Sketches of the Life of the Late Rev. Samuel Hopkins, D.D.* (Hartford, Conn., 1805).

16. Samuel G. Goodrich, *Recollections of a Lifetime, or Men and Things I Have Seen* (New York, 1857), p. 216. I am indebted to Richard Shiels, "The Democratization of Christianity: The View from New England" (unpublished paper, 1990), for the Goodrich reference.

17. Butler, "Enthusiasm Described and Decried," p. 308.

18. *The Spirit of the Pilgrims* began publication in 1828. Of particular importance are two series of letters dealing with New England and American religious history: Beecher's "Letters on the Introduction and Progress of Unitarianism in New England," which ran between 1829 and 1831, and Ebenezer Porter's "Letters on Revivalism," which ran between 1831 and 1833. On historical consciousness and the process of cultural invention in New England letters that produced such things as mythologizing of the Pilgrim forefathers, see Lawrence E. Buell, *New England Literary Culture: From Revolution through Renaissance* (New York, 1986), chap. 8.

19. "Life and Character of Rev. Jonathan Edwards," *Connecticut Evangelical Magazine and Religious Intelligencer* 1 (1808): 165–66. The journal was founded in 1800 as the *Connecticut Evangelical Magazine* and changed its name in 1808.

20. Benjamin Trumbull, *A Complete History of Connecticut, Civil and Ecclesiastical*, 2 vols. (1818; reprint, New London, Conn., 1898), 2:122.

21. Ibid., pp. 123–25.

22. Ibid., p. 145.

23. Ibid., pp. 201–3.

24. The religious periodical press was important to this process. See, for example, the *Christian Spectator* and its successor the *Quarterly Christian Spectator*, where essays such as the following appeared: "'Review' of the *Works of President Edwards*, edited by Samuel Austin" (1821): 298–315, 357–65; and [Noah Porter], "President Edwards on Revivals" (June 1827): 295–308.

25. See Leonard Woods, *History of the Andover Theological Seminary* (Boston, 1885), pp. 168–69.

26. Hatch, *Democratization of American Christianity*, p. 11. On the religious print culture of the Second Great Awakening, see also R. Laurence Moore, *Selling God: American Religion in the Marketplace of Culture* (New York, 1994), chap. 1.

27. Charles G. Finney, *Lectures on Revivals of Religion*, ed. William G. McLoughlin (Cambridge, Mass., 1960), p. 289.

28. Quoted in William G. McLoughlin, *Revivals, Awakenings, and Reform* (Chicago, 1978), p. 123. Also on Finney, see McLoughlin, *Modern Revivalism* (New York, 1959), chaps. 1–2; *Autobiography of Charles G. Finney* (New York, 1876); and Keith Hardiman, *Charles Grandison Finney, 1792–1875* (New York, 1987).

29. McLoughlin, *Modern Revivalism*, pp. 32–36; Finney, *Lectures on Revivals*, pp. xvi–xx.

30. *Letters of the Rev. Dr. Beecher and Rev. Mr. Nettleton on the "New Measures" in Conducting Revivals of Religion* (New York, 1828); *The Autobiography of Lyman Beecher*, ed. Barbara M. Cross, 2 vols. (Cambridge, Mass., 1961), 2:66–80. See also [Noah Porter], "President Edwards on Revivals," *Christian Spectator* 1 (June 1827): 295–308.

31. "Traditions of the Elders," in *Sermons on Various Subjects*, by Rev. Charles G. Finney (New York, 1835), esp. p. 62.

32. *Autobiography of Lyman Beecher*, 2:68–70.

33. Ibid., pp. 67–68.

34. Charles G. Finney, *True and False Repentance* (1836; reprint, Grand Rapids, Mich., 1966), esp. 31–51; McLoughlin, *Modern Revivalism*, p. 35.

35. Charles Spaulding, *Edwards on Revivals* (New York, 1832), p. viii.

36. Sprague, *Lectures on Revivals*, p. 34; Miller, quoted in ibid., Appendix p. 29; [Porter], "President Edwards on Revivals," p. 295.

37. Beecher and Nettleton, *Letters . . . on "New Measures,"* p. 13. See also [Beecher], "Letters on the Introduction and Progress of Unitarianism in New England," *Spirit of the Pilgrims* 2 (March 1829): 121–28.

38. Jonathan Edwards, *Some Thoughts Concerning the Present Revival of Religion*, ed. C. C. Goen, vol. 4 of *Works of Jonathan Edwards* (New Haven, Conn., 1972), pp. 409, 412.

39. Samuel Miller, quoted in Sprague, *Lectures on Revivals*, Appendix p. 29; [Porter], "President Edwards on Revivals," p. 296. See also S. E. Dwight, *The Life of President Edwards*, vol. 1 of *The Works of President Edwards, with a Memoir*, ed. Sereno E. Dwight, 10 vols. (New York, 1829), chap. 15, and Spaulding, *Edwards on Revivals*, pp. ix–xvi.

40. Beecher and Nettleton, *Letters . . . on "New Measures,"* p. 29. Spaulding, *Edwards on Revivals,* ix–xvi; Sprague, *Lectures on Revivals,* Appendix; [Porter], "President Edwards on Revivals," esp. p. 70; and [Beecher], "Letters on Unitarianism in New England," p. 125.

41. Albert Dod, "Finney's Lectures," *Biblical Repertory and Theological Review* 7 (October 1835): 657. See also Dod, "Finney's Sermons," ibid. (July 1835): 482–527.

42. Dwight, *Life of Edwards,* pp. 603–9; Samuel Miller, *Life of Jonathan Edwards,* vol. 8 of *The Library of American Biography,* ed. Jared Sparks (New York, 1837), pp. 196–97; "Edwards as a Sermonizer," *Christian Review* 10 (March 1845): esp. 44; and W. A. Stearns, "The American Pulpit," *Bibliotheca Sacra* 4 (May 1847): esp. 257. See also "Rev. Jonathan Edwards," in J. B. Waterbury, *Sketches of Eloquent Preachers* (New York 1864), pp. 151–62.

43. See Joseph A. Conforti, *Samuel Hopkins and the New Divinity Movement: Calvinism, the Congregational Ministry, and Reform in New England between the Great Awakenings* (Grand Rapids, Mich., 1981), chaps. 2, 11, and Donald M. Scott, *From Office to Profession: The New England Ministry, 1750–1850* (Philadelphia, 1978), chaps. 1–4.

44. Miller, *Life of Edwards,* pp. 39–40.

45. Sprague, *Lectures on Revivals,* Appendix. See also the introduction to Spaulding, *Edwards on Revivals,* pp. ix–xvi.

46. Finney, *Sermons on Various Subjects,* p. 77, and *Lectures on Revivals,* pp. 259–61. In addition to the works of McLoughlin, also helpful on Finney are Whitney R. Cross, *The Burned-Over District* (1950; reprint, New York, 1965), chaps. 10–12, and Paul Johnson, *A Shopkeeper's Millennium: Society and Revivals in Rochester, New York, 1815–1937* (New York, 1978), chap. 5.

47. Perry Miller, *The Life of the Mind in America* (New York, 1965), p. 9.

48. Edwards, quoted in Finney, *Lectures on Revivals,* p. 295.

49. Ibid., p. 289.

50. Ibid., p. 291.

51. Ibid., pp. 261–76. Of course Finney stretched the historical record. Edwards endorsed lay exhortation, for example, only in certain restricted circumstances and was careful to protect ministerial authority. See Edwards, *Some Thoughts,* pp. 483–88.

52. Finney, *Lectures on Revivals,* p. 269.

53. Dod, "Finney's Lectures," p. 657.

54. Charles Hodge, *Constitutional History of the Presbyterian Church in the United States of America,* 2 vols. (Philadelphia, 1839), 2:63; see also Robert Baird, *Religion in the United States of America* (London, 1844), esp. pp. 473–74.

55. Hodge, *Constitutional History,* pp. 67–70; Dwight, *Life of Edwards,* p. 469.

56. Joseph Tracy, *The Great Awakening: A History of the Revival of Religion in the Time of Edwards and Whitefield* (Boston, 1841), p. iii.

57. Ibid., p. 213.

58. Ibid., p. 240.

59. Ibid., pp. iii, 226, 427. For another interesting centennial retrospective essay, see "The Great Awakening," *Methodist Quarterly Review* 24 (1842): 594–615.

60. Butler, "Enthusiasm Described and Decried," p. 307, and *Awash in a Sea of Faith,* pp. 164–65.

61. John E. Smith, ed., *Religious Affections,* vol. 2 of *Works of Jonathan Edwards* (New Haven, Conn., 1959), pp. 75–78, 80; see also W. Ellerby, *The Treatise of Religious Affections, by the Late Rev. Jonathan Edwards, . . .* (1817; reprint, Boston, 1821), pp. i–viii; "Edwards on the Religious Affections," *Christian Disciple* 4 (September–October 1822): 445–63; and Thomas Johnson, ed., *The Printed Writings of Jonathan Edwards: A Bibliography* (1940; reprint, New York, 1968), pp. 33–42.

62. Jonathan Edwards, *The Treatise on Religious Affections* (New York, [1833]), p. 113. The Tract Society worked from Ellerby's abridgment. I have made a detailed comparison between the Tract Society's edition and the Yale edition of the *Religious Affections* edited by John Smith.

63. Edwards, *Religious Affections,* ed. John E. Smith, vol. 2 of *Works of Jonathan Edwards* (New Haven, Conn., 1959), p. 272; compare with the Tract Society's *Religious Affections,* p. 154.

64. John Wesley, "To the Reader," *The Work of the Holy Spirit in the Human Heart by Rev. Jonathan Edwards* (New York, 1853), p. 87. Robert C. Monk, *John Wesley: His Puritan Heritage* (New York and Nashville, 1966), pp. 48–52.

65. Smith, *Religious Affections,* pp. 253–54. My comments are based on a comparison of the Wesley and Smith editions. On Wesley and Edwards, see Monk, *John Wesley: His Puritan Heritage;* "Jonathan Edwards and John Wesley," *National Magazine* 3 (October 1853): 308–11; and Charles A. Rogers, "John Wesley and Jonathan Edwards," *Duke Divinity School Review* 31 (Winter 1966): 20–38.

66. Johnson, *Printed Writings of Edwards,* pp. 33–42; Smith, *Religious Affections,* pp. 73–82.

67. [E. H. Byington], "The Theology of Edwards, as Shown in His Treatise Concerning Religious Affections," *American Theological Review* 1 (May 1859): 199–220; see also George M. Marsden, *The Evangelical Mind and the New School Presbyterian Experience: A Case Study of Thought and Theology in Nineteenth-Century America* (New Haven, Conn., 1970), p. 118ff. On the continuing analyses of the Edwardsian revivalistic legacy in the 1840s and 1850s, see, for example, [William H. Channing], "Edwards and the Revivalists," *Christian Examiner* 43 (November 1844): 374–94; Edward Beecher, "The Works of Samuel Hopkins," *Bibliotheca Sacra* 10 (January 1853): 63–82; and A. P. Marvin, "Three Eras of Revivals in the United States," ibid. 16 (April 1859): 279–301.

68. [Beecher], "Letters on Unitarianism in New England," p. 132.

69. Eric Hobsbawm and Terrence Ranger, eds., *The Invention of Tradition* (New York, 1983), pp. 1–14.

70. For a very different view of the New England and American revival tradition from what I have presented, see Michael J. Crawford, *Seasons of Grace: Colonial New England's Revival Tradition in Its British Context* (New York, 1991), esp. pp. 240–50. Crawford's interpretation of revivals as deus ex machina (chap. 2) is very different from mine. Jon Butler also uses the term "deus ex machina"; see "Enthusiasm Described and Decried," p. 322.

CHAPTER TWO

1. The excellent collection of essays edited by Nathan O. Hatch and Harry S. Stout that broadly examines Edwards's influence does not address his importance to and in the Second Great Awakening, though Mark A. Noll offers some suggestive comments. See Noll, "Jonathan Edwards and Nineteenth-Century Theology," in *Jonathan Edwards and the American Experience*, ed. Nathan O. Hatch and Harry S. Stout (New York, 1988), pp. 260–87.

2. Edwards A. Park, *Memoir of the Life and Character of Samuel Hopkins, D.D. . . .* (Boston, 1852), p. 217. On Edwards and Scotland, see Harold P. Simonson, "Jonathan Edwards and His Scottish Connections," *Journal of American Studies* 21 (1987): 353–76. For reactions to Edwards's death and on his eighteenth-century reputation, see Donald Louis Weber, "The Image of Jonathan Edwards in American Culture" (Ph.D. diss., Columbia University, 1978), chap. 1, esp. p. 69f.; see also Daniel B. Shea, "Jonathan Edwards: The First Two Hundred Years," *Journal of American Studies* 14 (August 1980): 181–97.

3. This is the estimate of Thomas Johnson, ed., *The Printed Writings of Jonathan Edwards: A Bibliography* (1940; reprint, New York, 1968), p. xi.

4. Noll, "Edwards and Nineteenth-Century Theology," p. 260. Allen C. Guelzo, *Edwards on the Will: A Century of American Theological Debate* (Middletown, Conn., 1989), pp. 147, 276. My discussion of Edwards as a cultural icon has been influenced by Guelzo's suggestive comments, but I disagree with his notion that Edwards became little more than a kind of cultural artifact by the late 1820s.

5. One important exception was the publication together in 1765 of Edwards's dissertations on *The Nature of True Virtue* and *Concerning the End for Which God Created the World*.

6. Samuel Hopkins, *The Life and Character of the Late Reverend Mr. Jonathan Edwards*, in *Jonathan Edwards: A Profile*, ed. David Levin (New York, 1969), p. 2.

7. S. E. Dwight, *The Life of President Edwards*, vol. 1 of *The Works of President Edwards, with a Memoir*, ed. Sereno E. Dwight, 10 vols. (New York, 1829).

8. Ibid., p. 624.

9. See, for example, Noah Porter, "Review of the Works of President Edwards," *Quarterly Christian Spectator* 3 (September 1831): 337–51; American Sunday School Union's *The Life of President Edwards* (Philadelphia, 1832); and Samuel Miller, *Life of Jonathan Edwards*, vol. 8 of *The Library of American Biography*, ed. Jared Sparks (New York, 1837).

10. "'Review' of the *Works of President Edwards*, edited by Samuel Austin," *Christian Spectator* 3 (June 1821): 300.

11. Guelzo offers the best discussion of theological efforts to co-opt the New Divinity. See *Edwards on the Will*, esp. pp. 221–22, 228–29, 242–43.

12. See, for example, "Life and Character of Rev. Jonathan Edwards," *Connecticut Evangelical Magazine and Religious Intelligencer* 1 (May 1808): 161–78 and (June 1808): 201–12; Euopius, "On a Resolution of President Edwards," *Christian Spectator* 7 (January 1825): 14ff.; "Interesting Conversions: Jonathan Edwards," *Religious Monitor and*

Evangelical Repository 6 (February 1830): 414ff.; American Sunday School Union's *Life of Edwards*, esp. chap. 3; and William B. Sprague, *Annals of the American Pulpit*, 9 vols. (New York, 1857–69), 1:330.

13. *Conversion of President Edwards* (New York, [1827]); Johnson, *Printed Writings of Edwards*, p. 95.

14. Joseph Emerson, *Articles of Faith, and Form of Covenant, Adopted by the Third Congregational Church in Beverly, at Its Formation, November 9, 1801 . . . To Which Are Added Resolutions of President Edwards*. Published by Order of the Church for the use of the Members (Boston, 1807); Johnson, *Printed Writings of Edwards*, p. 101f.

15. Jonathan Edwards, *Religious Affections*, ed. John E. Smith, vol. 2 of *Works of Jonathan Edwards*, 13 vols. (New Haven, Conn., 1959), p. 311.

16. Edwards, quoted in Dwight, *Life of Edwards*, p. 311.

17. Ibid., pp. 69, 71. All seventy resolutions are reprinted on pp. 68–73.

18. Ibid., p. 71.

19. Ibid., p. 73.

20. American Sunday School Union's *Life of Edwards*, p. 26; see also Porter, "Review of the Works of Edwards," p. 342f.; Miller, *Life of Edwards*, esp. p. 190; and Joseph P. Thompson, "Jonathan Edwards, His Character, Teaching, and Influence," *Bibliotheca Sacra* 18 (October 1861): 813ff.

21. Manly is quoted and described in Anne C. Loveland, *Southern Evangelicals and the Social Order, 1800–1860* (Baton Rouge, La., 1980), p. 15.

22. Dwight, *Life of Edwards*, p. 587; Erasmus Middleton, "Jonathan Edwards, D.D.," in *Evangelical Biography*, 4 vols. (Philadelphia, 1798), 1:429; Miller, *Life of Edwards*, pp. 172, 190; "Edwards as a Sermonizer," *Christian Review* 10 (March 1845): 37; and [George MaGoun], "President Edwards as a Reformer," *Congregational Quarterly* 1 (April 1869): 265. On nineteenth-century evangelicals and the commonsense philosophy, see William G. McLoughlin, ed., *The American Evangelicals, 1800–1900* (New York, 1968), pp. 1–10; Mark A. Noll, "Common Sense Traditions and American Evangelical Thought," *American Quarterly* 37 (Summer 1985): 216–38; and Noll, *Princeton in the Republic, 1768–1822: The Search for a Christian Enlightenment in the Era of Samuel Stanhope Smith* (Princeton, N.J., 1989).

23. Middleton, "Jonathan Edwards, D.D.," p. 429.

24. Michael J. Crawford, *Seasons of Grace: Colonial New England's Revival Tradition in Its British Context* (New York, 1991), pp. 124, 189.

25. Johnson, *Printed Writings of Edwards*, pp. 4–15, lists the editions of the *Faithful Narrative*. In 1736, what was to become the *Faithful Narrative* was published in part as an appendix to another American work. But the 1737 English edition was the first complete edition. Bennett Tyler, the influential Edwardsian minister, edited revival narratives from the *Connecticut Evangelical Magazine* and the Massachusetts Sabbath School Society and published them in an important volume. See *New England Revivals, as They Existed at the Close of the Eighteenth, and the Beginning of the Nineteenth Centuries. Compiled Principally from Narratives First Published in the Connecticut Evangelical Magazine* (Boston, 1846). Thomas Prince published transatlantic revival narratives during the era of the so-called "great" awakening. But his *Church History*

(Boston, 1743–45) was a short-lived effort that did not establish the revival narrative in evangelical culture.

26. [Lyman Beecher], "Letters on the Introduction and Progress of Unitarianism in New England," *Spirit of the Pilgrims* 2 (March 1829): 122.

27. [MaGoun], "Edwards as a Reformer," p. 265.

28. Ibid.; see also "Edwards as a Sermonizer," esp. p. 53; "Review of Edwards on the Affections," *Christian Review* 6 (December 1841): 492; and Joseph Tracy, *The Great Awakening: A History of the Revival of Religion in the Time of Edwards and Whitefield* (Boston, 1841), esp. pp. 1–18.

29. Charles Spaulding, *Edwards on Revivals* (New York, 1832), p. x.

30. Rev. W. D. Snodgrass, quoted in ibid., p. vii.

31. Ibid., p. xi; see also William B. Sprague, *Lectures on Revivals of Religion* (Albany, 1832), passim.

32. Robert C. Monk, *John Wesley: His Puritan Heritage* (New York and Nashville, 1966), p. 221; Frank Baker, *From Wesley to Asbury: Studies in American Methodism* (Durham, N.C., 1976), esp. p. 71; "Edwards and Wesley," *National Magazine* 3 (October 1853): 308–11.

33. Johnson, *Printed Writings of Edwards*, p. 31; Sprague, *Lectures on Revivals*, p. 218f.

34. "Review of Edwards on the Affections," p. 501f.; "President Edwards on Charity and Its Fruits," *New Englander* 10 (May 1852): 227; John Brazer, "Essays on the Doctrine of Divine Influences," *Christian Examiner* 18 (March 1835): 52; and see also [E. H. Byington], "The Theology of Edwards, as Shown in His Treatise Concerning Religious Affections," *American Theological Review* 1 (May 1859): 199.

35. Crawford, *Seasons of Grace*, p. 132.

36. Jonathan Edwards, *A History of the Work of Redemption. Containing the Outline of a Body of Divinity in a Method Entirely New* (Edinburgh, 1774), p. ii.

37. Johnson, *Printed Writings of Edwards*, pp. 85–94.

38. Edwards W. Grinfield, *The Nature and Extent of the Christian Dispensation with Reference to the Salvability of the Heathen* (London, 1827), p. 427. I am indebted to John F. Wilson for this reference. See "Editor's Introduction," in Jonathan Edwards, *A History of the Work of Redemption*, ed. John F. Wilson, vol. 9 of *Works of Jonathan Edwards* (New Haven, Conn., 1989), pp. 87–88.

39. Edwards, *History of Redemption*, p. 116.

40. Chapter 4 discusses Mary Lyon's combination of Edwardsian millennialism, revivalism, and disinterested benevolence in the service of missionary work. I have found John Wilson's brief discussion (pp. 79–83) of the nineteenth-century reception of the *History of Redemption* useful. But I disagree that Edwards's ideas became so "diffused" that they were hardly Edwardsian. I also disagree with Wilson's similar assessment (pp. 83–84) of Edwards's more strictly theological legacy, namely, that debate "over technical points among ecclesiastics . . . took on a life of its own" largely divorced from Edwards. In one case, the appropriation of Edwards becomes too generalized and in the other too specialized.

41. [MaGoun], "Edwards as a Reformer," p. 269. The term "morphology" of revival is Crawford's; see *Seasons of Grace*, chap. 9.

42. Guelzo, *Edwards on the Will*, chaps. 7, 8. Also see Bruce Kuklick, *Churchmen and Philosophers: From Jonathan Edwards to John Dewey* (New Haven, Conn., 1985), and James Hoopes, *Consciousness in New England: From Puritanism and Ideas to Psycho-analysis and Semiotics* (Baltimore, Md., 1989).

43. Alexander, quoted in Guelzo, *Edwards on the Will*, p. 207. See also George M. Marsden, *The Evangelical Mind and the New School Presbyterian Experience: A Case Study of Thought and Theology in Nineteenth-Century America* (New Haven, Conn., 1970), and Earl Pope, *New England Calvinism and the Disruption of the Presbyterian Church* (New York, 1987).

44. These included Princeton (1812), Harvard (1815), Bangor (1816), Auburn (1818), General (1819), Yale (1822), Union of Virginia (1824), Western (1827), Columbia (1828), Lane (1829), McCormick (1830), East Windsor (1834), and Union of New York (1836). In *The Spiritual Self in Everyday Life: The Transformation of Personal Religious Experience in Nineteenth-Century New England* (Boston, 1989), Richard Rabinowitz offers suggestive discussions of the New Divinity, the relegation of theology to seminaries, and alterations in nineteenth-century evangelical religious sensibilities.

45. Nettleton, quoted in Guelzo, *Edwards on the Will*, p. 271. My discussion of the appropriation of Edwards's theology has been influenced by Guelzo and Noll, "Edwards and Nineteenth-Century Theology," pp. 260–87.

46. Curtis Manning Geer, *The Hartford Theological Seminary, 1834–1934* (Hartford, Conn., 1934), pp. 62–63.

47. John T. Wayland, *The Theological Development of Yale College, 1822–1858* (1933; reprint, New York, 1987), p. 238. For this reference I am indebted to Douglas Sweeney, "Nathaniel William Taylor and the Edwardsian Tradition: A Reassessment," a paper presented at the conference on "The Writings of Jonathan Edwards: Text and Context," Indiana University, June 1994.

48. Miller, *Life of Edwards*, p. 215.

49. Guelzo offers several perceptive comments on Edwards as a cultural icon that suggests how some nineteenth-century polemicists appropriated his figure but not necessarily his theology. See *Edwards on the Will*, pp. 147–48.

50. See Richard Brodhead's discussion of the nineteenth-century canonization of Hawthorne's work and his creative American genius in *The School of Hawthorne* (New York, 1986).

51. [MaGoun], "Edwards as a Reformer," p. 265; Porter, "Review of the Works of Edwards," p. 300; Increase N. Tarbox, "Jonathan Edwards," *Bibliotheca Sacra* 26 (April 1869): 245; William Tyler, "Genius," *Bibliotheca Sacra* 12 (April 1855): 296; Timothy Dwight, *Travels in New England and New York*, 4 vols. (New Haven, Conn., 1823), 4:323–28; and Shea, "Jonathan Edwards," p. 188f.

52. Stewart made this statement in *A General View of the Progress of Metaphysical, Ethical, and Political Philosophy Since the Revival of Letters in Europe: First Dissertation* (Boston, 1822), part 2, p. 256; references to Stewart's assessment are too numerous to cite, but some representative examples may be found in Dwight, *Life of Edwards*, p. 603; American Sunday School Union's *Life of Edwards*, p. 133; and Miller, *Life of Edwards*, p. 183.

53. William B. Sprague, "Jonathan Edwards," in *Annals of the American Pulpit*, ed. William B. Sprague, 9 vols. (New York, 1857–69), 1:334; Miller, *Life of Edwards*, p. 172; Tarbox, "Jonathan Edwards," p. 246; and [MaGoun], "Edwards as a Reformer," p. 265.

54. Porter, "Review of the Works of Edwards," p. 299.

55. Tarbox, "Jonathan Edwards," pp. 255, 261ff.; see also Dwight, *Life of Edwards*, pp. 9, 603.

56. Charles Osgood, "Jonathan Edwards and the New Calvinism," in *Studies in Christian Biography or Hours with Theologians and Reformers* (New York, 1850), p. 352.

57. Dwight, *Life of Edwards*, p. 587; Tarbox, "Jonathan Edwards," p. 259; Miller, *Life of Edwards*, p. 8; and American Sunday School Union's *Life of Edwards*, p. 11. See also Evert A. Duyckinck and George L. Duyckinck, *Cyclopedia of American Literature*, 2 vols. (New York, 1856), 1:92, and Benjamin Silliman, "Juvenile Observations of President Edwards on Spiders," *American Journal of Science and Arts* 21 (January 1832): 109–15.

58. Sprague, "Jonathan Edwards," p. 329; see also "Life of Edwards," *Connecticut Evangelical Magazine*, p. 162; Dwight, *Life of Edwards*, pp. 33–40; and Porter, "Review of the Works of Edwards," pp. 338–42. Wallace Anderson argues that Locke was probably not even available to Edwards when he was thirteen. See Anderson, ed., *Scientific and Philosophical Writings*, vol. 6 of *Works of Jonathan Edwards* (New Haven, Conn., 1980), pp. 16–18.

59. Miller, *Life of Edwards*, p. 191.

60. *The Autobiography of Lyman Beecher*, ed. Barbara M. Cross, 2 vols. (Cambridge, Mass., 1961), 2:177.

61. Dwight's description of Edwards appeared in *The Triumph of Infidelity: A Poem* (1788) and was quoted by nineteenth-century evangelicals. See, for example, Edwards A. Park, "New England Theology," *Bibliotheca Sacra* 9 (January 1852): 182.

62. Harriet Beecher Stowe, *The Minister's Wooing* (Boston, 1859; reprint, New York, 1967), p. 245.

63. Stowe, quoted in Charles H. Foster, *The Rungless Ladder: Harriet Beecher Stowe and New England Puritanism* (Durham, N.C., 1954), pp. 101–2; see also Lawrence E. Buell, "Calvinism Romanticized: Harriet Beecher Stowe, Samuel Hopkins, and *The Minister's Wooing*," *Emerson Society Quarterly* 24 (1978): 119–32.

64. W. Frothingham, "Jonathan Edwards and the Old Clergy," *Continental Monthly* 1 (March 1862): 210; see also Park, "New England Theology," pp. 184–85, and Edward Beecher, "The Works of Samuel Hopkins," *Bibliotheca Sacra* 10 (January 1853): 63–82.

65. Frothingham, "Jonathan Edwards and the Old Clergy," p. 265. Memoirs and collected works of New Divinity men included the following: Jonathan Edwards, Jr. (1842), Joseph Bellamy (1850), Samuel Hopkins (1852), and Nathanael Emmons (1861).

66. John Todd, *Address at the Laying of the Corner Stone of the Edwards Church in Northampton, Mass., July 4, 1833* (Northampton, Mass., 1834), pp. 50, 55; see also Todd, *The Pulpit – Its Influence upon Society: A Sermon Delivered at the Dedication of the Edwards Church in Northampton, Mass., December 25, 1833* (Northampton, Mass., 1834). On Edwards's theological followers as Farmer Metaphysicians, see Joseph A. Conforti, *Samuel Hopkins and the New Divinity Movement: Calvinism, the Congregational Min-*

istry, and Reform in New England between the Great Awakenings (Grand Rapids, Mich., 1981), p. 10.

67. The admirable Yankee emerges in works like Timothy Dwight's *Greenfield Hill* (1794), Jedidiah Morse's *American Geography* (1789), which was widely used in the nineteenth century, and numerous stories and books of Stowe. On the figure of the Yankee in art, see Sarah Burns, "Jonathans," in *Pastoral Inventions: Rural Life in Nineteenth-Century Art and Culture* (Philadelphia, 1989), pp. 149−67; and Elizabeth Johns, "An Image of Pure Yankeeism," in *American Genre Painting: The Politics of Everyday Life* (New Haven, Conn., 1991), pp. 24−59.

68. A. P. Marvin, "Three Eras of Revivals in the U.S.," *Bibliotheca Sacra* 16 (April 1859): 290f.; see also [MaGoun], "Edwards as a Reformer," p. 265, and Spaulding, *Edwards on Revivals,* esp. p. vii.

69. Dwight, *Life of Edwards,* p. 298.

70. See Joseph A. Conforti, "Edwardsians, Unitarians, and the Memory of the Great Awakening," in *American Unitarianism, 1805–1865,* ed. Conrad Edick Wright (Boston, 1989), pp. 31–50.

71. [James Walker], "The Revival under Whitefield," *Christian Examiner* 4 (1827): 465, 480−81.

72. Ibid., pp. 468−69.

73. Ibid., pp. 490−91.

74. Dwight, *Life of Edwards,* pp. 428, 593. Patricia J. Tracy, *Jonathan Edwards, Pastor: Religion and Society in Eighteenth-Century Northampton* (New York, 1989), offers a provocative social history of Edwards's ministry including his dismissal.

75. Dwight, *Life of Edwards,* p. 435.

76. Ibid., p. 436.

77. Miller, *Life of Edwards,* p. 431.

78. Dwight, *Life of Edwards,* p. 431f.

79. Ibid., p. 447.

80. Porter, "Review of the Works of Edwards," p. 349f.

81. Todd, *Address at Edwards Church,* p. 51.

CHAPTER THREE

1. John F. Sears, *Sacred Places: American Tourist Attractions in the Nineteenth Century* (New York, 1989), pp. 49−56; Peter Briggs, "Timothy Dwight Composes a Landscape for New England," *American Quarterly* 40 (September 1988): 359−77.

2. William B. Sprague, *Annals of the American Pulpit,* 9 vols. (New York, 1858), 3:116.

3. Gordon, quoted in Ernest B. Gordon, *Adoniram Judson Gordon: A Biography,* 2d ed. (New York, 1896), p. 85.

4. Elmer T. Clark, ed., *The Journal and Letters of Francis Asbury,* 3 vols. (Nashville, 1958), 2:154, 486, and 3:218; Gardiner Spring, *Memoir of Samuel John Mills* (1820; reprint, New York, 1842), p. 10; Francis Wayland, "The Ministry of Brainerd," *American Presbyterian and Theological Review* 3 (July 1865): 395. See also Joseph A. Conforti,

"Jonathan Edwards's Most Popular Work: 'The Life of David Brainerd' and Nineteenth-Century Evangelical Culture," *Church History* 54 (June 1985): 188–201.

5. Sereno E. Dwight, *Memoirs of David Brainerd: . . . by Rev. Jonathan Edwards . . .* (New Haven, Conn., 1822), p. 8; Sprague, *Annals of the American Pulpit*, 3:116.

6. William B. O. Peabody, *David Brainerd*, vol. 8 of *The Library of American Biography*, ed. Jared Sparks (New York, 1837).

7. The full title is *An Account of the Life of the Late Reverend Mr. David Brainerd, Minister of the Gospel, Missionary to the Indians, from the Honourable Society in Scotland, for the Propagation of Christian Knowledge, and Pastor of a Church of Christian Indians in New-Jersey, Who Died at Northampton in New England, Octob. 9th 1747 in the 30th Year of His Age: Chiefly Taken from His Own Diary, and Other Private Writings, Written for His Own Use; and Now Published, by Jonathan Edwards, A.M. Minister of the Gospel at Northampton* (Boston, 1749).

8. William Warren Sweet, *The Story of Religion in America* (New York, 1930), p. 236; Perry Miller, review of *The Life and Diary of David Brainerd*, ed. Philip E. Howard, Jr., *New England Quarterly* 23 (1950): 277. See also Ola Winslow, *Jonathan Edwards, 1703–1758: A Biography* (New York, 1940), p. 273, and R. Pierce Beaver, ed., *Pioneers in Missions: The Early Missionary Ordination Sermons, Charges, and Institutions* (Grand Rapids, Mich., 1966), p. 105.

9. For example, Alan Heimert devoted only a few pages of his massive *Religion and the American Mind from the Great Awakening to the Revolution* (Cambridge, Mass., 1966) to Brainerd and Edwards's *Life of Brainerd*; and Philip Greven, in *The Protestant Temperament: Patterns of Childrearing, Religious Experience, and the Self in Early America* (New York, 1977), paid only cursory attention to the *Life of Brainerd* and ignored its contribution as a major work that helped shape evangelical values. Existing studies of Brainerd are admiring accounts written from an evangelical perspective. See Jesse Page, *David Brainerd: The Apostle to the North American Indians* (London, 1891); Richard Ellsworth Day, *Flagellant on Horseback: The Life Story of David Brainerd* (Philadelphia, 1950); and David Wynbeek, *David Brainerd, Beloved Yankee* (Grand Rapids, Mich., 1961); also see Don O. Shelton, "David Brainerd," in *Heroes of the Cross in America* (New York, 1904), pp. 1–83; George McLean Harper, "David Brainerd, A Puritan Saint," in *John Morley and Other Essays* (Princeton, 1920), pp. 134–62; and Clyde S. Kilby, "David Brainerd," in *Heroic Colonial Christians*, ed. Russell T. Hitt (Philadelphia, 1966), pp. 155–206. Especially helpful is the biographical information contained in the introduction to Jonathan Edwards, *The Life of David Brainerd*, ed. Norman Pettit, vol. 7 of *Works of Jonathan Edwards*, 13 vols. (New Haven, Conn., 1985), esp. pp. 32–71. All citations of *Life of Brainerd* will be from the Yale edition.

10. Franklin B. Dexter, *Biographical Sketches of the Graduates of Yale College, with Annals of the College History*, 6 vols. (New Haven, Conn., 1885–1912), 1:661. Pettit's introduction to the Yale edition of *Life of Brainerd* offers biographical information as well as a description of activities at Yale; see esp. pp. 32–57.

11. Jonathan Edwards, *The Great Awakening: Distinguishing Marks of a Work of the Spirit of God*, ed. C. C. Goen, vol. 4 of *Works of Jonathan Edwards* (New Haven, Conn., 1972), p. 242.

12. See Pettit, *Life of Brainerd*, pp. 41–57, and Pettit, "Prelude to Mission: David Brainerd's Expulsion from Yale," *New England Quarterly* 59 (1986): 28–50.

13. Brainerd's activities are outlined in Pettit, *Life of Brainerd*, pp. 51–71.

14. The quotation is in David Brainerd's *Journal*, which was published in two parts. Part 1 is titled *Mirabilia Dei inter Indicos; or the Rise and Progress of a Remarkable Work of Grace, Among a Number of Indians . . . Justly Represented in a Journal, Kept . . . by David Brainerd*. Part 2 is titled *Divine Grace Displayed. . . .* Hereafter, I will refer to this work as the *Journal*. I have used the original edition (Philadelphia, 1746). The quotation is in part 2, p. 6.

15. *Life of Brainerd*, pp. 254n, 288. For an interesting discussion of the influence of Native Americans on Brainerd's mission work, see Richard W. Pointer, "'Poor Indians' and the 'Poor in Spirit': The Indian Impact on David Brainerd," *New England Quarterly* 67 (September 1994): 403–26.

16. Brainerd, *Journal*, part 2, pp. 71–72, 226–27; *Life of Brainerd*, pp. 298–428.

17. *Life of Brainerd*, p. 475.

18. S. E. Dwight, *The Life of President Edwards*, vol. 1 of *The Works of President Edwards, with a Memoir*, ed. Sereno E. Dwight, 10 vols. (New York, 1829), pp. 250–51.

19. Thomas Johnson, ed., *The Printed Writings of Jonathan Edwards: A Bibliography* (1940; reprint, New York, 1968), pp. ix, 47–60.

20. *Works of John Wesley*, ed. Thomas Jackson, 14 vols. (Grand Rapids, Mich., 1960), 3:294.

21. Ibid., 7:328; Johnson, *Printed Writings of Edwards*, pp. 48–54; Dwight, *Memoirs of Brainerd*, p. 8; Beaver, *Pioneers in Missions*, p. 106; Robert C. Monk, *John Wesley: His Puritan Heritage* (New York and Nashville, 1966), p. 221. In England, Brainerd's influence was not restricted to the Wesleyan movement, for the *Life of Brainerd* was equally popular among Baptists. William Carey, Andrew Fuller, John Ryland, and Henry Martyn, prominent Baptists of the late eighteenth and early nineteenth centuries, all described the inspiration they drew from this work. To Carey, one of the first Baptist missionaries to India, the *Life of Brainerd* was "almost a second bible." Martyn claimed that he was drawn into missionary work through reading the *Life of Brainerd*. He paraphrased a line from Brainerd's diary and used it as his missionary motto: "Let me burn out for God!" Ryland was so moved by the American missionary that he named one of his sons David Brainerd Ryland (he named another son after Jonathan Edwards). Carey and Martyn are quoted in E. A. Payne, "The Evangelical Revival and the Beginnings of the Modern Missionary Movement," *Congregational Quarterly* 21 (1943): 228. On Ryland, see Kilby, "David Brainerd," p. 200.

22. John Styles, *The Life of David Brainerd, Missionary to the Indians, with an Abridgment of His Diary and Journal* (Newport, Isle of Wight, 1808; reprint, Boston, 1812), preface.

23. Dwight, *Memoirs of Brainerd*, p. 8. Johnson, *Printed Writings of Edwards*, pp. 47–60.

24. See Pettit's discussion in the *Life of Brainerd*, p. 77.

25. *The Life of David Brainerd . . .* (New York [1833]). This edition was reprinted frequently but never with a date. See Johnson, *Printed Writings of Edwards*, p. 55.

26. B. B. Edwards, ed., *Memoir of the Rev. Elias Cornelius* (Boston, 1834), p. 230.

27. On other nineteenth-century editions of the *Life of Brainerd*, see Johnson, *Printed Writings of Edwards*, pp. 52–55, and Pettit, *Life of Brainerd*, pp. 77–78.

28. Wayland, "Ministry of Brainerd," p. 395. Other biographical sketches include the following: "David Brainerd," in *The Gospel Treasury: Containing Biography Compiled from the London Evangelical Magazine*, 4 vols. (Boston, 1811), 2:98–137; "David Brainerd," reprinted from the *Missionary Herald* (1834), in *The Life of John Brainerd, the Brother of David Brainerd and His Successor as Missionary to the Indians of New Jersey*, by Thomas Brainerd (Philadelphia, 1865); and Peabody, *David Brainerd*.

29. Spring, *Memoir of Mills*, p. 10; Brainerd, *Life of John Brainerd*, p. 465; Joan J. Brumberg, *Mission for Life: The Story of the Family of Adoniram Judson* (New York, 1980), pp. 25, 235; Shelton, *Heroes of the Cross*, p. 20; Day, *Flagellant on Horseback*, p. 248. Sermons that described Brainerd as one of the missionary heroes of America include Levi Parsons, "Farewell Address," in *Memoir of Levi Parsons, First Missionary to Palestine from the United States*, ed. Daniel O. Morton (Burlington, Vt., 1830), p. 407; Leonard Woods, "A Sermon Delivered at the Tabernacle in Salem, Feb. 6, 1812," in Beaver, *Pioneers in Missions*, p. 263; and Abiel Holmes, *A Discourse before the Society for Propagating the Gospel among the Indians and Others in North America, Delivered Nov. 3, 1808* (Boston, 1808), pp. 29–33.

30. I have borrowed this term from Charles E. Hambrick-Stowe, *The Practice of Piety: Puritan Devotional Disciplines in Seventeenth-Century New England* (Chapel Hill, 1982), which examines Puritan devotional exercises. Though Hambrick-Stowe analyzes seventeenth-century popular religious practices, I have found his excellent work also suggestive for later periods.

31. Compare, for example, Edwards's *Distinguishing Marks of a Work of the Spirit of God* with Brainerd's "Some Signs of Godliness," in *Life of Brainerd*, p. 483.

32. Pettit, *Life of Brainerd*, p. 6.

33. Ibid., pp. 500–541. See also David L. Weddle, "The Melancholy Saint: Jonathan Edwards's Interpretation of David Brainerd as a Model of Evangelical Spirituality," *Harvard Theological Review* 81 (1988): 297–318.

34. For a negative view of this practice, see Barbara M. Cross, ed., *The Autobiography of Lyman Beecher*, 2 vols. (Cambridge, Mass., 1961), 1:29–30. For a positive view, see Leonard Woods, *History of the Andover Theological Seminary* (Boston, 1885), pp. 168–69.

35. *Life of Brainerd*, p. 402.

36. Ibid., p. 511.

37. Ibid., pp. 141–42; see also Heimert, *Religion and the American Mind*, p. 313.

38. This was especially true of John Styles's text. The Methodist preacher even extended Wesley's alterations of the text, abridging it not simply in the interests of shortening it and making it inexpensive. For the most recent analysis of Brainerd's gloominess, see Julius H. Rubin, *Religious Melancholy and Protestant Experience in America* (New York, 1994), pp. 94–98.

39. Adoniram Judson Gordon, quoted in Gordon, *Adoniram Judson Gordon*, p. 85.

40. Alvan Bond, *Memoir of the Rev. Pliny Fisk, A.M., Late Missionary to Palestine* (Boston, 1828), p. 249.

41. For example, during the antebellum period, college graduates from socially established backgrounds increasingly found careers in business, law, politics, and medicine more attractive than the ministry. See Daniel Calhoun, *Professional Lives in America: Structure and Aspiration, 1750–1850* (Cambridge, Mass., 1965), pp. 157–66; and Donald M. Scott, *From Office to Profession: The New England Ministry, 1750–1850* (Philadelphia, 1978), pp. 55–62.

42. *Life of Brainerd*, p. 531.

43. Woods, *History of Andover*, pp. 168–69.

44. Morton, *Memoir of Levi Parsons*, p. 42.

45. Bond, *Memoir of Pliny Fisk*, p. 182; Morton, *Memoir of Levi Parsons*, pp. 370–71; William E. Strong, *The Story of the American Board: An Account of the First Hundred Years of the American Board of Commissioners for Foreign Missions* (Boston, 1910), p. 36. The name may have also served to recognize David's brother John.

46. Jonathan Edwards, *Ethical Writings: The Nature of True Virtue*, ed. Paul Ramsey, vol. 8 of *Works of Jonathan Edwards* (New Haven, Conn., 1989), pp. 540–41.

47. This is Pettit's characterization; see *Life of Brainerd*, p. 13. Also see Joseph A. Conforti, "Samuel Hopkins and the New Divinity: Theology, Ethics, and Social Reform in Eighteenth-Century New England," *William and Mary Quarterly* 34 (October 1977): 572–89.

48. On the influence of the Edwardsian doctrine of disinterested benevolence, see Joseph A. Conforti, *Samuel Hopkins and the New Divinity Movement: Calvinism, the Congregational Ministry, and Reform in New England between the Great Awakenings* (Grand Rapids, Mich., 1981), chaps. 7–9; and Wolfgang E. Lowe, "The First American Foreign Missionaries: The Students, 1810–1829: An Inquiry into Their Theological Motives" (Ph.D. diss., Brown University, 1962). Surprisingly, while noting the influence of the doctrine of disinterested benevolence, Lowe completely ignores Brainerd as a model of true virtue and missionary piety.

49. See the biographical sketches in Lowe, "First American Foreign Missionaries," Appendix, and in Leonard Woods, *Memoirs of the American Missionaries Formerly Connected with the Society of Inquiry Respecting Missions in the Andover Theological Seminary* (Boston, 1833).

50. Horatio Boardwell, *Memoir of Rev. Gordon Hall, A.M., One of the First Missionaries of the American Board of Commissioners for Foreign Missions at Bombay* (Andover, Mass., 1841), pp. 21–22; Morton, *Memoir of Levi Parsons*, p. 407. See also Bond, *Memoir of Pliny Fisk*, pp. 93, 182; Spring, *Memoir of Mills*, pp. 234–36; and John Holt Rice and Benjamin Holt Rice, *Memoir of James Brainerd Taylor* (New York, 1833), p. 301.

51. Joseph Tracy, *The Great Awakening: A History of the Revival of Religion in the Time of Edwards and Whitefield* (Boston, 1841), p. 238.

52. Brainerd, *Journal*, Part 2, p. 241.

53. James Axtell, *The European and the Indian: Essays in the Ethnohistory of North America* (New York, 1981), p. 68. Also, on the cultural bias and unimpressive record of

American missionaries, see Gregory Evans Dowd, *A Spirited Resistance: The North American Indian Struggle for Unity* (Baltimore, Md., 1992); Henry Warner Bowden, *American Indians and Christian Missions: Studies in Cultural Conflict* (Chicago, 1981); John A. Andrew III, *Rebuilding the Christian Commonwealth: New England Congregationalists and Foreign Missions* (Lexington, Ky., 1976), esp. chap. 9; and Robert F. Berkhofer, *Salvation and the Savage: An Analysis of Protestant Missions and American Indian Response, 1787–1862* (Lexington, Ky., 1965), esp. p. 152.

54. Brainerd, *Journal*, Part 2, pp. 208–48.

55. *Life of Brainerd*, pp. 259, 274.

56. Ibid., p. 285.

57. The Edwardsian view of missionary work as a test of disinterested benevolence – as a physical and spiritual ordeal that constituted an evangelical rite of passage – is illustrated not only by Edwards's spiritual sons, but also by an incident that occurred with his real son in 1755. At a time when Indian hostilities made the frontier unsafe, the theologian sent ten-year-old Jonathan Edwards, Jr., along with Indian missionary Gideon Hawley, into Iroquois country more than two hundred miles from Stockbridge. In a lengthy letter to his son, Edwards made no mention of the Indians but stressed the spiritual lessons and benefits that the boy would derive from his ordeal: "Never give your self any rest, unless you have good evidence that you are converted & become a new creature." Furthermore, Edwards wrote, "alwaies remember that Life is uncertain; you know not how soon you must die, & therefore had need to be alwaies ready." This letter is reprinted in Robert L. Ferm, *Jonathan Edwards the Younger, 1745–1801: A Colonial Pastor* (Grand Rapids, Mich., 1976), pp. 15–16.

58. *Life of Brainerd*, pp. 520, 531–32.

59. There are no satisfactory scholarly studies of the development and popularity of the missionary memoir. Two helpful works are Brumberg, *Mission for Life*, chap. 1, and Joanna Bowen Gillespie, "'The Clear Leadings of Providence': Pious Memoirs and the Problems of Self-Realization for Women in the Early Nineteenth Century," *Journal of the Early Republic* 5 (1985): 197–221. My generalizations about the missionary memoir are based on the works referred to throughout this essay. See especially note 64, below.

60. *Life of Brainerd*, p. 173. On the popularity of the pilgrim theme in Puritan devotional literature and private writings, see Hambrick-Stowe, *Practice of Piety*, chap. 3.

61. *Life of Brainerd*, p. 267.

62. Ibid., p. 204. On the Indian captivity narrative, see Mitchell Robert Breitwieser, *American Puritanism and the Defense of Mourning: Religion, Grief, and Ethnology in Mary White Rowlandson's Captivity Narrative* (Madison, Wis., 1990); Alden T. Vaughan and Edward W. Clark, eds., *Puritans among the Indians: Accounts of Captivity and Redemption, 1676–1724* (Cambridge, Mass., 1981); Hambrick-Stowe, *Practice of Piety*, pp. 256–65; and Richard S. Slotkin, *Regeneration through Violence: The Mythology of the American Frontier, 1600–1860* (Middletown, Conn., 1973).

63. *Life of Brainerd*, pp. 222, 536.

64. Morton, *Memoir of Levi Parsons*.

65. In addition to the memoirs of John Brainerd, Pliny Fisk, Samuel J. Mills, Levi

Parsons, Gordon Hall, and James Brainerd Taylor, already cited, see James Barnett Taylor, *Memoir of Luther Rice, One of the First American Missionaries to the East* (Baltimore, 1840), and the numerous memoirs of Adoniram Judson, who was raised as a Congregationalist, graduated from Andover, and became a Baptist missionary. The Judson hagiography is described in Brumberg, *Mission for Life*, pp. 11–13; see also the inspirational biographies of missionary women, such as James D. Knowles, *Life of Mrs. Ann H. Judson* (Philadelphia, 1830), and Miron Winslow, *A Memoir of Mrs. Harriet Wadsworth Winslow, Thirteen Years a Member of the American Mission in Ceylon* (Boston, 1835).

66. Bond, *Memoir of Pliny Fisk*, p. 259.

67. Johnson, *Printed Writings of Edwards*, pp. 56–59; *Life of Brainerd*, p. 77.

68. Leonard Bacon, *Thirteen Historical Discourses, on the Completion of Two Hundred Years from the Beginning of the First Church in New Haven* (New Haven, Conn., 1839), p. 245.

69. Archibald Alexander, *Biographical Sketches of the Founder and Principal Alumni of the Log College: Together with an Account of the Revivals under Their Ministry* (Philadelphia, 1851), pp. 77–78; *Life of Brainerd*, pp. 55–56.

70. For recent discussions of the rise of this literature, see Nathan O. Hatch, *The Democratization of American Christianity* (New Haven, Conn., 1989), pp. 141–46; R. Laurence Moore, "Religion, Secularization and the Shaping of the Culture Industry in Antebellum America," *American Quarterly* 41 (1989): 216–42; and Brumberg, *Mission for Life*, chap. 3.

71. Richard Rabinowitz, *The Spiritual Self in Everyday Life: The Transformation of Personal Religious Experience in Nineteenth-Century New England* (Boston, 1989), pp. 105–20; David S. Reynolds, "From Doctrine to Narrative: The Rise of Pulpit Storytelling in America," *American Quarterly* 32 (1980): 479–98. See also Cathy N. Davidson, *Revolution and the Word: The Rise of the Novel in America* (New York, 1986).

72. Clark, *Journal and Letters of Francis Asbury*, 1:300; Frank Baker, *From Wesley to Asbury: Studies in Early American Methodism* (Durham, N.C., 1976), p. 71.

73. Quoted in Brumberg, *Missions for Life*, p. xii.

74. See Robert H. Abzug, *Passionate Liberator: Theodore Dwight Weld and the Dilemma of Reform* (New York, 1980), p. 16.

CHAPTER FOUR

1. Kathryn Kish Sklar, "The Founding of Mount Holyoke College," in *Women of America: A History*, ed. Carol Ruth Berkin and Mary Beth Norton (Boston, 1979), pp. 177–201. On women and the Second Great Awakening, see Nancy F. Cott, *The Bonds of Womanhood: "Women's Sphere" in New England, 1780–1835* (New Haven, Conn., 1977); Barbara Leslie Epstein, *The Politics of Domesticity: Women, Evangelism, and Temperance in Nineteenth-Century America* (Middletown, Conn., 1981); Mary P. Ryan, *Cradle of the Middle Class: The Family in Oneida County, New York, 1790–1865* (New York, 1981); Richard D. Shiels, "The Feminization of American Congregational-

ism, 1730–1835," *American Quarterly* 33 (1981): 46–62; and Susan Juster, "'In a Different Voice': Male and Female Narratives of Religious Conversion in Post-Revolutionary America," ibid. 41 (1989): 34–62.

2. Elizabeth Alder Green, *Mary Lyon and the Founding of Mount Holyoke* (Hanover, N.H., 1979), pp. 337–38. Older studies of Lyon also ignore or downplay her Edwardsianism. See, for example, Beth Bradford Gilchrist, *The Life of Mary Lyon* (Boston, 1910). One has to return to mid-nineteenth-century interpretations of Lyon's life to begin to recover the evangelical subculture that profoundly influenced her.

3. Arthur C. Cole, *A Hundred Years of Mount Holyoke College: The Evolution of an Educational Ideal* (New Haven, Conn., 1940), pp. 102–3. A useful recent social history of Mount Holyoke's first students completely ignores the Edwardsian orientation of Lyon and the seminary and sees her as a disciple of Charles G. Finney. See Lisa Natale Drakeman, "Seminary Sisters: Mount Holyoke's First Students, 1837–1849" (Ph.D. diss., Princeton University, 1988).

4. Green, *Mary Lyon and Mount Holyoke*, p. 6. Nineteenth-century works have been particularly helpful in understanding Lyon's life. See, for example, Edward Hitchcock, *The Power of Christian Benevolence Illustrated in the Life and Labors of Mary Lyon* (1851; reprint, Northampton, Mass., 1855), and William Thayer, *Poor Girl and True Woman: or, Elements of Woman's Success Drawn from the Life of Mary Lyon and Others* (Boston, 1859).

5. Joseph A. Conforti, *Samuel Hopkins and the New Divinity Movement: Calvinism, the Congregational Ministry, and Reform in New England between the Great Awakenings* (Grand Rapids, Mich., 1981), chap. 3.

6. Green, *Mary Lyon and Mount Holyoke*, p. 6.

7. Quoted in Sklar, "Founding of Mount Holyoke," p. 6.

8. See earlier pp. 41–42; on Emerson's life, see Ralph Emerson, *Life of Rev. Joseph Emerson, Pastor of the Third Congregational Church in Beverly, Mass., and Subsequently Principal of a Female Seminary* (Boston, 1834).

9. Joseph Emerson, *The Evangelical Primer, Containing a Minor Doctrinal Catechism and a Minor Historical Catechism* . . . (Charlestown, Mass., 1809; reprint, Boston, 1824); Emerson, *Life of Joseph Emerson*, p. 192.

10. Quoted in Sklar, "Founding of Mount Holyoke College," p. 185.

11. Emerson, *Life of Joseph Emerson*, p. 284. See also Fidelia Fisk, *Recollections of Mary Lyon, with Selections from Her Instruction to the Pupils in Mt. Holyoke Female Seminary* (Boston, 1866), pp. 1, 47–50.

12. Green, *Mary Lyon and Mount Holyoke*, pp. 27, 162; Hitchcock, *Power of Christian Benevolence*, p. 389; Emerson, *Life of Joseph Emerson*, p. 154.

13. Hitchcock, *Power of Christian Benevolence*, p. 261; Emerson, *Life of Joseph Emerson*, p. 421. See also Joseph Emerson, *Female Education: A Discourse Delivered at the Dedication of the Seminary Hall in Saugus, January 15, 1822* (Boston, 1822).

14. Green, *Mary Lyon and Mount Holyoke*, p. 26.

15. Sarah D. Stow, *History of Mount Holyoke Seminary, South Hadley, Mass., during the First Half Century, 1837–1887* (South Hadley, Mass., 1887), p. 45; Green, *Mary Lyon and Mount Holyoke*, pp. 127–28. Todd had delivered addresses when the cornerstone

for the Edwards Church was laid and when the building was dedicated. The addresses heaped praise on Edwards (see Chapter 2).

16. Theodore Cuyler, "Mount Holyoke and Mary Lyon," in *Reminiscences of Mary Lyon* (Chicago, 1880), p. 36. Lyon's clerical supporters and fund-raising activities are detailed in Hitchcock, *Power of Christian Benevolence*, pp. 187–238. For an interesting history of the origins and early development of New England men's colleges, including the activities of the evangelical American Education Society (for which Amherst's Heman Humphrey served as president), see David F. Allmendinger, Jr., *Paupers and Scholars: The Transformation of Student Life in Nineteenth-Century New England* (New York, 1975).

17. Hitchcock, *Power of Christian Benevolence*, p. 466.

18. Leonard I. Sweet, *The Minister's Wife: Her Role in Nineteenth-Century American Evangelicalism* (Philadelphia, 1983), p. 38.

19. Jay Leyda, ed., *The Years and Hours of Emily Dickinson*, 2 vols. (New Haven, Conn., 1960), 1:129. On applications and enrollment, see Green, *Mary Lyon and Mount Holyoke*, pp. 170–219, and Fisk, *Recollections of Mary Lyon*, p. 115. On the backgrounds of Mount Holyoke students, see Stow, *History of Mount Holyoke*, p. 21; Drakeman, "Seminary Sisters," pp. 239–52; and David F. Allmendinger, "Mount Holyoke Students Encounter the Need for Life Planning, 1837–1850," *History of Education Quarterly* 19 (1979): 27–43; see also Allmendinger, *Paupers and Scholars*, for the modest social backgrounds of students at New England's provincial men's colleges.

20. Quoted in Louise Porter Thomas, *Seminary Militant: An Account of the Missionary Movement at Mount Holyoke Seminary and College* (South Hadley, Mass., 1937), p. 25.

21. Heman Humphrey, *The Shining Path: A Sermon Preached in South Hadley at the Funeral of Miss Mary Lyon, March 8, 1849* (Northampton, Mass., 1849), p. 14; Allmendinger, *Paupers and Scholars*, p. 119.

22. Hitchcock, *Power of Christian Benevolence*, pp. 23, 132–57; Green, *Mary Lyon and Mount Holyoke*, p. 26.

23. Fisk, *Recollections of Mary Lyon*, pp. 77–78.

24. Ibid., p. 260; see also Cuyler, *Reminiscences of Mary Lyon*, p. 30.

25. Fisk, *Recollections of Mary Lyon*, pp. 93, 104; Hitchcock, *Power of Christian Benevolence*, p. 453.

26. Quoted in Drakeman, "Seminary Sisters," p. 86; see also Fisk, *Recollections of Mary Lyon*, pp. 103–4, 148–79; and Green, *Mary Lyon and Mount Holyoke*, pp. 279–81.

27. Quoted in Drakeman, "Seminary Sisters," p. 95.

28. Quoted in Green, *Mary Lyon and Mount Holyoke*, p. 285; see also Leyda, *Emily Dickinson*, 1:136–40.

29. Quoted in Drakeman, "Seminary Sisters," p. 141; see also Green, *Mary Lyon and Mount Holyoke*, pp. 247–48.

30. Hitchcock, *Power of Christian Benevolence*, p. 247; Fisk, *Recollections of Mary Lyon*, pp. 183–84. On Fisk, alumna, teacher, and the first single woman from Mount Holyoke to become a foreign missionary, see D. T. Fiske, *Faith Working by Love: A Memoir of Miss Fidelia Fiske* (Boston, 1868).

31. Hitchcock, *Power of Christian Benevolence*, p. 483.

32. Quoted by Leyda, *Emily Dickinson*, 1:132. I am indebted to Drakeman for her suggestive discussion of Lyon as a moral philosopher at Mount Holyoke; see "Seminary Sisters," pp. 45–47. Unfortunately, Drakeman completely ignores the Edwardsian Calvinist foundations of Lyon's moral philosophy. Amherst's Edward Hitchcock offers the most accurate description of Lyon's theology: "Her doctrinal system was that of Calvinism, as explained by the ablest American divines. Her expositions to her school, however, were highly practical, and she took no great interest in discussions merely speculative. In the skeletons of her discourses you see but few formal statements and defenses of doctrines. But these formed the foundation on which rested her instructions, and from which she drew her strongest appeals" (*Power of Christian Benevolence*, p. 454).

33. Fisk, *Recollections of Mary Lyon*, p. 104.

34. Ann Douglas, *The Feminization of American Culture* (New York, 1977). Susan Juster has recently argued, after analyzing conversion narratives written during the Second Great Awakening, that the religious "process of self-abasement and unconditional surrender" to the Divine may be seen as an "allegorical rendering of prevailing notions of gender and authoritarian relations." Evangelical men, far more than women, appear to have been attracted to a legalistic, contractual, "rule-governed" approach to salvation consistent with the piety to moralism transition in American theology. See Juster, "'In a Different Voice,'" pp. 34, 39, 47. See also Richard Rabinowitz's discussion of female devotionalism and quest for personal holiness in *The Spiritual Self in Everyday Life: The Transformation of Personal Religious Experience in Nineteenth-Century New England* (Boston, 1989), pp. 153–216.

35. See Abigail Hutchinson's and Sarah Edwards's conversions in Jonathan Edwards, *The Great Awakening: A Faithful Narrative*, ed. C. C. Goen, vol. 4 of *Works of Jonathan Edwards*, 13 vols. (New Haven, Conn., 1972), pp. 191–99, 331–41. On Edwards's promotion of female spirituality, see the discussion in Carol F. Karlsen and Laurie Crumpacker, eds., *The Journal of Esther Edwards Burr, 1754–1757* (New Haven, Conn., 1984), pp. 6–7, 21, and Amanda Porterfield, *Feminine Spirituality in America: From Sarah Edwards to Martha Graham* (Philadelphia, 1980), esp. 42–44; see also Porterfield, *Female Piety in Puritan New England* (New York, 1992). On Hopkins, see Edwards A. Park, *Memoir of the Life and Character of Samuel Hopkins, D.D. . . .* (Boston, 1852), p. 21; S. E. Dwight, *The Life of President Edwards*, vol. 1 of *The Works of President Edwards, with a Memoir*, ed. Sereno E. Dwight, 10 vols. (New York, 1829), p. 176; also see Stephen West, ed., *Sketches of the Life of the Late Rev. Samuel Hopkins, D.D.* (Hartford, Conn., 1805), pp. 41–42; and Charles E. Hambrick-Stowe, "The Spiritual Pilgrimage of Sarah Osborn (1714–1796)," *Church History* 61 (December 1992): 408–21.

36. Conforti, *Samuel Hopkins and the New Divinity Movement*, chaps. 7–8; Mark Valeri, "The Economic Thought of Jonathan Edwards," *Church History* 60 (1991): 54. For a suggestive recent work that explores the relationship between evangelical religion and a changing economic order, see David G. Hackett, *The Rude Hand of Innovation: Religion and Social Order in Albany, New York, 1652–1836* (New York, 1991).

37. Hitchcock, *Power of Christian Benevolence*, p. 235. Hitchcock reprinted Lyon's fund-raising circulars.

38. Ibid.

39. Quoted in Sklar, "Founding of Mount Holyoke College," p. 196.

40. Hitchcock, *Power of Christian Benevolence*, pp. 212–13.

41. Lyon, *A Missionary Offering, or Christian Sympathy, Personal Responsibility, and the Present Crisis in Foreign Missions* (Boston, 1843), p. 48.

42. Green, *Mary Lyon and Mount Holyoke*, p. 285.

43. Lyon, *A Missionary Offering*, pp. 58–59.

44. Drakeman, "Seminary Sisters," pp. 66–102, offers a good description of how Mount Holyoke was organized as a household. Helen Lefkowitz Horowitz argues that the architecture of the Seminary differed from buildings at male colleges. The seminary building "followed the form of a large dwelling house." The architecture helped establish the seminary as a "hierarchical," "well-governed home" that restricted individual autonomy. In Horowitz's view Lyon created a "total institution" that drew its inspiration from the nineteenth-century asylum. See *Alma Mater: Design and Experience in the Women's Colleges from Their Nineteenth-Century Beginnings to the 1930s* (New York, 1984), pp. 21–22, 25. I see Lyon's efforts far less rooted in a nineteenth-century environmental-institutional approach to reform than in a traditional, even reactionary, framework derived from her own social and religious experience.

45. Fisk, *Recollections of Mary Lyon*, pp. 37, 108.

46. Leyda, *Emily Dickinson*, 1:129; see also Drakeman, "Seminary Sisters," esp. pp. 65–77.

47. This is Leonard Sweet's term; see *The Minister's Wife*, p. 91. Thomas, *Seminary Militant*, is a helpful study of missionary activity at Mount Holyoke.

48. Lyon, *A Missionary Offering*, pp. 16, 27.

49. Jonathan Edwards, *A History of the Work of Redemption*, ed. John F. Wilson, vol. 9 of *Works of Jonathan Edwards* (New Haven, Conn., 1989), p. 472.

50. Ibid., p. 483. On Edwards's globalism, see Gerald R. McDermott, *One Holy and Happy Society: The Public Theology of Jonathan Edwards* (University Park, Pa., 1992).

51. Lyon, *A Missionary Offering*, p. 27; Fisk, *Recollections of Mary Lyon*, p. 171. For the reference to the hanging of maps and for a helpful discussion of Lyon's attraction to Edwards's millennialism, I am indebted to the unpublished work of Amanda Porterfield, including "Mount Holyoke Missionaries, 1840–1860," a paper presented at the annual meeting of the American Academy of Religion, Washington, D.C., November 1993.

52. Lyon, *A Missionary Offering*, pp. 52–53, 83, 95–96.

53. Ibid., p. 16. Harriet Newell, nineteen-year-old missionary wife who died in 1812 en route to India, was one early evangelical heroine. See Leonard Woods, *Sermon Preached at Haverhill, Mass., in Remembrance of Mrs. Harriet Newell . . . To Which Are Added Memoirs of Her Life* (Boston, 1814).

54. E. W. Hooker, *The Cultivation of the Missionary Spirit in Our Literary and Theological Institutions* (Boston, 1845), p. 10. For one female missionary who left a record of the influence of Edwards's writings and piety on her, see [Louisa Hawes],

Memoir of Mrs. Mary E. Van Lennep, Only Daughter of the Rev. Joel Hawes, D.D., and Wife of the Rev. Henry J. Van Lennep, Missionary in Turkey, by Her Mother (Hartford, 1847), pp. 78–79, 179. Van Lennep's popular memoir went through six editions by 1854.

55. Norman Pettit, ed., *The Life of Brainerd*, vol. 7 of *Works of Jonathan Edwards* (New Haven, Conn., 1985), pp. 70–73, 474n.

56. David Dudley Field, *The Genealogy of the Brainerd Family in the United States* (New York, 1857), p. 283. The romanticizing of the Brainerd-Jerusha relationship is discussed in Patricia J. Tracy, "The Romance of David Brainerd and Jerusha Edwards," in *Three Essays in Honor of the Publication of "The Life of David Brainerd,"* ed. Wilson H. Kimnach (New Haven, Conn., 1985), pp. 28–36. On Mount Holyoke students' "excursions to the gravesite," see Green, *Mary Lyon and Mount Holyoke*, p. 285.

57. Patricia Grimshaw, *Paths of Duty: American Missionary Wives in Nineteenth-Century Hawaii* (Honolulu, 1989), esp. chap. 1; see also Mary Zwiep, *Pilgrim Path: The First Company of Women Missionaries to Hawaii* (Madison, Wis., 1991); and R. Pierce Beaver, *American Protestant Women in World Mission: History of the First Feminist Movement in North America* (Grand Rapids, Mich., 1968).

58. See, for example, William B. O. Peabody, *David Brainerd*, vol. 8 of *The Library of American Biography*, ed. Jared Sparks (New York, 1837), pp. 363–65.

59. Joan J. Brumberg, *Mission for Life: The Story of the Family of Adoniram Judson* (New York, 1980), pp. 41–42.

60. Quoted in Thomas, *Seminary Militant*, p. 35.

61. Drakeman, "Seminary Sisters," chap. 6; Green, *Mary Lyon and Mount Holyoke*, pp. 252–55; and Fisk, *Recollections of Mary Lyon*, pp. 172–73.

62. Quoted in Thomas, *Seminary Militant*, p. 41.

63. Grimshaw, *Paths of Duty*, p. 9.

64. Fisk, *Recollections of Mary Lyon*, pp. 161–74; Hitchcock, *Power of Christian Benevolence*, pp. 346–71; Cuyler, "Mount Holyoke and Mary Lyon," p. 36; Thomas, *Seminary Militant*, pp. 29–35.

65. Jonathan Edwards, *Account of Abigail Hutchinson, A Young Woman, Hopefully Converted at Northampton, Mass., 1734* (Andover, Mass., 1816); Thomas Johnson, ed., *The Printed Writings of Jonathan Edwards: A Bibliography* (1940; reprint, New York, 1968), pp. 103–4.

66. American Sunday School Union, *The Life of President Edwards* (Philadelphia, 1832), p. 123; Dwight, *Life of Edwards*, pp. 171–89; Samuel Miller, *Life of Jonathan Edwards*, vol. 8 of *Library of American Biography*, ed. Sparks (New York, 1837), pp. 12, 55–56. The "companion" description is used by Leonard Sweet, who also quotes the marriage manual; see *The Minister's Wife*, p. 26.

67. This female hagiography included missionary memoirs and works such as the following: T. Sharp, *The Heavenly Sisters, or Biographical Sketches of the Lives of Eminently Pious Females . . .* (New Haven, Conn., 1822); Samuel L. Knapp, *Female Biography: Containing Notices of Distinguished Women in Different Nations and Ages* (New York, 1834); and Sarah Josepha Hale, *Women's Record: or Sketches of Distinguished Women, from Creation to A.D. 1854* (New York, 1854).

68. See *Memorial: Twenty-Fifth Anniversary of the Mount Holyoke Female Seminary* (South Hadley, Mass., 1862).

69. Sklar, "Founding of Mount Holyoke College," p. 198.

70. Lyon, *A Missionary Offering*, pp. 65, 84; Green, *Mary Lyon and Mount Holyoke*, pp. 258–59.

71. Quoted in Green, *Mary Lyon and Mount Holyoke*, p. 305.

CHAPTER FIVE

1. Donald M. Scott, *From Office to Profession: The New England Ministry, 1750–1850* (Philadelphia, 1978), esp. chaps. 4, 7; Bruce Kuklick, *Churchmen and Philosophers: From Jonathan Edwards to John Dewey* (New Haven, Conn., 1985), chap. 14; and Daniel Calhoun, *Professional Lives in America: Structure and Aspiration, 1750–1850* (Cambridge, Mass., 1965), pp. 135–45, 157–66.

2. Charles Hodge, "Professor Park and the Princeton Review," *Biblical Repertory and Princeton Review* 23 (October 1851): 687.

3. Thomas Johnson, ed., *The Printed Writings of Jonathan Edwards: A Bibliography* (1940; reprint, New York, 1968), pp. 64–71; Mark A. Noll, "Jonathan Edwards and Nineteenth-Century Theology," in *Jonathan Edwards and the American Experience*, ed. Nathan O. Hatch and Harry S. Stout (New York, 1988), esp. p. 270.

4. This is the judgment, for example, of Allan C. Guelzo's otherwise superb *Edwards on the Will: A Century of American Theological Debate* (Middletown, Conn., 1989), chaps. 6, 7.

5. Park composed "Autobiographical Fragments," which are now lost but were quoted by Frank H. Foster, *The Life of Edwards Amasa Park* (New York, 1936). The quotation is on p. 31. The most recent biographical study of Park is Anthony C. Cecil, Jr., *The Theological Development of Edwards Amasa Park: Last of the "Consistent Calvinists"* (Missoula, Mont., 1974). Helpful biographical material is also found in R. S. Storrs, *Professor Park and His Pupils . . .* (Boston, 1899); Storrs, *Edwards A. Park: A Memorial Address* (Boston, 1900); and Alexander McKenzie, *Memoir of Professor Edwards Amasa Park* (Cambridge, Mass., 1901).

6. See Park, "Miscellaneous Reflections of a Visitor upon the Character of Dr. Emmons," in *The Works of Nathanael Emmons*, ed. Jacob Ide, 7 vols. (Boston, 1842), 1:cxxvii–clxxii.

7. Storrs, *Edwards A. Park*, pp. 27–30.

8. Leonard Woods, *History of the Andover Theological Seminary* (Boston, 1885), p. 134. See also Park, *A Memorial of the Semi-Centennial Celebration of the Founding of the Theological Seminary at Andover* (Andover, Mass., 1859); Henry K. Rowe, *History of Andover Seminary* (Newton, Mass., 1933); and Harold Young Vanderpool, "The Andover Conservatives: Apologetics, Biblical Criticism and Theological Change at Andover Theological Seminary, 1808–1880" (Ph.D. diss., Harvard University, 1971).

9. Woods, *History of Andover*, pp. 31–43.

10. Storrs, *Memorial Address*, pp. 36–37. Park replaced Storrs's father, a family

friend who had taken a temporary leave to work for the Home Missionary Society.

11. Scholars, such as Bruce Kuklick in *Churchmen and Philosophers*, pp. 209–14, have overemphasized Park's debt to Taylor and therefore downplayed his extension of and dependence on New Divinity tradition. Cecil, *Theological Development of Park*, seems unsure, even confused at times about Park's relationship to Taylor; he concludes (pp. 268–73) that Park was both an Edwardsian and a Taylorite. Cecil's interpretation of Park's theological development is marred by his seeming unfamiliarity with New Divinity theology after Edwards. In "Nestor of Orthodoxy, New England Style: A Study in the Theology of Edwards Amasa Park, 1808–1900" (Ph.D. diss., Drew University, 1969), Kenneth Rowe examines Park's theology in relationship to the familiar piety to moralism thesis. Frank H. Foster's view is more helpful, though he – like all students of Park – was hampered by the fact that Park never published works of systematic theology. Foster argued that in spite of Taylor's influence, Park held to the "previous certainty of all events which actually occur. To maintain this, he also maintained Edwards's theory of the Will, not following Taylor into his modification in the interest of freedom." See Foster, "The New England Theology," in *The New Schaff-Herzog Encyclopedia of Religious Knowledge*, ed. Samuel McCauley Jackson, 12 vols. (New York, 1910), 8:139. In *A Genetic History of New England Theology* (Chicago, 1907), a sometimes confusing and wordy discussion of Park's theology, Foster acknowledges Taylor's influence. Foster, though a student of Park, was writing from a post-Calvinist perspective sympathetic to Taylor. Foster concluded that Park allowed the "overshadowing influence of Edwards" to undermine "the constructive process so actively proceeding." As a result, after Taylor, Park "maintain[ed] the historic attitude at the expense of perfect clearness and dogmatic success" (Foster, *A Genetic History*, p. 258).

12. Porter, *Letters on the Religious Revivals which Prevailed about the Beginning of the Present Century* (Boston, 1858). This was a reprint of Porter's letters that had appeared in the *Spirit of the Pilgrims* between 1832 and 1833. For Park's view of doctrine and preaching, see "Connection between Theological Study and Pulpit Eloquence," *American Biblical Repository* 10 (July 1837): 169–91.

13. Quoted in Frank Luther Mott, *A History of American Magazines, 1741–1850*, 5 vols. (Cambridge, Mass., 1957), 1:740. See also Cecil, *Theological Development of Park*, pp. 25–26.

14. Quoted in Mott, *History of American Magazines*, 1:740.

15. These figures are taken from Glenn T. Miller, *Piety and Intellect: The Aims and Purposes of Ante-Bellum Theological Education* (Atlanta, Ga., 1990), p. 201. Woods, *History of Andover*, p. 138, contains enrollment figures down to 1846.

16. Jay Leyda, ed., *The Years and Hours of Emily Dickinson*, 2 vols. (New Haven, Conn., 1960), 1:287. For one seminary professor's recruitment trips to New England colleges, see the account in *The Autobiography of Enoch Pond, D.D. . . .* , edited and with an introduction by Rev. Edwin Pond Parker, D.D. (Boston, 1883), p. 73.

17. See the suggestive figures in Scott, *From Office to Profession*, p. 114. "Of the matriculants of Andover Theological Seminary from 1815 through 1835," Scott notes,

"only 48 of 631, or 6 percent, held a single clerical post of any kind for their entire clerical career, and about 40 percent of these were nonpastoral positions, particularly pro-
fessorships and foreign missionary assignments." See also Woods, *History of Andover*,
pp. 198–202, and the biographical information in *General Catalogue of the Theological
Seminary, Andover, Massachusetts, 1808–1908* (Boston, 1909), pp. 241–302, for students of the 1850s.

18. The most suggestive discussion of the history of the term "New England theology" is found in Enoch Pond, *Sketches of the Theological History of New England*
(Boston, 1880), esp. p. 58. Compare his account of theological developments behind
the founding of Andover with Woods's *History of Andover*, chap. 2. See also Edwards
A. Park, "New England Theology," *Bibliotheca Sacra* 9 (January 1852): 174–76.

19. See, for example, Park, "The Duties of a Theologian," *American Biblical Repository* 2 (October 1839): 374, 380.

20. See, for example, Edward Beecher, "The Works of Samuel Hopkins," *Bibliotheca
Sacra* 10 (January 1853): 63–82; Daniel Fiske, "New England Theology," ibid. 22 (July
1865): 467–512, and (October 1865): 568–88.

21. The best introduction to Pond's activities and to the history of Bangor Seminary
is in *Autobiography of Pond*; see esp. chaps. 6 and 7.

22. See *Sketches of Theological History*, pp. 60–70, for Pond's doctrinal summary of
the New England theology.

23. Park, "Duties of a Theologian," p. 354.

24. Ibid., p. 380; Fiske, "New England Theology," p. 469.

25. Noll, "Edwards and Nineteenth-Century Theology," p. 263.

26. Noah Porter, "The Princeton Review on Dr. Taylor and the Edwardean Theology," *New Englander* 18 (August 1860): 739. George Park Fisher became Yale's most
perceptive critic of both Park and Princeton. Several of his major essays on the New
England theology that appeared in the *New Englander* were reprinted in *Discussions in
History and Theology* (New York, 1880).

27. Park, "New England Theology," p. 175; Pond, *Sketches of Theological History*,
chap. 3.

28. Lawrence Buell, *New England Literary Culture: From Revolution through Renaissance* (New York, 1986), chaps. 8, 9.

29. Park, "Duties of a Theologian," p. 348. See also [Edwards A. Park and B. B. Ed-
wards], "Thoughts on the State of Theological Science and Education in Our Country," *Bibliotheca Sacra* 1 (November 1844): 735–67, and Cecil, *Theological Development
of Park*, chap. 3.

30. Park, "Theology of the Intellect and That of the Feelings," *Bibliotheca Sacra* 7
(July 1850): 545.

31. Ibid., pp. 537, 551; see also [Edwards A. Park and B. B. Edwards], "Natural Theology," *Bibliotheca Sacra* 3 (May 1846): 241–76; on the commonsense philosophy in the
nineteenth century, see Mark A. Noll, "Common Sense Traditions and American
Evangelical Thought," *American Quarterly* 37 (Summer 1985): 216–38.

32. For Hodge's initial response, which touched off the controversy, see "Review of

Professor Park's Discourse," *Biblical Repertory and Princeton Review* 22 (October 1850): 642–74. The dispute is detailed in Cecil, *Theological Development of Park*, chap. 6, and Noll, "Edwards and Nineteenth-Century Theology," pp. 262–69.

33. Joseph Haroutunian, *Piety versus Moralism: The Passing of the New England Theology* (New York, 1932), pp. xxx, 305n. Foster, *A Genetic History of New England Theology*, is another standard work. A more recent attempt at a general history is a derivative, disappointing work; see Robert C. Whittemore, *The Transformation of the New England Theology* (New York, 1987).

34. Recent revisionist work includes William K. Breitenbach, "The Consistent Calvinism of the New Divinity Movement," *William and Mary Quarterly* 41 (April 1984): 241–64; Breitenbach, "Unregenerate Doings: Selflessness and Selfishness in New Divinity Theology," *American Quarterly* 34 (Winter 1982): 479–502; Breitenbach, "Piety *and* Moralism: Edwards and the New Divinity," in *Jonathan Edwards and the American Experience*, ed. Hatch and Stout, pp. 177–204; Guelzo, *Edwards on the Will*, esp. chaps. 3, 4; and Mark Valeri, *Law and Providence in Joseph Bellamy's New England: The Origins of the New Divinity in Revolutionary America* (New York, 1994). See also Donald Louis Weber, *Rhetoric and History in Revolutionary New England* (New York, 1988).

35. Edwards A. Park, *Memoir of Nathanael Emmons, with Sketches of His Friends and Pupils* (Boston, 1861), p. 430.

36. Park, "New England Theology," p. 212. For similar statements about the balance of divine sovereignty and moral accountability in the New England theology, see Pond, *Sketches of Theological History*, pp. 60–62, and Fiske, "New England Theology," pp. 472–95, 584.

37. Jonathan Edwards, *The Freedom of the Will*, ed. Paul Ramsey, vol. 1 of *Works of Jonathan Edwards*, 13 vols. (New Haven, Conn., 1957), pp. 156–57, 159.

38. Ibid., pp. 156, 159.

39. Park, "New England Theology," pp. 177, 178; Park, "Unity amid Diversities of Belief, Even on Imputed and Involuntary Sin," *Bibliotheca Sacra* 8 (July 1851): 604–5; Enoch Pond, "Review of Edwards on the Will," *Literary and Theological Review* 1 (December 1834): 523–39; and Pond, "Natural and Moral Ability and Inability," *New Englander* 13 (May 1855): 387–96. The best discussions of the impact of *Freedom of the Will* on the New Divinity men are Guelzo, *Edwards on the Will*, esp. 122, and Breitenbach, "Consistent Calvinism," pp. 256–64.

40. Fiske, "New England Theology," p. 506.

41. Park, *Memoir of Emmons*, p. 341; Park, "New England Theology," p. 179.

42. Park, "New England Theology," p. 175; Park "Unity amid Diversities," p. 605.

43. C. A. Salmond, *Charles and A. A. Hodge, with Class and Table Talk of Hodge the Younger* (New York, n.d.), p. 177n; see also Hodge, "Park and the Princeton Review," p. 693; and for an earlier Princeton critique of the New England emphasis on natural ability, see "The Power of the Contrary Choice," *Biblical Repertory and Princeton Review* 12 (October 1840): 532–49.

44. Park, "New England Theology," p. 188; see also Pond, "Natural and Moral Ability," pp. 387–96.

45. Guelzo, *Edwards on the Will*, p. 16.

46. Fiske, "New England Theology," pp. 494–95; see also the discussion in Breitenbach, "Consistent Calvinism," pp. 250–52; for a still useful general history, see H. Shelton Smith, *Changing Conceptions of Original Sin: A Study in American Theology Since 1750* (New York, 1955).

47. Park, "New England Theology," pp. 193, 206; Park, "Remarks on the Biblical Repertory and Princeton Review," *Bibliotheca Sacra* 8 (January 1851): 166–67.

48. Jonathan Edwards, *The Great Doctrine of Original Sin*, ed. Clyde Holbrook, vol. 3 of *Works of Jonathan Edwards* (New Haven, Conn., 1970), pp. 96, 389, 408.

49. Park, "New England Theology," p. 205; Pond, *Sketches of Theological History*, pp. 60–63.

50. Samuel Hopkins, *System of Doctrines Contained in Divine Revelation, Explained and Defended, with a Treatise on the Millennium*, 2 vols. (Boston, 1793), 1:268.

51. For the heavy use of Hopkins's works to develop the New England view of original sin, see Park, "New England Theology," pp. 200–201, and Fiske, "New England Theology," pp. 498–500.

52. Hopkins, *System of Doctrines*, 1:268.

53. Lyman Atwater, "Old Orthodoxy, New Divinity and Unitarianism," *Biblical Repertory and Princeton Review* 29 (October 1857): 568. Two early New England critics of Park's interpretation of the New England theology were Daniel Dana, Old Calvinist minister in Newburyport, and Nathan Lord, president of Dartmouth College. Dana wrote a series of articles critical of Park in the 1850s; see, for example, "Andover Theological Seminary," *Congregationalist* 2 (July 12, 1850): 109, 110. Lord authored *A Letter to the Rev. Daniel Dana on Professor Park's Theology of New England* (Boston, 1852).

54. Guelzo, *Edwards on the Will*, p. 134, offers a good discussion of the connection between natural ability and the new view of the atonement. For a general history, see Dorus Paul Rudisill, *The Doctrine of the Atonement in Jonathan Edwards and His Successors* (New York, 1971).

55. Joseph Bellamy, *True Religion Delineated*, in *Works of Joseph Bellamy, D.D. . . . with a Memoir of His Life and Character*, ed. Tryon Edwards, 2 vols. (Boston, 1850), 1:292. Edwards A. Park, *The Atonement: Discourses and Treatises by Edwards, Smalley, Maxcy, Emmons, Griffin, Burge and Weeks, with an Introductory Essay* (Boston, 1859), pp. x–xi; see also Park, "The Prominence of the Atonement," in *Discourses on Some Theological Doctrines Related to the Religious Character* (Andover, Mass., 1885), pp. 45–68.

56. Park, *The Atonement*, p. lxiv. For the younger Edwards's development of the governmental theory, see *Three Sermons on the Necessity of the Atonement, and Its Consistency with Free Grace in Forgiveness*, in *The Works of Jonathan Edwards, D.D., with a Memoir of His Life and Character*, ed. Tryon Edwards, 2 vols. (Andover, Mass., 1842), 2:11–52; see also Robert L. Ferm, *Jonathan Edwards the Younger, 1745–1801: A Colonial Pastor* (Grand Rapids, Mich., 1976), chap. 7.

57. Park, *The Atonement*, pp. xi–xii. For one historical interpretation of the atonement that drew heavily on Park, see Fiske, "New England Theology," pp. 577–84.

58. Park, *The Atonement*, p. xlvii; Bellamy, *True Religion Delineated*, pp. 259, 285,

292. The best treatment of Bellamy's theology is in Valeri, *Law and Providence in Joseph Bellamy's New England,* chaps. 2, 4; on the possible New Divinity influence on Edwards's views of the atonement, see Guelzo, *Edwards on the Will,* pp. 134–35.

59. Park, *The Atonement,* pp. lxii–lxiii; see also Hopkins, *System of Doctrines,* 1:398, 408; 2:60, 61.

60. Parson Cooke, "Edwards on the Atonement," *American Theological Review* 2 (February 1860): 107, 108. See also [Cooke], *Views in New England Theology No. I: The New England Theology Contrasted with the New Arminianism* (Boston, 1859), and [Cooke], *Views in New England Theology No. II: The New Apostasy, or a Word to the Laodiceans* (Boston, 1860).

61. See George Park Fisher, "Professor Park's Memoir of Dr. Emmons," *New Englander* 19 (July 1861): 720–21.

62. Park, *Memoir of the Life and Character of Samuel Hopkins, D.D. . . .* (Boston, 1852), p. 211; Park, "Remarks on the Biblical Repertory and Princeton Review," p. 163; and Park, *Memoir of Emmons,* pp. 394–96. On Hopkins's doctrine of disinterested benevolence and the willingness to be damned, see Joseph A. Conforti, *Samuel Hopkins and the New Divinity Movement: Calvinism, the Congregational Ministry, and Reform in New England between the Great Awakenings* (Grand Rapids, Mich., 1981), chap. 7.

63. Park, "New England Theology," p. 189n.

64. Park, *Memoir of Emmons,* p. 365; Fiske, "New England Theology," p. 492; see also Park's careful discussion of the epigram in "New England Theology," pp. 192–95, where he attempted to counter what he saw as Princeton's interpretation of "moral exercises" as "moral acts." Helpful recent discussions of the exercise-taste controversy are James Hoopes, "Calvinism and Consciousness from Edwards to Beecher," in *Jonathan Edwards and the American Experience,* ed. Hatch and Stout, pp. 216–18; Guelzo, *Edwards on the Will,* pp. 109–10, 214–15; and Kuklick, *Churchmen and Philosophers,* pp. 55–59.

65. Park, *Memoir of Hopkins,* p. 200.

66. See Nathanael Emmons, "Man's Activity and Dependence Illustrated" and "God Sovereign in Man's Formation," in *Works,* ed. Jacob Ide, 7 vols. (Boston, 1842), 4:355–56, 366, 373, 387, 397. See also E. Smalley, "The Theology of Emmons," *Bibliotheca Sacra* 7 (April 1850): 253–80 and (July 1850): 479–501.

67. Edwards incorporated the idea of "continual creation" into *Original Sin,* where he argued that God creates all things "out of nothing at each moment of their existence" (p. 401).

68. See Park's discussion of Burton in *Memoir of Emmons,* p. 378. Foster, *A Genetic History* (p. 259), claims that Park adopted the threefold division, but he offers no evidence to support his claims, though Park's views may have changed by the mid-1870s when Foster was his student. Foster also seems unable to decide (pp. 504–6) whether Park was a taster or an exerciser.

69. Park, "New England Theology," p. 198. For the background of Edwards's criticism of this type of circular reasoning, see Kuklick, *Churchmen and Philosophers,* p. 57.

70. Park, "New England Theology," p. 201; see Hopkins's views in *Two Discourses:*

I. On the Necessity of the Knowledge of the Law of God, in Order to the Knowledge of Sin. II. A Particular and Critical Inquiry into the Cause, Nature, and Means of That Change in Which Men Are Born of God (Boston, 1768), pp. 38, 48, 50.

71. Park, "New England Theology," pp. 203–5; Park, "Unity amid Diversities," p. 627; Park, *Memoir of Emmons*, pp. 412–13.

72. Park, "New England Theology," p. 197.

73. Fiske, "New England Theology," p. 484; Park, "New England Theology," pp. 196, 200; [Park et al.], "President Edwards's Dissertation on the Nature of True Virtue," *Bibliotheca Sacra* 10 (October 1853): 717.

74. Fiske, "New England Theology," p. 569; Park, "New England Theology," p. 202; Park, *Memoir of Emmons*, pp. 405–6.

75. Hopkins, *An Inquiry Concerning the Promises of the Gospel: Whether Any of Them Are Made to the Exercises and Doings of Persons in an Unregenerate State . . .* (Boston, 1765), pp. 54, 78–79; Fiske, "New England Theology," p. 574.

76. Bruce Kuklick, for example, insists that Park was essentially a Taylorite. He draws heavily on Henry Boynton Smith's review of Park's *Memoir of Emmons* and concludes that the Abbot Professor was trying to associate the great exerciser with Taylor (*Churchmen and Philosophers*, pp. 59n, 212–15). In fact, Park attempted to disassociate Emmons from the New Haven theology; see *Memoir of Emmons*, pp. 383, 403n, 420. As a Hopkinsian, Park obviously had difficulty with Taylor's acceptance of self-love and other New Haven positions.

77. Park to Bancroft, quoted in Donald Louis Weber, "The Image of Jonathan Edwards in American Culture" (Ph.D. diss., Columbia University, 1978), p. 156n. Stowe is quoted in Joan Hedrick, *Harriet Beecher Stowe: A Life* (New York, 1994), p. 284. On the designation "Hopkinsian," see Henry Boynton Smith, "The Theological System of Emmons," *American Theological Review* 13 (January 1862): 49–53. Smith tries to distinguish between "old" and "New" or "modern" Hopkinsians.

78. These biographical sketches are too numerous to cite. See the bibliography in Cecil, *Theological Development of Park*, pp. 297–300. Park also contributed essays on New England theology to these works. See, for example, "New England Theology," in *A Religious Encyclopaedia; or, Dictionary of Biblical, Historical, and Practical Theology*, 3d ed., ed. Philip Schaff, 10 vols. (New York, 1891), 3:1634–38.

79. See the advertising publication list at the end of Park's *The Atonement*. The memoirs mentioned have already been cited, except for the two on Hopkins that preceded Park's work; see John Ferguson, *Memoir of the Life and Character of the Rev. Samuel Hopkins, D.D. . . . .* (Boston, 1830), and William Patten, *Reminiscences of the Late Rev. Samuel Hopkins, D.D. . . . .* (Boston, 1843).

80. Park, *Memoir of Hopkins*, p. 200.

81. This is Edward Beecher in his *Bibliotheca Sacra* review of Park's edition of Hopkins's *Works*, summarizing the Princeton perspective; "The Works of Samuel Hopkins," p. 63. See also Hodge, "Park and the Princeton Review," pp. 674–94.

82. Park, *Memoir of Hopkins*, p. 116; Park was quoting the Quaker poet-abolitionist John Greenleaf Whittier. For the less than heroic context of Hopkins's antislavery activities, see Conforti, *Samuel Hopkins and the New Divinity Movement*, pp. 126–28.

83. Leonard Bacon, "Prof. Park's Memoir of Hopkins," *New Englander* 10 (August 1852): 471.

84. Beecher, "Works of Samuel Hopkins," p. 66.

85. Park, *Memoir of Hopkins*, p. 110.

86. In addition to the sympathetic reviews of Bacon and Beecher cited above, see the negative Unitarian review by George E. Ellis, "Prof. Park's Memoir of Hopkins," *Christian Examiner and Religious Miscellany* 54 (January 1853): 123–30.

87. Smith, "Theological System of Emmons," p. 9.

88. Park, *Memoir of Emmons*, pp. 32–33, 60, 176–88, 355.

89. Ibid., pp. 215, 263; sketches of Emmons's students are on pp. 222–62.

90. Enoch Pond, *Lectures on Christian Theology* (Boston, 1867). The only extended study of Emmons is John Terrence Dahlquist, "Nathanael Emmons: His Life and Work" (Ph.D. diss., Boston University, 1963).

91. Smith, "Theological System of Emmons," p. 13; see also Fiske, "New England Theology," p. 492.

92. Park, *Memoir of Emmons*, pp. 384, 408, 411.

93. Ibid., pp. 387, 402.

94. Ibid., pp. 386, 417.

95. Ibid., pp. 379, 412.

96. Enoch Pond, "The Life and Character of Emmons," *American Theological Review* 3 (October 1861): 633; other reviews include Smith, "Theological System of Emmons"; Fisher, "Memoir of Emmons"; and George E. Ellis, "Memoir of Nathanael Emmons," *Christian Examiner and Religious Miscellany* 61 (September 1861): 287–91.

97. See Foster, *Life of Park*, pp. 87, 169; Cecil, *Theological Development of Park*, p. 55.

98. [Lyman Atwater], "Modern Explanations of the Doctrine of Ability," *Biblical Repertory and Princeton Review* 26 (April 1854): 219; Atwater, "Jonathan Edwards and the Successive Forms of the New Divinity," ibid. 30 (October 1858): 589, 599; see also Atwater, "Old Orthodoxy, New Divinity, and Unitarianism," pp. 561–98.

99. Edward Lawrence, "New England Theology Historically Considered," *American Theological Review* 2 (May 1860): 210–11; Lawrence, "The Old School in New England Theology," *Bibliotheca Sacra* 20 (April 1863): 312; Lawrence, "The New England Theology: The Edwardean Period," *American Theological Review* 3 (January 1861): 37, 64; Charles Hodge, "Professor Park's Remarks on the Princeton Review," *Biblical Repertory and Princeton Review* 23 (April 1851): 347.

100. Lawrence, "New England Theology: The Edwardean Period," p. 37.

101. Ibid., p. 61; Cooke, "Edwards on the Atonement," p. 99; Atwater, "Edwards and the New Divinity," p. 603; and Smith, "Theological System of Emmons," p. 14.

102. Cooke, "Edwards on the Atonement," pp. 99–107; Smith, "Theological System of Emmons," p. 40n. For a Unitarian perspective on the dispute over Edwards and the New England theology, see R. P. S., "The Andover and Princeton Theologies," *Christian Examiner and Religious Miscellany* 54 (May 1852): 309–35; and Christopher Tappan Thayer, "Heresy in Andover Seminary," ibid. 55 (July 1853): 80–87.

103. Smith, "Theological System of Emmons," pp. 48–51; Atwater, "Modern Explanations of the Doctrine of Ability," p. 236; Hodge, "Park and the Princeton Review,"

p. 693. In *Churchmen and Philosophers* (pp. 212–14), Bruce Kuklick simply adopts Smith's perspective that Park and the New England theology were close to Taylorism. He also suggests that Park was trying to deny that Emmons was as an exerciser. My disagreements with this interpretation should be clear. For the Yale perspective on the dispute over natural ability, see Noah Porter, "Princeton Review on Taylor and Edwardean Theology," pp. 726–73; and Fisher, *Discussions in Theology and History*, pp. 285–384.

104. Atwater, "Edwards and the New Divinity," pp. 589, 614, 619; see also the discussion in Noll, "Edwards and Nineteenth-Century Theology," pp. 264–66.

105. Edwards, "Improvements in Theology, Made by President Edwards, and Those Who Have Followed His Course of Thought," in *The Life of President Edwards*, by Sereno E. Dwight, vol. 1 of *The Works of President Edwards, with a Memoir*, ed. Sereno E. Dwight, 10 vols. (New York, 1829), pp. 613–24; and in *Works of Jonathan Edwards, D.D.*, 1:481–92.

106. This is Yale's Noah Porter summarizing the Princeton historical perspective in "The Princeton Review on Dr. Taylor and the Edwardean Theology," p. 740; see Atwater, "Edwards and the New Divinity," p. 513; and the anonymous "Review of the Works of Jonathan Edwards, D.D., late president of Union College," *Biblical Repertory and Princeton Review* 15 (January 1843): 42.

107. Guelzo, *Edwards on the Will*, p. 136; Breitenbach, "Edwards and the New Divinity," p. 191.

108. The changes are discussed in Cecil, *Theological Development of Park*, chap. 6, and Foster, *Life of Park*, chap. 14; see also Daniel Day Williams, *The Andover Liberals* (New York, 1941).

109. Quoted in Daniel B. Shea, "Jonathan Edwards: The First Two Hundred Years," *Journal of American Studies* 14 (August 1980): 197.

110. See the discussion of these manuscripts in Richard D. Pierce, "A Suppressed Edwards Manuscript on the Trinity," *The Crane Review* 1 (Winter 1959): 66–80. Pierce discusses a controversy surrounding Park's alleged suppression of a heterodox unpublished work of Edwards on the Trinity. Park presented his view in "Remarks of Jonathan Edwards on the Trinity," *Bibliotheca Sacra* 38 (January 1881): 147–87 and (April 1881): 333–69.

111. A copy of Park's extensive notes for the Edwards biography is in the Beinecke Rare Book and Manuscript Library, Yale University. The "Notebook" reveals both the ambitious scope of his project as well as the interpretive issues and struggles that he confronted.

112. Cecil, *Theological Development of Park*, pp. 172, 190.

113. Park, *The Associate Creed of Andover Theological Seminary* (Boston, 1883); Foster, *Life of Park*, chap. 16.

114. Johnson, *Printed Writings of Edwards*, p. xi; M. X. Lesser, *Jonathan Edwards: A Reference Guide* (Boston, 1981), pp. 69–90; and Noll, "Edwards and Nineteenth-Century Theology," pp. 275–77.

115. Quoted in Storrs, *Professor Park and His Pupils*, p. 74; George Boardman, *A History of New England Theology* (New York, 1899).

116. Foster, *A Genetic History*, pp. v–vi. It is important to keep in mind, however, that both Foster and Boardman were writing from a post-Calvinist perspective after the collapse of the New England theology. Their doctrinal sympathies were with Taylor, who emerges as the theological liberator in both books. Foster had difficulty dealing with Park, who remained heavily Edwardsian and came after Taylor. Foster concluded (p. 504) that "a new thought, new for Calvinism, was struggling in Park's mind, as yet not quite able to come to the birth. It was the idea of freedom."

117. Haroutunian, *Piety versus Moralism*, p. xxxi.

CHAPTER SIX

1. The colonial revival has been studied primarily in relationship to material culture – architecture, domestic interiors, and antiques – and to the centennial celebration of 1876. I am using the term to refer to a broad interest in the colonial past that was fueled by cultural nationalism and cultural reaction in the late nineteenth and early twentieth centuries. The colonial revival perspective on American culture was reflected in and constituted by a variety of artifacts and activities, both popular and elite, that are the subject of this chapter. My understanding of the colonial revival is informed by the suggestive essays in Alan Axelrod, ed., *The Colonial Revival in America* (New York, 1985). Also see Karal Ann Marling, *George Washington Slept Here: Colonial Revivals and American Culture* (Cambridge, Mass., 1988).

2. Harriet Beecher Stowe, *The Minister's Wooing* (Boston, 1859; reprint, New York, 1967), pp. 101, 245, 246.

3. Ibid., p. 18. On Stowe and Puritanism, see Lawrence E. Buell, *New England Literary Culture: From Revolution through Renaissance* (New York, 1986), chap. 11, and Charles H. Foster's still useful *The Rungless Ladder: Harriet Beecher Stowe and New England Puritanism* (Durham, N.C., 1954).

4. Stowe, *Oldtown Folks* (1869; reprint, New Brunswick, N.J., 1987), pp. 317, 318, 322.

5. Beecher, *Norwood; or, Village Life in New England* (New York, 1867), pp. 2–3. The description of Buell is from Beecher's preface to the 1887 edition. It is quoted in William G. McLoughlin, *The Meaning of Henry Ward Beecher: An Essay on the Shifting Values of Mid-Victorian America* (New York, 1970), p. 63.

6. Beecher, *Norwood*, p. 326.

7. Quoted in Buell, *New England Literary Culture*, p. 206.

8. This term is Buell's, who uses it to examine how antebellum views of the Puritan past were shaped by Calvinist-Unitarian disputes over theology and revivalism. See ibid., chap. 9.

9. The sketch of Edwards is reprinted in Oliver Wendell Holmes, *Pages from an Old Volume of Life: A Collection of Essays, 1857–1881* (Boston, 1883); the quotation is on p. 361.

10. Williston Walker, *A History of the Congregational Churches in the United States* (New York, 1894), pp. 397–98.

11. Ibid., p. 399. For the background and the "Burial Hill Declaration" itself, see

also Walker, *Creeds and Platforms of Congregationalism* (New York, 1893), pp. 553–69.

12. Henry Martyn Dexter, *The Congregationalism of the Last Three Hundred Years as Seen in Its Literature* (New York, 1880), p. 448; Albert E. Dunning, *Congregationalists in America: A Popular History of Their Origins, Belief, Polity, Growth and Work* (Boston, 1894), p. 263.

13. Dexter, *Congregationalism of the Last Three Hundred Years*, p. v; Dexter, *As to Roger Williams, and His "Banishment" from Massachusetts Plantations* (Boston, 1876).

14. Walker, *History of the Congregational Churches*, p. 438.

15. For background information on the Congregational Library Association, see ibid., pp. 384–85. Dr. Harold Worthley of the library has also furnished me with information about the association, the building, and the bas-reliefs.

16. For a suggestive discussion of Saint-Gaudens's work and of Puritan iconography, see Michael Kammen, *Mystic Chords of Memory: The Transformation of Tradition in American Culture* (New York, 1991), pp. 206–15. Kammen's brief discussion of the Puritan tradition in the late nineteenth century has informed my own analysis. Less helpful is Jan C. Dawson, *The Unusable Past: America's Puritan Tradition, 1830 to 1930* (Chico, Calif., 1984).

17. Quoted in Kammen, *Mystic Chords of Memory*, p. 212.

18. George Ellis, *The Puritan Age in Massachusetts, 1629–1685* (Boston, 1888). Among the biographies published were the following: Joseph H. Twichell, *John Winthrop, First Governor of the Massachusetts Colony* (New York, 1891); George L. Walker, *Thomas Hooker* (New York, 1891); Abijah Marvin, *The Life and Times of Cotton Mather* (Boston, 1892); Alice M. Earle, *Margaret Winthrop* (New York, 1895); and Nathan H. Chamberlain, *Samuel Sewall and the World He Lived In* (Boston, 1897). Of course antebellum religious controversies had stimulated historical interest in the Puritans. But the colonial revival surge of historical studies of the Puritans was broader and deeper and embraced secular scholarship emerging in colleges and universities.

19. Barrett Wendell, *Cotton Mather, The Puritan Priest* (1891; reprint, Cambridge, Mass., 1926), pp. 1, 78–79, 301, 305. In his introduction to a 1963 paperback edition of Wendell's biography, Alan Heimert comments on Mather and the strenuous life; see *Cotton Mather, The Puritan Priest* (New York, 1963), p. xviii. See also Wendell's views on the Puritans in *Stelligeri and Other Essays* (New York, 1893).

20. Ezra Byington, *The Puritan in England and New England*, 4th ed. (1900; reprint, New York, 1972), pp. x, 113, 335–81.

21. Ezra Byington, *The Puritan as a Colonist and Reformer* (Boston, 1899), pp. vii, 55, 273.

22. Lyman Abbott, "The New Puritanism," in *The New Puritanism*, ed. Lyman Abbott (New York, 1898), pp. 28, 33, 38.

23. Amory Bradford, "Puritan Principles in the Modern World," in ibid., pp. 85, 96, 99.

24. Alice M. Earle, *The Sabbath in Puritan New England* (1891; 8th ed., New York, 1898), p. 327. See "Alice Morse Earle," in *Dictionary of American Biography*, ed. Allen Johnson and Dumas Malone, 10 vols. (New York, 1927–36), 3:593–94. Earle is a crucial figure in the colonial revival construction of an early American past, but she receives

only passing mention in works such as Kammen's *Mystic Chords of Memory* and Axelrod's *Colonial Revival in America*. Earle's publications were more influential than similar works, such as Mary Caroline Crawford's *The Romance of Old New England Churches* (Boston, 1903), which contained a chapter on the Edwards family. Earle's books even reached a wider audience than colonial revival novels, such as Frank Samuel Child's *A Puritan Wooing: A Tale of the Great Awakening* (New York, 1898).

25. Quoted in M. X. Lesser, *Jonathan Edwards: A Reference Guide* (Boston, 1981), p. 136.

26. Adams, *The Emancipation of Massachusetts* (Boston, 1886). See also Dawson, *The Unusable Past*, pp. 94–97.

27. John Fiske, *The Beginnings of New England* (Boston, 1889), pp. viii, 105, 148, 278. Another dissenting Adams responded to Fiske. See Charles Francis Adams, Jr., *Three Episodes of Massachusetts History* (Boston, 1892) and *Massachusetts: Its Historians and Its History* (Boston, 1893).

28. Holmes, "Jonathan Edwards," in *Pages from an Old Volume*, pp. 368, 387, 389, 394, 395; for the reference to Edwards as a Protestant saint and for criticism of Holmes's essay by his literary circle, see Mrs. John T. Sargent, ed., *Sketches and Reminiscences of the Radical Club of Chestnut Street, Boston* (Boston, 1880), pp. 362–75.

29. See the advertisement and list of publications at the end of the first edition of Allen's biography (Boston, 1889).

30. Allen, *Jonathan Edwards*, p. vi.

31. Ibid., pp. 7, 22, 32, 111.

32. Ibid., pp. 52, 55, 116, 299.

33. Ibid., pp. 104, 116.

34. Williston Walker, "Jonathan Edwards," in *Ten New England Leaders* (New York, 1901), p. 236. See also Walker, "Jonathan Edwards," in *Great Men of the Christian Church* (Chicago, 1908), pp. 339–53, and I. N. Tarbox, "Jonathan Edwards as a Man, and the Ministers of the Last Century," *New Englander*, n.s., 7 (September 1884): 615–31.

35. Allen, *Jonathan Edwards*, pp. 160, 246.

36. Walker, *Ten New England Leaders*, p. 243. Hopkins was one of the ten leaders whose lives and careers Walker sympathetically chronicled.

37. Allen, *Jonathan Edwards*, pp. 68, 219, 299, 386, 388.

38. Ibid., p. 68.

39. Egbert Smyth, "Professor Allen's 'Jonathan Edwards,'" *Andover Review* 13 (March 1890): 285–304; George Park Fisher, "Review of Professor Allen's Life of Jonathan Edwards," *New Englander and Yale Review* 52 (January 1890): 85–88; J. W. Wellman, "A New Biography of Jonathan Edwards," *Our Day* 5 (March and April 1890): 195–219, 288–307.

40. Nina Baym, "Early Histories of American Literature: A Chapter in the Institutionalization of New England," *American Literary History* 1 (Fall 1989): 460. See also Kermit Vanderbilt, *American Literature and the Academy* (Philadelphia, 1986), chaps. 6–8, and Richard Brodhead, *The School of Hawthorne* (New York, 1986), esp. chap. 3.

41. Philip F. Gura uses the word "prologue" to describe the long-standing approach

to early American literature that examines colonial writing not on its own terms but primarily in its relationship to nineteenth-century literature. See "The Study of Colonial American Literature, 1966–1987: A Vade Mecum," *William and Mary Quarterly* 45 (April 1988): 308. Wendell coined the term the "Renaissance of New England," in *A Literary History of America* (1900; reprint, New York, 1968), p. 9.

42. Quoted in Michael Kammen, "Moses Coit Tyler: The First Professor of American History in the United States," in *Selvages and Biases* (Ithaca, N.Y., 1987), p. 227. In addition to Kammen's essay, Kermit Vanderbilt's chapter on Tyler is also helpful; see *American Literature and the Academy*, chap. 6.

43. Tyler, *A History of American Literature*, 2 vols. (1878; reprint, New York, 1895). Volume 1 covered 1607–76 and volume 2, 1676–1765.

44. Tyler, *History of American Literature*, 1:94–95, 98.

45. Ibid., pp. 101, 109.

46. Ibid., pp. 113–14.

47. Ibid., 2:178, 180, 186.

48. Ibid., pp. 188, 190, 192.

49. Charles F. Richardson, *American Literature, 1607–1885*, 2 vols. (New York, 1887), 1:ix, xvii. See also Vanderbilt's helpful discussion of Richardson's background and professional life in *American Literature and the Academy*, chap. 7.

50. Wendell, *Literary History of America*, pp. 36, 82; see also Wendell, *Stelligeri and Other Essays*, p. 121.

51. Frances Underwood, *The Builders of American Literature* (Boston, 1893), pp. 3–4, 40. See also Underwood, *Quabbin: The Story of a Small Town with Outlooks on Puritan Life* (1893; reprint, Boston, 1986). Robert Gross's introduction to this reprint offers an excellent analysis of Underwood's life and historical perspective.

52. Donald G. Mitchell, *American Land and Letters* (New York, 1897), pp. 60–61; Walter C. Bronson, *A Short History of American Literature* (1900; reprint, Boston, 1906), p. 33; and Henry S. Pancoast, *An Introduction to American Literature* (New York, 1898), p. 66. See also Henry A. Beers, *Initial Studies in American Letters* (Cleveland, Ohio, 1895), pp. 34–36; F. V. N. Painter, *Introduction to American Literature* (Boston, 1897), pp. 51–58; Lorenzo Sears, *American Literature in the Colonial Period* (Boston, 1902), pp. 3–4, 91–94; and Charles Wells Moulton, ed., *The Library of Literary Criticism of English and American Authors*, 8 vols. (Buffalo, N.Y., 1901–4), 3:380–95.

53. Edwin Bacon, *Historic Pilgrimages in New England* (New York, 1900). The advertisement is in the back of Bacon, *Literary Pilgrimages in New England* (New York, 1902).

54. Bacon, *Literary Pilgrimages*, p. 2. For an excellent analysis of the colonial revival interest in the homes of famous people, which led to the creation of house museums, see Celia Betsky, "Inside the Past: The Interior and the Colonial Revival in American Art and Literature, 1860–1914," in *Colonial Revival in America*, ed. Axelrod, pp. 241–77.

55. Bacon, *Literary Pilgrimages*, pp. 432–38, 460–61.

56. Nathaniel Eggleston, *In Memoriam: A Discourse Preached November 1, 1868, on the Occasion of the Erection of Tablets in the Old Church at Stockbridge, Mass., In Mem-*

ory of Its Former Pastors, John Sergeant, Jonathan Edwards, Stephen West, David D. Field (New York, 1869), pp. 9–10, 33. On the history of Stockbridge, see Sarah Cabot Sedgwick and Christina Sedgwick Marquand, *Stockbridge, 1739–1939, A Chronicle* (Great Barrington, Mass., 1939).

57. Theodore Dwight Woolsey, "Commemorative Address," in *Memorial Volume of the Edwards Family Meeting at Stockbridge, Mass., September 6–7 A.D. 1870* (Boston, 1871), p. 72.

58. I. N. Tarbox, "On the Early Life of Jonathan Edwards," in ibid., p. 86.

59. Edwards A. Park, "Characteristics of Edwards," in ibid., pp. 119–20.

60. Henry Gale, "Remarks," in ibid., p. 197.

61. *Memorial Volume*, pp. 22, 163–65, 184.

62. Kammen, *Mystic Chords of Memory*, p. 222.

63. *Memorial Volume*, pp. 13, 177.

64. Ibid., p. 183. Other historical markers included an Indian monument dedicated to "The Friends of Our Fathers," a memorial chime tower at the First Church, and a memorial grove to the Reverend David Dudley Field, minister from 1819 to 1837.

65. "Jonathan Edwards Celebrations," *Congregational and Christian World* 88 (October 17, 1903): 537; see also "Jonathan Edwards Memorial Sundial in Front of the Riggs Foundation," typescript, Stockbridge Library. On Stockbridge as a resort after the Civil War, see Sedgwick and Marquand, *Stockbridge, 1739–1939*, chap. 12. On the "colonializing" of another western New England resort town in the late nineteenth century, see William Butler, "Another City upon a Hill: Litchfield, Connecticut, and the Colonial Revival," in *Colonial Revival in America*, ed. Axelrod, pp. 15–51.

66. The colonial revival in Salem led, among other things, to the extensive preservation work of the Essex Institute, the restoration of the House of Seven Gables, and the erection of a Puritan statue to Roger Conant. There is no study of which I am aware of the colonial revival in Salem, but such historicizing activities are mentioned in William B. Rhoads, "The Colonial Revival and the Americanization of Immigrants," in *Colonial Revival in America*, ed. Axelrod, pp. 349–50, and in Jane Holtz Kay, *Preserving New England* (New York, 1986), pp. 38, 45.

67. Z. Eastman, "Jonathan Edwards About His Elms," *Hampshire Gazette* (August 19, 1879), p. 1. In addition to the new monument to Edwards, there was an earlier memorial to him placed next to the gravestones of David Brainerd and Jerusha Edwards; see "In Bridge Cemetery," *Hampshire Gazette* (November 13, 1894), p. 2. On the two churches, see Donald Keyes, *The First Church of Christ in Northampton: A Centennial Celebration of the Fifth Meeting House, 1878–1978* (Northampton, Mass., 1978), esp. p. 28. On the Edwards homesite and Whitney Mansion, see "False Impression Held About House in Northampton," *Springfield Union and Sunday Republican* (August 30, 1931), p. 4A (clipping in Edwards File, Northampton Historical Society); and Charles J. Dean, "Finds the Whitney House and the Jonathan Edwards House Were Not the Same," *Hampshire Gazette* (February 14, 1936), pp. 9, 13.

68. See Archibald V. Galbraith, "Industrial History, 1860–1900," Leo Leopold, "Northampton Labor Unions," and Harold Faulkner, "How Our People Lived," in

The Northampton Book, Chapters from 300 Years in the Life of a New England Town, 1654–1954 (Northampton, Mass., 1954), pp. 233–39, 260–67, 268–76.

69. John Francis Manfredi, "Immigration to Northampton," Virginia Corwin, "Religious Life in Northampton, 1800–1954," and John Smith, "The Origin and Development of the Parochial School System," in *The Northampton Book*, pp. 331–36, 383–93, 194–200. For the larger context of native Yankee response to these changes, see Barbara Miller Solomon's classic study, *Ancestors and Immigrants: A Changing New England Tradition* (Chicago, 1956).

70. "Celebration – Northampton 250th" (File, Historical Society, Northampton, Mass.); see also *Northampton Historical Localities Illustrated, 1654–1904*, compiled by the Committee on Historical Localities for the 250th Anniversary of the Settlement of the Town, June 5, 6, 7 (Northampton, Mass., 1904), and "False Impression Held About House in Northampton," p. 4A.

71. "Edwards Tablets," *Hampshire Gazette* (October 6, 1905), p. 3; "False Impression Held About House in Northampton," p. 4A.

72. James Russell Trumbull, *History of Northampton, Massachusetts from Its Settlement in 1654*, 2 vols. (Northampton, Mass., 1898, 1902). See also *Prospectus of Meadow City Quarter-Millennial Book* (Northampton, Mass., 1904), p. viii.

73. See *Hampshire Gazette* (August 2, 1898), p. 6. Later the original stepping stone of the First Church was hauled to the site of the present church and placed in the front with a plaque. Also, a stone marker was placed at the original site of the First Church. See *Hampshire Gazette* (November 11, 1912), p. 3, (October 18, 1917), p. 4, and (July 30, 1920), p. 3.

74. On the development of Edwards Square and the building of the armory, see "Inventory of Historic Houses," nos. 610, 611 (Historical Society, Northampton, Mass.). On the history of armories, see Robert N. Fogelson, *America's Armories: Architecture, Society, and the Public Order* (Cambridge, Mass., 1989).

75. Background information on the commemoration is contained in the "Report" of the chairman of the memorial committee in *Jonathan Edwards: A Retrospect*, ed. H. Norman Gardiner (Boston, 1901), pp. 165–68. See also *Hampshire Gazette* (June 23, 1900), pp. 1, 8.

76. *Jonathan Edwards: A Retrospect*, p. ix.

77. Alexander V. G. Allen, "The Place of Edwards in History," Egbert Smyth, "The Influence of Edwards on the Spiritual Life of New England," George Park Fisher, "Greetings from Yale University," Henry Rose, "Edwards in Northampton," in ibid., pp. 10, 12, 16, 48, 78, 79, 96.

78. "An American Philosopher of the Eighteenth Century," editorial, *New York Times* (June 11, 1900), p. 6; "Tablet to Jonathan Edwards," ibid. (June 23, 1900), p. 7; "The Jonathan Edwards Memorial," *Harper's Weekly* 44 (June 23, 1900): 574. I am indebted to M. X. Lesser, *Jonathan Edwards: A Reference Guide*, for calling my attention to these notices.

79. The history of the Hall of Fame is detailed in George Cary Eggleston, *The American Immortals* (New York, 1901). The quotations are on p. x, and pp. 337–49 contain a

biographical sketch of Edwards. See also Henry Mitchell MacCracken, *The Hall of Fame* (New York, 1901).

80. Eggleston, *The American Immortals*, pp. xi, xv; Lesser, *Jonathan Edwards: A Reference Guide*, p. 103.

81. Reports and material generated by this commemoration are far too numerous to cite. A good summary may be found in "Jonathan Edwards Celebrations," *Congregationalist and Christian World* 88 (October 17, 1903): 537; see also Lesser, *Jonathan Edwards: A Reference Guide*, pp. 111–20. The Andover and Stockbridge commemorations led to the publication of books; see *Exercises Commemorating the Two-Hundredth Anniversary of the Birth of Jonathan Edwards, Held at Andover Theological Seminary, October 4 and 5, 1903* (Andover, Mass., 1904) and *Jonathan Edwards: The Two Hundredth Anniversary of his Birth. Union Meeting of the Berkshire North and South Conferences, Stockbridge, Mass., October Fifth, 1903* (Stockbridge, Mass., 1903). On the commemoration in California, see Henry Kingman, *Jonathan Edwards: A Commemorative Address in Observance of the Bicentenary of His Birth, at the First Congregational Church, Berkeley, California, October 5, 1903* (Berkeley, 1904).

82. John DeWitt, "Jonathan Edwards: A Study," in *Exercises* at the Stockbridge commemoration, pp. 39–40.

83. Rev. Newton Hall, quoted in *Springfield Daily Republican* (October 5, 1903), p. 4. Racial elements in the commemoration of Edwards were part of the larger Anglo-Saxon complex in the assessment of the Puritan heritage. Edwards even became a case study in eugenics at the turn of the century that gained currency and found favor with some bicentennial commemorators. In *Jukes-Edwards: A Study in Education and Heredity* (Harrisburg, Pa., 1900), A. E. Winship compared the hereditary genius and success of Edwards's descendants with the descendants of a clan of "degenerates" who were dubbed the Jukes. "The whole teaching of the culture of animals and plants," Winship concluded, "leaves no room to question the persistency of character, and this is so grandly exemplified in the descendants of Mr. Edwards that it is interesting to see what inheritances were focused in him" (p. 20).

84. See the material on the parade in "Celebrations – Northampton 250th"; on the Polish National Church and the historical marker, see "False Impression Held About House in Northampton," p. 4A, and "King Street," (File, Historical Society, Northampton, Mass.).

EPILOGUE

1. William Harder Squires, ed., *The Edwardean: A Quarterly Devoted to the History of Thought in America* (1903–4; reprint, Lewiston, N.Y., 1991), pp. 4, 33–44.

2. See M. X. Lesser, *Jonathan Edwards: A Reference Guide* (Boston, 1980), pp. 125–30.

3. *Historic Pageant of Northampton, Mass.* (Northampton, 1911), p. 27. On the popularity and historical significance of these pageants, see David Glassberg, *American Historical Pageantry: The Uses of Tradition in the Early Twentieth Century* (Chapel Hill,

N.C., 1990). When the second Edwards elm fell in 1913, a slice of it was preserved, framed, and hung in the reference room of the Forbes Library. It is presently held in storage at the library. See "Famous Old Elm Gone," *New York Times* (August 22, 1913), p. 7.

4. William Peterfield Trent et al., *The Cambridge History of American Literature*, 3 vols. (1917; reprint, New York, 1940), 1:ix.

5. Ibid., pp. 31, 35, 43, 53.

6. Ibid., pp. 60, 65, 69; Charles Beard, *The Rise of American Civilization* (1927; reprint, New York, 1959), p. 148.

7. Parrington, *Main Currents in American Thought*, 2 vols. (New York, 1927), 1:151, 153, 165.

8. Ibid., pp. 159, 164.

9. Henry Parkes, *Jonathan Edwards: The Fiery Puritan* (New York, 1930), pp. 23, 252, 253, 254.

10. See Henry F. May, "The Recovery of American Religious History," *American Historical Review* 70 (October 1964): 79–92; and Donald Louis Weber, "The Recovery of Jonathan Edwards," in *Jonathan Edwards and the American Experience*, ed. Nathan O. Hatch and Harry S. Stout (New York, 1988), pp. 62–66.

11. A. C. McGiffert, Jr., *Jonathan Edwards* (New York, 1932). For the reviewer's description of this work, see *American Literature* 4 (1932–33): 317.

12. Joseph Haroutunian, *Piety versus Moralism: The Passing of the New England Theology* (New York, 1932), p. xxxiii, and *Wisdom and Folly in Religion: A Study in Chastened Protestantism* (New York, 1940), p. 82. It is also interesting that Yale established Jonathan Edwards College in 1933.

13. Haroutunian, *Piety versus Moralism*, p. xxx.

14. H. Richard Niebuhr, *The Kingdom of God in America* (New York, 1937), pp. 99, 137–38.

15. C. C. Goen, "Jonathan Edwards: A New Departure in Eschatology," *Church History* 28 (1959): 25–40; Ernest Lee Sandeen, *Redeemer Nation: The Idea of America's Millennial Role* (Chicago, 1968). Perry Miller served as link between Niebuhr and subsequent interpretations of Edwards's millennialism. Miller suggested in an essay first published in 1951 that Edwards was a postmillennialist who located the millennium before the apocalypse. See Miller, "The End of the World," in *Errand into the Wilderness* (1956; reprint, New York, 1964), pp. 233–35.

16. Niebuhr, *Kingdom of God in America*, pp. xiii, 10.

17. Thomas Johnson, ed., *The Printed Writings of Jonathan Edwards: A Bibliography* (1940; reprint, New York, 1968). Five years earlier Johnson and Clarence Faust had contributed a major work on Edwards to an "American Writers Series." See *Jonathan Edwards: Representative Selections, with Introduction, Bibliography, and Notes* (New York, 1935). Faust and Johnson authored an excellent and lengthy introduction which made no attempt to assess Edwards's legacy.

18. Perry Miller, "From Edwards to Emerson," in *Errand into the Wilderness*, pp. 184–203. In the same year that Miller published his famous essay, Ola Winslow

published *Jonathan Edwards, 1703–1758: A Biography* (New York, 1940), which won the Pulitzer Prize.

19. Miller, *Jonathan Edwards* (New York, 1949), pp. 270–71.

20. Perry Miller, "General Editor's Note," *Freedom of the Will*, ed. Paul Ramsey, vol. 1 of *Works of Jonathan Edwards*, 13 vols. (New Haven, Conn., 1957), pp. vii–viii.

21. On doctoral dissertations on Edwards, see the entries in Lesser, *Jonathan Edwards: A Reference Guide*. Influential Edwards scholars trained at Yale included C. C. Goen, who not only authored "Jonathan Edwards: A New Departure in Eschatology," but also edited the Yale edition of Edwards's writings on the Great Awakening; Roland A. Delattre, whose *Beauty and Sensibility in the Thought of Jonathan Edwards: An Essay in Aesthetics and Theological Ethics* (New Haven, Conn., 1968) remains an important work; and Clyde A. Holbrook, author of *The Ethics of Jonathan Edwards: Morality and Aesthetics* (Ann Arbor, Mich., 1973) and editor of the Yale edition of *Original Sin*. H. Richard Niebuhr was a key Yale faculty member who supervised dissertations on Edwards and who served on the editorial board of the *Works of Edwards*. I have found the analyses of Donald Weber on Miller and Niebuhr very helpful; see Weber, "The Recovery of Jonathan Edwards," in *Jonathan Edwards and the American Experience*, ed. Hatch and Stout, pp. 61–66; Weber, "Perry Miller and the Recovery of Jonathan Edwards," introduction to Perry Miller, *Jonathan Edwards* (Amherst, Mass., 1981). See also Leo Sandon, Jr., "Jonathan Edwards and H. Richard Niebuhr," *Religious Studies* 12 (1976): 101, 115; and Joseph A. Conforti, "Jonathan Edwards and American Studies," *American Quarterly* 41 (March 1989): 165–71.

22. Conrad Cherry, *The Theology of Jonathan Edwards: A Reappraisal* (Garden City, N.Y., 1966), pp. 6, 77.

23. Miller, "From the Covenant to the Revival," in *The Shaping of American Religion*, ed. James Ward Smith and A. Leland Jamison (Princeton, N.J., 1961), pp. 322–50.

24. Alan Heimert, *Religion and the American Mind from the Great Awakening to the Revolution* (Cambridge, Mass., 1966), pp. 14, 98–99, 457. Heimert and Miller also produced the most comprehensive anthology on the awakening with an introduction that restated their views; see *The Great Awakening: Documents Illustrating the Crisis and Its Consequences* (Indianapolis and New York, 1967).

25. Hatch and Stout, *Jonathan Edwards and the American Experience*; see especially the essays by Norman Fiering, John F. Wilson, Stephen Stein, Harry S. Stout, William Breitenbach, and Bruce Kuklick; see also William J. Scheick, ed., *Critical Essays on Jonathan Edwards* (Boston, 1980). Two recent attempts to revise, but also salvage, key elements of Heimert's analysis are Donald Louis Weber, *Rhetoric and History in Revolutionary New England* (New York, 1988), and Gerald R. McDermott, *One Holy and Happy Society: The Public Theology of Jonathan Edwards* (University Park, Pa., 1992).

SELECTED BIBLIOGRAPHY

NINETEENTH-CENTURY RELIGIOUS PERIODICALS

American Biblical Repository, 1839–44

American Presbyterian Review (*American Theological Review*), 1859–71

Biblical Repertory and Princeton Review, 1857–71

Biblical Repertory and Theological Review, 1827–36

Biblical Repository, 1831–38

Bibliotheca Sacra, 1844–81

Christian Disciple, 1813–23

Christian Examiner, 1824–69

Christian Spectator, 1819–28

Congregationalist, 1815–60

Congregational Quarterly, 1859–78

Connecticut Evangelical Magazine, 1800–1807

Connecticut Evangelical Magazine and Religious Intelligencer, 1808–15

Literary and Theological Review, 1834–39

Massachusetts Missionary Magazine, 1803–7

Methodist Quarterly Review, 1849–84

Missionary Herald, 1821–50

New Englander, 1843–92

Panoplist, 1803–8

Panoplist and Missionary Magazine, 1809–20

Quarterly Christian Spectator, 1829–38

Spirit of the Pilgrims, 1828–33

OTHER PRIMARY SOURCES

Abbott, Lyman, ed. *The New Puritanism*. New York, 1898.

Adams, Brooks. *The Emancipation of Massachusetts*. Boston, 1886.

Adams, Charles Francis, Jr. *Three Episodes of Massachusetts History*. Boston, 1892.

Allen, Alexander V. G. *Jonathan Edwards*. Boston, 1889.

Asbury, Francis. *Journal and Letters*. Edited by Elmer T. Clark. 3 vols. Nashville, 1958.

Bacon, Edwin. *Historic Pilgrimages in New England*. New York, 1900.

———. *Literary Pilgrimages in New England*. New York, 1902.

Bacon, Leonard. *Thirteen Historical Discourses, on the Completion of Two Hundred Years from the Beginning of the First Church in New Haven.* New Haven, Conn., 1839.

——. *A Commemorative Discourse on the Completion of Fifty Years from the Founding of the Seminary at Andover.* Andover, Mass., 1858.

Baird, Robert. *Religion in the United States of America.* London, 1844.

Beaver, R. Pierce, ed. *Pioneers in Missions: The Early Missionary Ordination Sermons, Charges, and Institutions.* Grand Rapids, Mich., 1966.

Beecher, Henry Ward. *Norwood; or, Village Life in New England.* New York, 1867.

Beecher, Lyman. *The Autobiography of Lyman Beecher.* Edited by Barbara M. Cross. 2 vols. Cambridge, Mass., 1961.

Beers, Henry A. *Initial Studies in American Letters.* Cleveland, Ohio, 1895.

Bellamy, Joseph. *Works.* 3 vols. New York, 1811–12.

——. *Works, with a Memoir of His Life and Character.* Edited by Tryon Edwards. 2 vols. Boston, 1850.

Boardwell, Horatio. *Memoir of Rev. Gordon Hall, A.M., One of the First Missionaries of the American Board of Commissioners for Foreign Missions at Bombay.* Andover, Mass., 1841.

Bond, Alvan. *Memoir of the Rev. Pliny Fisk, A.M., Late Missionary to Palestine.* Boston, 1828.

Brainerd, David. *Mirabilia Dei inter Indicos; or the Rise and Progress of a Remarkable Work of Grace, Among a Number of Indians . . . Justly Represented in a Journal, Kept . . . by David Brainerd.* Philadelphia, 1746.

——. *Divine Grace Displayed. . . .* Philadelphia, 1746.

Brainerd, Thomas. *The Life of John Brainerd, the Brother of David Brainerd and His Successor as Missionary to the Indians of New Jersey.* Philadelphia, 1865.

Bronson, Walter C. *A Short History of American Literature.* 1900. Reprint, Boston, 1906.

Byington, Ezra. *The Puritan as a Colonist and Reformer.* Boston, 1899.

——. *The Puritan in England and New England.* 4th ed. 1900. Reprint, New York, 1972.

"Celebration – Northampton 250th." File: Historical Society, Northampton, Mass.

Chamberlain, Nathan H. *Samuel Sewall and the World He Lived In.* Boston, 1897.

Child, Frank Samuel. *A Puritan Wooing: A Tale of the Great Awakening.* New York, 1898.

Circular Letter Containing an Invitation to the Ministers of Every Christian Denomination in the United States to Unite in Their Endeavours to Carry into Execution the Humble Attempt of President Edwards. Concord, N.H., 1798.

[Cooke, Parson.] *Views in New England Theology No. I: The New England Theology Contrasted with the New Arminianism.* Boston, 1859.

——. *Views in New England Theology No. II: The New Apostasy, or a Word to the Laodiceans.* Boston, 1860.

Crawford, Mary Caroline. *The Romance of Old New England Churches.* Boston, 1903.

Dexter, Henry Martyn. *As to Roger Williams, and His "Banishment" from Massachusetts Plantations.* Boston, 1876.

————. *The Congregationalism of the Last Three Hundred Years as Seen in Its Literature.* New York, 1880.

Dunning, Albert E. *Congregationalists in America: A Popular History of Their Origins, Belief, Polity, Growth and Work.* Boston, 1894.

Dwight, Sereno E. *Memoirs of David Brainerd: . . . by Rev. Jonathan Edwards. . . .* New Haven, Conn., 1822.

Dwight, Timothy. *Travels in New England and New York.* 4 vols. New Haven, Conn., 1823.

Earle, Alice M. *Margaret Winthrop.* New York, 1895.

————. *The Sabbath in Puritan New England.* 1891. 8th ed., New York, 1898.

Edwards, B. B., ed. *Memoir of the Rev. Elias Cornelius.* Boston, 1834.

Edwards, Jonathan. *An Account of the Life of the Late Reverend Mr. David Brainerd. . . .* Boston, 1749.

————. *A History of the Work of Redemption. Containing the Outline of a Body of Divinity in a Method Entirely New.* Edinburgh, 1774.

————. *A Humble Attempt to Promote Explicit Agreement and Visible Union of God's People, in Extraordinary Prayer, for the Revival of Religion and the Advancement of Christ's Kingdom on Earth, Pursuant to Scripture-Promises and Prophecies Concerning the Last Time.* Elizabethtown, N.J., 1794.

————. *Works.* Edited by Edward Williams and Edwards Parson. 8 vols. Leeds, England, 1806–11.

————. *Works.* 8 vols. Worcester, Mass., 1808.

————. *Account of Abigail Hutchinson, A Young Woman, Hopefully Converted at Northampton, Mass., 1734.* Andover, Mass., 1816.

————. *Works, with a Memoir.* Edited by Sereno E. Dwight. 10 vols. New York, 1829–30.

————. *Works.* Edited by Edward Hickman. 2 vols. London, 1834.

————. *Works.* 4 vols. New York and Boston, 1843.

————. *Charity and Its Fruits; or, Christian Love as Manifested in the Heart and Life.* Edited by Tryon Edwards. New York, 1852.

————. *Selections from the Unpublished Writings of Jonathan Edwards.* Edited by Alexander B. Grossart. Edinburgh, 1865.

————. *The Nature of True Virtue* (1765) with a foreword by William K. Frankena. Ann Arbor, Mich., 1960.

————. *Works.* Edited by Perry Miller (1957–64), John E. Smith (1964–93), and Harry S. Stout (1993–94). 13 vols. New Haven, Conn., 1957–94.

Edwards, Jonathan, Jr. *Works, with a Memoir of His Life and Character.* Edited by Tryon Edwards. 2 vols. Andover, Mass., 1842.

Eggleston, Nathaniel. *In Memoriam: A Discourse Preached November 1, 1868, on the Occasion of the Erection of Tablets in the Old Church at Stockbridge, Mass., In Memory of Its Former Pastors, John Sergeant, Jonathan Edwards, Stephen West, David D. Field.* New York, 1869.

Ellis, George. *The Puritan Age in Massachusetts, 1629–1685.* Boston, 1888.

Emerson, Joseph. *Articles of Faith, and Form of Covenant, Adopted by the Third*

Congregational Church in Beverly, at Its Formation, November 9, 1801 . . . To Which Are Added Resolutions of President Edwards. Boston, 1807.

————. *Female Education: A Discourse Delivered at the Dedication of the Seminary Hall in Saugus, January 15, 1822.* Boston, 1822.

————. *The Evangelical Primer, Containing a Minor Doctrinal Catechism and a Minor Historical Catechism. . . .* Charlestown, Mass., 1809. Reprint, Boston, 1824.

Emerson, Ralph. *Life of Rev. Joseph Emerson, Pastor of the Third Congregational Church in Beverly, Mass., and Subsequently Principal of a Female Seminary.* Boston, 1834.

Emmons, Nathanael. *Works.* Edited by Jacob Ide. 7 vols. Boston, 1842.

————. *Works.* Edited by Edwards A. Park. 6 vols. Boston, 1861.

Exercises Commemorating the Two-Hundredth Anniversary of the Birth of Jonathan Edwards, Held at Andover Theological Seminary, October 4 and 5, 1903. Andover, Mass., 1904.

Faust, Clarence, and Thomas Johnson, eds. *Jonathan Edwards: Representative Selections, with Introduction, Bibliography, and Notes.* New York, 1935.

Ferguson, John. *Memoir of the Life and Character of the Rev. Samuel Hopkins, D.D. . . .* Boston, 1830.

Finney, Charles G. *Sermons on Various Subjects.* New York, 1835.

————. *True and False Repentance.* 1836. Reprint, Grand Rapids, Mich., 1966.

————. *Autobiography of Charles G. Finney.* New York, 1876.

————. *Lectures on Revivals of Religion.* Edited by William G. McLoughlin. Cambridge, Mass., 1960.

Fisher, George Park. *Discussions in History and Theology.* New York, 1880.

Fisk, Fidelia. *Recollections of Mary Lyon, with Selections from Her Instruction to the Pupils in Mt. Holyoke Female Seminary.* Boston, 1866.

Fiske, D. T. *Faith Working by Love: A Memoir of Miss Fidelia Fiske.* Boston, 1868.

Fiske, John. *The Beginnings of New England.* Boston, 1889.

Foster, Frank. *A Genetic History of New England Theology.* Chicago, 1907.

Gardiner, H. Norman, ed. *Jonathan Edwards: A Retrospect.* Boston, 1901.

General Catalogue of the Theological Seminary, Andover, Massachusetts, 1808–1908. Boston, 1909.

Goodrich, Samuel G. *Recollections of a Lifetime, or Men and Things I Have Seen.* New York, 1857.

The Gospel Treasury: Containing Biography Compiled from the London Evangelical Magazine. 4 vols. Boston, 1811.

Hampshire, Massachusetts, *Gazette*, 1870–1905.

[Hawes, Louisa.] *Memoir of Mrs. Mary E. Van Lennep, Only Daughter of the Rev. Joel Hawes, D.D., and Wife of the Rev. Henry J. Van Lennep, Missionary in Turkey, by Her Mother.* Hartford, 1847.

Historic Pageant of Northampton, Mass. Northampton, Mass., 1911.

Hitchcock, Edward. *The Power of Christian Benevolence Illustrated in the Life and Labors of Mary Lyon.* 1851. Reprint, Northampton, Mass., 1855.

Hodge, Charles. *Constitutional History of the Presbyterian Church in the United States of America.* 2 vols. Philadelphia, 1839.

Holmes, Abiel. *A Discourse before the Society for Propagating the Gospel among the Indians and Others in North America, Delivered Nov. 3, 1808.* Boston, 1808.

Holmes, Oliver Wendell. *Pages from an Old Volume of Life: A Collection of Essays, 1857–1881.* Boston, 1883.

Hooker, E. W. *The Cultivation of the Missionary Spirit in Our Literary and Theological Institutions.* Boston, 1845.

Hopkins, Samuel. *An Inquiry Concerning the Promises of the Gospel: Whether Any of Them Are Made to the Exercises and Doings of Persons in an Unregenerate State.* Boston, 1765.

———. *Two Discourses: I. On the Necessity of the Knowledge of the Law of God, in Order to the Knowledge of Sin. II. A Particular and Critical Inquiry into the Cause, Nature, and Means of That Change in Which Men Are Born of God.* Boston, 1768.

———. *System of Doctrines Contained in Divine Revelation, Explained and Defended, with A Treatise on the Millennium.* 2 vols. Boston, 1793.

———. *Works.* Edited by Edwards A. Park. 3 vols. Boston, 1852.

Humphrey, Heman. *The Shining Path: A Sermon Preached in South Hadley at the Funeral of Miss Mary Lyon, March 8, 1849.* Northampton, Mass., 1849.

———. *Revival Sketches and Manual.* New York, 1859.

Jonathan Edwards: The Two Hundredth Anniversary of his Birth. Union Meeting of the Berkshire North and South Conferences, Stockbridge, Mass., October Fifth, 1903. Stockbridge, Mass., 1903.

Karlsen, Carol F., and Laurie Crumpacker, eds. *The Journal of Esther Edwards Burr, 1754–1757.* New Haven, Conn., 1984.

Kingman, Henry. *Jonathan Edwards: A Commemorative Address in Observance of the Bicentenary of His Birth, at the First Congregational Church, Berkeley, California, October 5, 1903.* Berkeley, Calif., 1904.

Knowles, James D. *Life of Mrs. Ann H. Judson.* Philadelphia, 1830.

Letters of the Rev. Dr. Beecher and Rev. Mr. Nettleton on the "New Measures" in Conducting Revivals of Religion. New York, 1828.

Lord, Nathan. *A Letter to the Rev. Daniel Dana on Professor Park's Theology of New England.* Boston, 1852.

Lyon, Mary. *A Missionary Offering, or Christian Sympathy, Personal Responsibility, and the Present Crisis in Foreign Missions.* Boston, 1843.

Marvin, Abijah. *The Life and Times of Cotton Mather.* Boston, 1892.

Matthews, Lyman. *Memoir of the Life and Character of Ebenezer Porter, D.D., Late President of the Theological Seminary, Andover.* Boston, 1837.

McLoughlin, William G., ed. *The American Evangelicals, 1800–1900.* New York, 1968.

Memorial: Twenty-Fifth Anniversary of the Mount Holyoke Female Seminary. South Hadley, Mass., 1862.

Memorial Volume of the Edwards Family Meeting at Stockbridge, Mass., September 6–7 A.D. 1870. Boston, 1871.

Miller, Samuel. *Life of Jonathan Edwards.* Vol. 8 of *The Library of American Biography,* edited by Jared Sparks. New York, 1837.

Mitchell, Donald G. *American Land and Letters*. New York, 1897.

Morton, Daniel O., ed. *Memoir of Levi Parsons, First Missionary to Palestine from the United States*. Burlington, Vt., 1830.

Moulton, Charles Wells, ed. *The Library of Literary Criticism of English and American Authors*. 8 vols. Buffalo, N.Y., 1901–4.

Northampton Historical Localities Illustrated, 1654–1904. Compiled by the Committee on Historical Localities for the 250th Anniversary of the Settlement of the Town, June 5, 6, 7th. Northampton, Mass., 1904.

Osgood, Charles. *Studies in Christian Biography or Hours with Theologians and Reformers*. New York, 1850.

Page, Jesse. *David Brainerd: The Apostle to the North American Indians*. London, 1891.

Painter, F. V. N. *Introduction to American Literature*. Boston, 1897.

Pancoast, Henry S. *An Introduction to American Literature*. New York, 1898.

Park, Edwards A. *The Theology of the Intellect and That of the Feelings: A Discourse Delivered before the Convention of the Congregational Ministers of Massachusetts . . . May 30, 1850*. Boston, 1850.

———. *Memoir of the Life and Character of Samuel Hopkins, D.D. . . .* Boston, 1852.

———. *New England Theology: With Comments on a Third Article in the Princeton Review, Relating to a Convention Sermon*. Andover, Mass., 1852.

———. *A Memorial of the Semi-Centennial Celebration of the Founding of the Theological Seminary at Andover*. Andover, Mass., 1859.

———. *The Atonement: Discourses and Treatises by Edwards, Smalley, Maxcy, Emmons, Griffin, Burge and Weeks, with an Introductory Essay*. Boston, 1859.

———. *Memoir of Nathanael Emmons, with Sketches of His Friends and Pupils*. Boston, 1861.

———. *The Associate Creed of Andover Theological Seminary*. Boston, 1883.

———. *Discourses on Some Theological Doctrines Related to the Religious Character*. Andover, Mass., 1885.

———. "Notebook for a Biography of Jonathan Edwards." Ms., Yale University Library.

Patten, William. *Reminiscences of the Late Rev. Samuel Hopkins, D.D. . . .* Boston, 1843.

Peabody, William B. O. *David Brainerd*. Vol. 8 of *The Library of American Biography*, edited by Jared Sparks. New York, 1837.

Pond, Enoch. *Lectures on Christian Theology*. Boston, 1867.

———. *Sketches of the Theological History of New England*. Boston, 1880.

———. *The Autobiography of Enoch Pond, D.D. . . .* Edited with an introduction by Rev. Edwin Pond Parker, D.D. Boston, 1883.

Porter, Ebenezer. *Letters on the Religious Revivals which Prevailed about the Beginning of the Present Century*. Boston, 1858.

Prospectus of Meadow City Quarter-Millennial Book. Northampton, Mass., 1904.

Rice, John Holt, and Benjamin Holt Rice. *Memoir of James Brainerd Taylor*. New York, 1833.

Richardson, Charles F. *American Literature, 1607–1885*. 2 vols. New York, 1887.

Sargent, Mrs. John T., ed. *Sketches and Reminiscences of the Radical Club of Chestnut Street, Boston.* Boston, 1880.

Schaff, Philip, ed. *A Religious Encyclopedia; or, Dictionary of Biblical, Historical, and Practical Theology.* 3d ed. 10 vols. New York, 1891.

Sears, Lorenzo. *American Literature in the Colonial Period.* Boston, 1902.

Shelton, Don O. *Heroes of the Cross in America.* New York, 1904.

Sherman, David. *Sketches of New England Divines.* New York, 1860.

Spaulding, Charles. *Edwards on Revivals.* New York, 1832.

Sprague, William B. *Lectures on Revivals of Religion.* Albany, N.Y., 1832.

————. *Annals of the American Pulpit.* 9 vols. New York, 1857–69.

Spring, Gardiner. *Memoir of Samuel John Mills.* 1820. Reprint, New York, 1842.

Squires, William Harder, ed. *The Edwardean: A Quarterly Devoted to the History of Thought in America.* 1903–4. Reprint, Lewiston, N.Y., 1991.

Stiles, Ezra. *The Literary Diary of Ezra Stiles, D.D. LL.D.* Edited by Franklin B. Dexter. 3 vols. New York, 1901.

Storrs, R. S. *Professor Park and His Pupils. . . .* Boston, 1899.

————. *Edwards A. Park: A Memorial Address.* Boston, 1900.

Stowe, Harriet Beecher. *The Minister's Wooing.* Boston, 1859. Reprint, New York, 1967.

————. *Oldtown Folks.* 1869. Reprint, New Brunswick, N.J., 1987.

Styles, John. *The Life of David Brainerd, Missionary to the Indians, with an Abridgement of His Diary and Journal.* New Port, Isle of Wight, 1808. Reprint, Boston, 1812.

Taylor, James Barnett. *Memoir of Luther Rice, One of the First American Missionaries to the East.* Baltimore, 1840.

Taylor, Nathaniel William. *Concio ad Clerum.* New Haven, Conn., 1828.

Thayer, William. *Poor Girl and True Woman: or, Elements of Women's Success Drawn from the Life of Mary Lyon and Others.* Boston, 1859.

Todd, John. *Address at the Laying of the Corner Stone of the Edwards Church in Northampton, Mass., July 4, 1833.* Northampton, Mass., 1834.

————. *The Pulpit – Its Influence upon Society: A Sermon Delivered at the Dedication of the Edwards Church in Northampton, Mass., December 25, 1833.* Northampton, Mass., 1834.

Tracy, Joseph. *The Great Awakening: A History of the Revival of Religion in the Time of Edwards and Whitefield.* Boston, 1841.

Trent, William Peterfield, et al. *The Cambridge History of American Literature.* 3 vols. 1917. Reprint, New York, 1940.

Trumbull, Benjamin. *A Complete History of Connecticut Civil and Ecclesiastical.* 2 vols. 1818. Reprint, New London, Conn., 1898.

Trumbull, James Russell. *History of Northampton, Massachusetts from Its Settlement in 1654.* 2 vols. Northampton, Mass., 1898, 1902.

Twichell, Joseph H. *John Winthrop, First Governor of the Massachusetts Colony.* New York, 1891.

Tyler, Bennett. *New England Revivals, as They Existed at the Close of the Eighteenth, and the Beginning of the Nineteenth Centuries. Compiled Principally from Narratives First Published in the Connecticut Evangelical Magazine.* Boston, 1846.

Tyler, Moses Coit. *A History of American Literature.* 2 vols. 1878. Reprint, New York, 1895.

Underwood, Frances. *The Builders of American Literature.* Boston, 1893.

———. *Quabbin: The Story of a Small Town with Outlooks on Puritan Life.* 1893. Reprint, Boston, 1986.

Vaughan, Alden T., and Edward W. Clark, eds. *Puritans among the Indians: Accounts of Captivity and Redemption, 1676–1724.* Cambridge, Mass., 1981.

Walker, George L. *Thomas Hooker.* New York, 1891.

Walker, Williston. *Creeds and Platforms of Congregationalism.* New York, 1893.

———. *A History of the Congregational Churches in the United States.* New York, 1894.

———. *Ten New England Leaders.* New York, 1901.

———. *Great Men of the Christian Church.* Chicago, 1908.

Waterbury, J. B. *Sketches of Eloquent Preachers.* New York, 1864.

Wendell, Barrett. *Stelligeri and Other Essays.* New York, 1893.

———. *Cotton Mather, The Puritan Priest.* 1891. Reprint, Cambridge, Mass., 1926.

———. *A Literary History of America.* 1900. Reprint, New York, 1968.

Wesley, John. *The Work of the Holy Spirit in the Human Heart by Rev. Jonathan Edwards.* New York, 1853.

———. *Works.* Edited by Thomas Jackson. 14 vols. Grand Rapids, Mich., 1960.

West, Stephen, ed. *Sketches of the Life of the Late Rev. Samuel Hopkins, D.D.* Hartford, Conn., 1805.

Winship, A. E. *Jukes-Edwards: A Study in Education and Heredity.* Harrisburg, Pa., 1900.

Winslow, Miron. *A Memoir of Mrs. Harriet Wadsworth Winslow, Thirteen Years a Member of the American Mission in Ceylon.* Boston, 1835.

Woods, Leonard. *Sermon Preached at Haverhill, Mass., in Remembrance of Mrs. Harriet Newell . . . To Which Are Added Memoirs of Her Life.* Boston, 1814.

———. *Memoirs of the American Missionaries Formerly Connected with the Society of Inquiry Respecting Missions in the Andover Theological Seminary.* Boston, 1833.

———. *History of the Andover Theological Seminary.* Boston, 1885.

SECONDARY SOURCES

Abzug, Robert H. *Passionate Liberator: Theodore Dwight Weld and the Dilemma of Reform.* New York, 1980.

Alexander, Archibald. *Biographical Sketches of the Founder and Principal Alumni of the Log College: Together with an Account of the Revivals under Their Ministry.* Philadelphia, 1851.

Allmendinger, David F. *Paupers and Scholars: The Transformation of Student Life in Nineteenth-Century New England.* New York, 1975.

————. "Mount Holyoke Students Encounter the Need for Life Planning, 1837–1850." *History of Education Quarterly* 19 (1979): 27–43.

Anderson, Glenn P. "Joseph Bellamy (1719–1790): The Man and His Work." Ph.D. dissertation, Boston University, 1971.

Andrew, John A., III. *Rebuilding the Christian Commonwealth: New England Congregationalists and Foreign Missions.* Lexington, Ky., 1976.

Axelrod, Alan, ed. *The Colonial Revival in America.* New York, 1985.

Axtell, James. *The European and the Indian: Essays in the Ethnohistory of North America.* New York, 1981.

Baker, Frank. *From Wesley to Asbury: Studies in Early American Methodism.* Durham, N.C., 1976.

Baym, Nina. "Early Histories of American Literature: A Chapter in the Institutionalization of New England." *American Literary History* 1 (Fall 1989): 459–84.

Beard, Charles. *The Rise of American Civilization.* 1927. Reprint, New York, 1959.

Berkhofer, Robert F. *Salvation and the Savage: An Analysis of Protestant Missions and American Indian Response, 1787–1862.* Lexington, Ky., 1965.

Birdsall, Richard D. "The Second Great Awakening and the New England Social Order." *Church History* 39 (1970): 345–64.

Boardman, George. *A History of New England Theology.* New York, 1899.

Bowden, Henry Warner. *American Indians and Christian Missions: Studies in Cultural Conflict.* Chicago, 1981.

Boylan, Anne M. *Sunday School: The Formation of an American Institution.* New Haven, Conn., 1988.

Breen, Timothy. *Imagining the Past: East Hampton Histories.* Reading, Mass., 1989.

Breitenbach, William K. "The New Divinity and the Idea of Moral Accountability." Ph.D. dissertation, Yale University, 1978.

————. "Unregenerate Doings: Selflessness and Selfishness in New Divinity Theology." *American Quarterly* 34 (Winter 1982): 479–502.

————. "The Consistent Calvinism of the New Divinity Movement." *William and Mary Quarterly* 41 (April 1984): 241–64.

Breitwieser, Mitchell Robert. *American Puritanism and the Defense of Mourning: Religion, Grief, and Ethnology in Mary White Rowlandson's Captivity Narrative.* Madison, Wis., 1990.

Briggs, Peter. "Timothy Dwight Composes a Landscape for New England." *American Quarterly* 40 (September 1988): 359–77.

Brodhead, Richard. *The School of Hawthorne.* New York, 1986.

Brumberg, Joan J. *Mission for Life: The Story of the Family of Adoniram Judson.* New York, 1980.

Buell, Lawrence E. "Calvinism Romanticized: Harriet Beecher Stowe, Samuel Hopkins, and *The Minister's Wooing.*" *Emerson Society Quarterly* 24 (1978): 119–32.

————. *New England Literary Culture: From Revolution through Renaissance.* New York, 1986.

Burns, Sarah. *Pastoral Inventions: Rural Life in Nineteenth-Century Art and Culture.* Philadelphia, 1989.

Butler, Jon. "Enthusiasm Described and Decried: The Great Awakening as Interpretive Fiction." *Journal of American History* 69 (1982): 305–25.

———. *Awash in a Sea of Faith: Christianizing the American People.* Cambridge, Mass., 1990.

Calhoun, Daniel. *Professional Lives in America: Structure and Aspiration, 1750–1850.* Cambridge, Mass., 1965.

Cecil, Anthony C., Jr. *The Theological Development of Edwards Amasa Park: Last of the "Consistent Calvinists."* Missoula, Mont., 1974.

Cherry, Conrad. *The Theology of Jonathan Edwards: A Reappraisal.* Garden City, N.Y., 1966.

Clifford, James. *The Predicament of Culture.* Cambridge, Mass., 1988.

Clifford, James, and George Marcus, eds. *Writing Culture: The Poetics and Politics of Ethnography.* Berkeley, Calif., 1986.

Cole, Arthur C. *A Hundred Years of Mount Holyoke College: The Evolution of an Educational Ideal.* New Haven, Conn., 1940.

Conforti, Joseph A. "Samuel Hopkins and the New Divinity: Theology, Ethics, and Social Reform in Eighteenth-Century New England." *William and Mary Quarterly* 34 (October 1977): 572–89.

———. *Samuel Hopkins and the New Divinity Movement: Calvinism, the Congregational Ministry, and Reform in New England between the Great Awakenings.* Grand Rapids, Mich., 1981.

———. "Joseph Bellamy and the New Divinity Movement." *New England Historical and Genealogical Register* 137 (1983): 126–38.

———. "Jonathan Edwards's Most Popular Work: 'The Life of David Brainerd' and Nineteenth-Century Evangelical Culture." *Church History* 54 (June 1985): 188–201.

———. "Jonathan Edwards and American Studies." *American Quarterly* 41 (March 1989): 165–71.

Cott, Nancy F. *The Bonds of Womanhood: "Women's Sphere" in New England, 1780–1835.* New Haven, Conn., 1977.

Crawford, Michael J. *Seasons of Grace: Colonial New England's Revival Tradition in Its British Context.* New York, 1991.

Cross, Whitney R. *The Burned-Over District.* 1950. Reprint, New York, 1965.

Dahlquist, John Terrence. "Nathanael Emmons: His Life and Work." Ph.D. dissertation, Boston University, 1963.

Davidson, Cathy N. *Revolution and the Word: The Rise of the Novel in America.* New York, 1986.

Dawson, Jan C. *The Unusable Past: America's Puritan Tradition, 1830 to 1930.* Chico, Calif., 1984.

Day, Richard Ellsworth. *Flagellant on Horseback: The Life Story of David Brainerd.* Philadelphia, 1950.

Delattre, Roland. *Beauty and Sensibility in the Thought of Jonathan Edwards: An Essay in Aesthetics and Theological Ethics.* New Haven, Conn., 1968.

Dexter, Franklin B. *Biographical Sketches of the Graduates of Yale College, with Annals of the College History.* 6 vols. New Haven, Conn., 1885–1912.

Douglas, Ann. *The Feminization of American Culture.* New York, 1977.

Dowd, Gregory Evans. *A Spirited Resistance: The North American Indian Struggle for Unity.* Baltimore, Md., 1992.

Drakeman, Lisa Natale. "Seminary Sisters: Mount Holyoke's First Students, 1837–1849." Ph.D. dissertation, Princeton University, 1988.

Drummond, Andrew L. *The Story of Protestantism.* London, 1949.

Duyckinck, Evert A., and George L. Duyckinck. *Cyclopedia of American Literature.* 2 vols. New York, 1856.

Eggleston, George Cary. *The American Immortals.* New York, 1901.

Eggleston, Percy C. *A Man of Bethlehem, Joseph Bellamy, D.D., and His Divinity School.* New London, Conn., 1908.

Epstein, Barbara Leslie. *The Politics of Domesticity: Women, Evangelism, and Temperance in Nineteenth-Century America.* Middletown, Conn., 1981.

Ferm, Robert L. *Jonathan Edwards the Younger, 1745–1801: A Colonial Pastor.* Grand Rapids, Mich., 1976.

Fitzmier, John R. "The Godly Federalism of Timothy Dwight, 1752–1817: Society, Doctrine and Religion in the Life of New England's 'Moral Legislator.'" Ph.D. dissertation, Princeton University, 1986.

Fogelson, Robert N. *America's Armories: Architecture, Society, and the Public Order.* Cambridge, Mass., 1989.

Foster, Charles H. *The Rungless Ladder: Harriet Beecher Stowe and New England Puritanism.* Durham, N.C., 1954.

Foster, Frank H. *The Life of Edwards Amasa Park.* New York, 1936.

Geer, Curtis Manning. *The Hartford Theological Seminary, 1834–1934.* Hartford, Conn., 1934.

Geertz, Clifford. *The Interpretation of Cultures: Selected Essays.* New York, 1973.

———. *Local Knowledge: Further Essays in Interpretive Anthropology.* New York, 1983.

Gilchrist, Beth Bradford. *The Life of Mary Lyon.* Boston, 1910.

Gillespie, Joanna Bowen. "'The Clear Leadings of Providence': Pious Memoirs and the Problems of Self-Realization for Women in the Early Nineteenth Century." *Journal of the Early Republic* 5 (1985): 197–221.

Ginzburg, Lori. *Women and the Work of Benevolence: Morality, Politics and Class in the Nineteenth-Century United States.* New Brunswick, N.J., 1990.

Glassberg, David. *American Historical Pageantry: The Uses of Tradition in the Early Twentieth Century.* Chapel Hill, N.C., 1990.

Goen, C. C. "Jonathan Edwards: A New Departure in Eschatology." *Church History* 28 (1959): 25–40.

Gordon, Ernest B. *Adoniram Judson Gordon: A Biography.* 2d ed. New York, 1896.

Green, Elizabeth Alder. *Mary Lyon and the Founding of Mount Holyoke.* Hanover, N.H., 1979.

Greven, Philip. *The Protestant Temperament: Patterns of Childrearing, Religious Experience, and the Self in Early America.* New York, 1977.

Grimshaw, Patricia. *Paths of Duty: American Missionary Wives in Nineteenth-Century Hawaii.* Honolulu, 1989.

Guelzo, Allen C. *Edwards on the Will: A Century of American Theological Debate.* Middletown, Conn., 1989.

Gura, Philip F. "The Study of Colonial American Literature, 1966–1987: A Vade Mecum." *William and Mary Quarterly* 45 (April 1988): 305–44.

Hackett, David G. *The Rude Hand of Innovation: Religion and Social Order in Albany, New York, 1652–1836.* New York, 1991.

Hambrick-Stowe, Charles E. *The Practice of Piety: Puritan Devotional Disciplines in Seventeenth-Century New England.* Chapel Hill, N.C., 1982.

———. "The Spiritual Pilgrimage of Sarah Osborn (1714–1796)." *Church History* 61 (December 1992): 408–21.

Haroutunian, Joseph. *Piety versus Moralism: The Passing of the New England Theology.* New York, 1932.

———. *Wisdom and Folly in Religion: A Study in Chastened Protestantism.* New York, 1940.

Hatch, Nathan O. *The Democratization of American Christianity.* New Haven, Conn., 1989.

Hatch, Nathan O., and Harry S. Stout, eds. *Jonathan Edwards and the American Experience.* New York, 1988.

Hedrick, Joan. *Harriet Beecher Stowe: A Life.* New York, 1994.

Heimert, Alan. *Religion and the American Mind from the Great Awakening to the Revolution.* Cambridge, Mass., 1966.

Heimert, Alan, and Perry Miller, eds. *The Great Awakening: Documents Illustrating the Crisis and Its Consequences.* Indianapolis and New York, 1967.

Henry, Stuart C. *Unvanquished Puritan: A Portrait of Lyman Beecher.* Grand Rapids, Mich., 1973.

Hitt, Russell, ed. *Heroic Colonial Christians.* Philadelphia, 1966.

Hobsbawm, Eric, and Terrence Ranger, eds. *The Invention of Tradition.* New York, 1983.

Holbrook, Clyde A. *The Ethics of Jonathan Edwards: Morality and Aesthetics.* Ann Arbor, Mich., 1973.

Hoopes, James. *Consciousness in New England: From Puritanism and Ideas to Psychoanalysis and Semiotics.* Baltimore, Md., 1989.

Horowitz, Helen Lefkowitz. *Alma Mater: Design and Experience in Women's Colleges from Their Nineteenth-Century Beginnings to the 1930s.* New York, 1984.

Hunt, Lynn, ed. *The New Cultural History.* Berkeley, Calif., 1989.

Jenson, Robert W. *America's Theologian: A Recommendation of Jonathan Edwards.* New York, 1988.

Johns, Elizabeth. *American Genre Painting: The Politics of Everyday Life.* New Haven, Conn., 1991.

Johnson, Paul. *A Shopkeeper's Millennium: Society and Revivals in Rochester, New York, 1815–1937*. New York, 1978.

Johnson, Thomas, ed. *The Printed Writings of Jonathan Edwards: A Bibliography*. 1940. Reprint, New York, 1968.

Juster, Susan. "'In a Different Voice': Male and Female Narratives of Religious Conversion in Post-Revolutionary America." *American Quarterly* 41 (1989): 34–62.

Kammen, Michael. *Selvages and Biases*. Ithaca, N.Y., 1987.

———. *Mystic Chords of Memory: The Transformation of Tradition in American Culture*. New York, 1991.

Kay, Jane Holtz. *Preserving New England*. New York, 1986.

Keller, Charles R. *The Second Great Awakening in Connecticut*. New Haven, Conn., 1942.

Keyes, Donald. *The First Church of Christ in Northampton: A Centennial Celebration of the Fifth Meeting House, 1878–1978*. Northampton, Mass., 1978.

Kimnach, Wilson, ed. *Three Essays in Honor of the Publication of "The Life of David Brainerd."* New Haven, Conn., 1985.

Kling, David W. *A Field of Divine Wonders: The New Divinity and Village Revivals in Northwestern Connecticut, 1792–1822*. University Park, Pa., 1993.

Kuklick, Bruce. *Churchmen and Philosophers: From Jonathan Edwards to John Dewey*. New Haven, Conn., 1985.

Lambert, Frank. *"Pedlar in Divinity": George Whitefield and the Transatlantic Revivals, 1737–1770*. Princeton, N.J., 1994.

Lesser, M. X. *Jonathan Edwards: A Reference Guide*. Boston, 1981.

———. *Jonathan Edwards, 1981–1993*. Westport, Conn., 1994.

Levin, David, ed. *Jonathan Edwards: A Profile*. New York, 1969.

Leyda, Jay, ed. *The Years and Hours of Emily Dickinson*. 2 vols. New Haven, Conn., 1960.

Loveland, Anne C. *Southern Evangelicals and the Social Order, 1800–1860*. Baton Rouge, La., 1980.

Lowe, Wolfgang E. "The First American Foreign Missionaries: The Students, 1810–1829: An Inquiry into Their Theological Motives." Ph.D. dissertation, Brown University, 1962.

MacCracken, Henry Mitchell. *The Hall of Fame*. New York, 1901.

Manspeaker, Nancy. *Jonathan Edwards: Bibliographical Synopses*. New York, 1981.

Marling, Karal Ann. *George Washington Slept Here: Colonial Revivals and American Culture*. Cambridge, Mass., 1988.

Marsden, George M. *The Evangelical Mind and the New School Presbyterian Experience: A Case Study of Thought and Theology in Nineteenth-Century America*. New Haven, Conn., 1970.

May, Henry F. "The Recovery of American Religious History." *American Historical Review* 70 (1964): 79–92.

McDermott, Gerald R. *One Holy and Happy Society: The Public Theology of Jonathan Edwards*. University Park, Pa., 1992.

McGiffert, Arthur C., Jr. *Jonathan Edwards*. New York, 1932.

McKenzie, Alexander. *Memoir of Professor Edwards Amasa Park*. Cambridge, Mass., 1901.

McLoughlin, William G. *Modern Revivalism*. New York, 1959.

———. *The Meaning of Henry Ward Beecher: An Essay on the Shifting Values of Mid-Victorian America*. New York, 1970.

———. *Revivals, Awakenings, and Reform: An Essay on Religion and Social Change in America, 1607–1977*. Chicago, 1978.

Mead, Sidney E. *Nathaniel William Taylor, 1786–1888, A Connecticut Liberal*. Chicago, 1942.

Miller, Glenn T. *Piety and Intellect: The Aims and Purposes of Ante-Bellum Theological Education*. Atlanta, Ga., 1990.

Miller, Perry. *Jonathan Edwards*. New York, 1949.

———. *Errand into the Wilderness*. Cambridge, Mass., 1956. Reprint, New York, 1964.

———. *The Life of the Mind in America*. New York, 1965.

Monk, Robert C. *John Wesley: His Puritan Heritage*. New York and Nashville, 1966.

Moore, R. Laurence. "Religion, Secularization and the Shaping of the Culture Industry in Antebellum America." *American Quarterly* 41 (1989): 216–42.

———. *Selling God: American Religion in the Marketplace of Culture*. New York, 1994.

Mott, Frank Luther. *A History of American Magazines, 1741–1850*. 2 vols. Cambridge, Mass., 1957.

Niebuhr, H. Richard. *The Kingdom of God in America*. New York, 1937.

Noll, Mark A. "Common Sense Traditions and American Evangelical Thought." *American Quarterly* 37 (Summer 1985): 216–38.

———. *Princeton in the Republic, 1768–1822: The Search for a Christian Enlightenment in the Era of Samuel Stanhope Smith*. Princeton, N.J., 1989.

The Northampton Book, Chapters from 300 Years in the Life of a New England Town, 1654–1954. Northampton, Mass., 1954.

Oberg, Barbara B., and Harry S. Stout, eds. *Benjamin Franklin, Jonathan Edwards, and the Representation of American Culture*. New York, 1993.

Parkes, Henry. *Jonathan Edwards: The Fiery Puritan*. New York, 1930.

Parrington, Vernon L. *Main Currents in American Thought*. 2 vols. New York, 1927.

Payne, E. A. "The Evangelical Revival and the Beginnings of the Modern Missionary Movement." *Congregational Quarterly* 21 (1943).

Pettit, Norman. "Prelude to Mission: David Brainerd's Expulsion from Yale." *New England Quarterly* 59 (1986): 28–50.

Pierce, Richard D. "A Suppressed Edwards Manuscript on the Trinity." *The Crane Review* 1 (Winter 1959): 66–80.

Pointer, Richard W. "'Poor Indians' and the 'Poor in Spirit': The Indian Impact on David Brainerd." *New England Quarterly* 67 (September 1994): 403–26.

Pope, Earl. *New England Calvinism and the Disruption of the Presbyterian Church*. New York, 1987.

Porterfield, Amanda. *Feminine Spirituality in America: From Sarah Edwards to Martha Graham*. Philadelphia, 1980.

Rabinowitz, Richard. *The Spiritual Self in Everyday Life: The Transformation of Personal Religious Experience in Nineteenth-Century New England.* Boston, 1989.

Reynolds, David S. "From Doctrine to Narrative: The Rise of Pulpit Storytelling in America." *American Quarterly* 32 (1980): 479–98.

Rogers, Charles A. "John Wesley and Jonathan Edwards." *Duke Divinity School Review* 31 (1966): 73–82.

Roth, Randolph A. *The Democratic Dilemma: Religion, Reform, and the Social Order in the Connecticut River Valley of Vermont, 1791–1850.* New York, 1987.

Rowe, Henry K. *History of Andover Seminary.* Newton, Mass., 1933.

Rowe, Kenneth E. "Nestor of Orthodoxy, New England Style: A Study in the Theology of Edwards Amasa Park, 1808–1900." Ph.D. dissertation, Drew University, 1969.

Rubin, Julius H. *Religious Melancholy and Protestant Experience in America.* New York, 1994.

Rudisill, Dorus Paul. *The Doctrine of the Atonement in Jonathan Edwards and His Successors.* New York, 1971.

Ryan, Mary P. *Cradle of the Middle Class: The Family in Oneida County, New York, 1790–1865.* New York, 1981.

Salmond, C. A. *Charles and A. A. Hodge, with Class and Table Talk of Hodge the Younger.* New York, n.d.

Scheick, William J., ed. *Critical Essays on Jonathan Edwards.* Boston, 1980.

Scott, Donald M. *From Office to Profession: The New England Ministry, 1750–1850.* Philadelphia, 1978.

Sears, John F. *Sacred Places: American Tourist Attractions in the Nineteenth Century.* New York, 1989.

Sedgwick, Sarah Cabot, and Christina Sedgwick Marquand. *Stockbridge, 1739–1939, A Chronicle.* Great Barrington, Mass., 1939.

Shea, Daniel B. "Jonathan Edwards: The First Two Hundred Years." *Journal of American Studies* 14 (1980): 181–97.

Shiels, Richard D. "The Connecticut Clergy in the Second Great Awakening." Ph.D. dissertation, Boston University, 1976.

———. "The Second Great Awakening in Connecticut: Critique of the Traditional Interpretation." *Church History* 49 (1980): 401–15.

———. "The Feminization of American Congregationalism, 1730–1835." *American Quarterly* 33 (1981): 46–62.

Sklar, Kathryn Kish. *Catharine Beecher: A Study in Domesticity.* New Haven, Conn., 1973.

———. "The Founding of Mount Holyoke College." In *Women of America: A History,* edited by Carol Ruth Berkin and Mary Beth Norton, pp. 177–201. Boston, 1979.

Slotkin, Richard S. *Regeneration through Violence: The Mythology of the American Frontier, 1600–1860.* Middletown, Conn., 1973.

Smith, H. Shelton. *Changing Conceptions of Original Sin: A Study in American Theology Since 1750*. New York, 1955.

Smith, John E. *Jonathan Edwards: Puritan, Preacher, Philosopher*. Notre Dame, Ind., 1993.

Sollors, Werner, ed. *The Invention of Ethnicity*. New York, 1989.

Solomon, Barbara Miller. *Ancestors and Immigrants: A Changing New England Tradition*. Chicago, 1956.

Staloff, Darren Marcus. "Intellectual History Naturalized: Materialism and the 'Thinking Class.'" *William and Mary Quarterly* 50 (April 1993): 406–17.

Stout, Harry S. *The Divine Dramatist: George Whitefield and the Rise of Modern Evangelicalism*. Grand Rapids, Mich., 1991.

Stow, Sarah D. *History of Mount Holyoke Seminary, South Hadley, Mass., during the First Half Century, 1837–1887*. South Hadley, Mass., 1887.

Strong, William E. *The Story of the American Board: An Account of the First Hundred Years of the American Board of Commissioners for Foreign Missions*. Boston, 1910.

Sweet, Leonard I. *The Minister's Wife: Her Role in Nineteenth-Century American Evangelicalism*. Philadelphia, 1983.

Sweet, William Warren. *The Story of Religion in America*. New York, 1930.

Thomas, Louise P. *Seminary Militant: An Account of the Missionary Movement at Mount Holyoke Seminary and College*. South Hadley, Mass., 1937.

Tracy, Patricia J. *Jonathan Edwards, Pastor: Religion and Society in Eighteenth-Century Northampton*. New York, 1989.

Valeri, Mark. "The Economic Thought of Jonathan Edwards." *Church History* 60 (1991): 37–54.

———. *Law and Providence in Joseph Bellamy's New England: The Origins of the New Divinity in Revolutionary America*. New York, 1994.

Vanderbilt, Kermit. *American Literature and the Academy*. Philadelphia, 1986.

Vanderpool, Harold Young. "The Andover Conservatives: Apologetics, Biblical Criticism and Theological Change at Andover Theological Seminary, 1808–1880." Ph.D. dissertation, Harvard University, 1971.

Vesser, Aram, ed. *The New Historicism*. New York, 1989.

———, ed. *The New Historicism Reader*. New York, 1994.

Walker, George Leon. *Some Aspects of the Religious Life of New England with Special Reference to the Congregationalists*. New York, 1897.

Walters, Ronald G. "Signs of the Times: Clifford Geertz and Historians." *Social Research* 47 (1980): 537–56.

Ward, W. R. *The Protestant Evangelical Awakening*. New York, 1992.

Wayland, John T. *The Theological Development of Yale College, 1822–1858*. 1933. Reprint, New York, 1987.

Weber, Donald Louis. "The Image of Jonathan Edwards in American Culture." Ph.D. dissertation, Columbia University, 1978.

———. *Rhetoric and History in Revolutionary New England*. New York, 1988.

Weddle, David L. "The Melancholy Saint: Jonathan Edwards's Interpretation of

David Brainerd as a Model of Evangelical Spirituality." *Harvard Theological Review*
81 (1988): 297–319.

Whittemore, Robert C. *The Transformation of the New England Theology.* New York,
1987.

Williams, Daniel Day. *The Andover Liberals.* New York, 1941.

Winslow, Ola. *Jonathan Edwards, 1703–1758: A Biography.* New York, 1940.

Wright, Conrad E., ed. *American Unitarianism, 1805–1865.* Boston, 1989.

Wynbeek, David. *David Brainerd, Beloved Yankee.* Grand Rapids, Mich., 1961.

Yarborough, Stephen R., and John C. Adams. *Delightful Convictions: Jonathan
Edwards and the Rhetoric of Conversion.* Westport, Conn., 1993.

Zwiep, Mary. *Pilgrim Path: The First Company of Women Missionaries to Hawaii.*
Madison, Wis., 1991.

INDEX

to American Hall of Fame, 183, 184; Progressive Era and, 190, 193–94; Richard Niebuhr on, 191–92; Alan Heimert on, 195–96

—theology of: Northampton revivals, 1, 13, 18, 58; doctrine of disinterested benevolence, 2, 60, 85, 86, 97, 129–30, 214 (n. 57); concert of prayer, 16, 101; "Sinners in the Hands of an Angry God" sermon, 19, 26, 94, 152, 155, 161, 162; on revivals, 23, 25–26, 29, 47–49; repudiation of antinomianism, 25, 29, 73; and experimental religion, 32–33, 41, 46, 79; signs of religious affections, 33, 34; personal piety of, 37, 41, 42, 44; evangelical humility, 42, 85; "Resolutions" on, 42–44; Calvinism, 50, 54, 109, 140, 162; on Yale revival, 65–66; on missionaries, 74, 214 (n. 57); on authentic holiness, 75–76, 129–30; and religious reform, 76, 85; and social reform, 86; and female spirituality, 97, 105; and capitalism, 97–98; social ethics, 98; and millennialism, 101; seminary study of, 109, 110; distinction of natural and moral necessity, 119, 120–21, 122, 139–40; and doctrine of imputation, 122, 123; and theory of the atonement, 124, 125–26, 140; and exercise-taste dispute, 127, 128, 129–31; continual creation, 128; Hopkins and, 131; "A Divine and Supernatural Light" sermon, 162, 181

—works: popularity of, xi, 9, 192; unpublished writings, xii, 1, 2; publication of, 2, 33, 37, 41–42, 46–47, 194; bibliographies of, 2, 192; and Emerson's transcendentalism, 3, 162, 195, 196; writing of *Life of Brainerd*, 63, 68, 72, 73–74; manuscript collection, 142, 170, 183, 194; as literature, 165–68, 187. *See also names of individual works*

Edwards, Jonathan, Jr., 48, 116, 121, 132; and theory of the atonement, 124, 125–26, 140; "Improvements in Theology," 140; as missionary, 214 (n. 57)

Edwards, Sarah Pierpont, 1, 40, 97, 105–6

Edwards, Tryon, 142

Edwards Church (Northampton), 61, 175

Edwards family reunion, 169–71

Eggleston, Nathaniel, 169

Eliot, John, 71, 79, 187; Rogers statue of, 152

Ellis, George: *The Puritan Age in Massachusetts*, 155

Emerson, Joseph, 41, 90–91, 94; *The Evangelical Primer*, 91

Emerson, Ralph Waldo, 3, 162, 167, 193, 196

Emmons, Nathanael, 5, 91, 110, 121, 141; training of ministers, 90, 116, 134–35, 146–47; influence on Park, 111–12; on Calvinism, 119; exercise theology, 127–28, 129, 135, 137, 139; Park's biography of, 132, 134–37

Enfield, Conn.: Edwards monument, 152

Erskine, John, 68

Eschatology, 47–48, 192

Evangelical humility, 42, 85

Exercise-taste controversy, 127, 140; Park and, 120, 128–31, 135, 137; Emmons exercise theology, 127–28, 135, 137, 139

Faithful Narrative of the Surprising Works of God (Edwards), 44–45, 46, 72, 97, 105

Finney, Charles Grandison, 49, 59; new-measures revivalism, 12, 16, 21–22, 56; and legacy of Edwards, 21, 22, 23, 28, 29–30, 202 (n. 51); Presbygational fight against, 22–23, 25–26, 27, 29, 46; *Lectures on Revivals*, 23, 28–30; "Traditions of the Elders" sermon, 28

Fisher, George Park, 181–83

Fisk, Fidelia, 94, 96

Fisk, Pliny, 74, 82

Fiske, John: *The Beginnings of New England*, 159